MADONNA
BLOND AMBITION

MADONNA BLOND AMBITION
Daryl Easlea & Eddi Fiegel

A BACKBEAT BOOK
First edition 2012
Published by Backbeat Books
An imprint of Hal Leonard Corporation
7777 West Bluemound Road
Milwaukee, WI 53213
www.backbeatbooks.com

Devised and produced for Backbeat Books by
Outline Press Ltd
2A Union Court, 20-22 Union Road,
London SW4 6JP, England

ISBN: 978-1-61713-034-2

Editor: Thomas Jerome Seabrook
Design: Paul Cooper Design

Printed by Regent Publishing Services Limited, China

12 13 14 15 16 5 4 3 2 1

CONTENTS

PART 1

MATERIAL GIRL

by Daryl Easlea

CHAPTER 1
THE EARLY YEARS

Madonna Louise Ciccone was born in Bay City, Michigan, on August 16 1958, the third child of Silvio 'Tony' Ciccone and Madonna Louise Ciccone Sr. She would go on to become a true icon of the entertainment industry, an international superstar, and a metaphor for the American dream.

The Ciccones were a moderately wealthy middle-class family. Tony was a second generation Italian American whose family originated from Pacentro in the central Abruzzo region of Italy. At the age of 16, Madonna's paternal grandfather, Gaetano, had moved to America looking for work. He returned to Pacentro to marry his childhood sweetheart, Michelina, and in 1919 moved with his wife to Pittsburgh to work in a foundry.

Tony was born in 1934, the youngest of six sons. He joined the Air Force after the Second World War and was stationed in Alaska during the Korean War. While on leave he met his friend Dale Fortin's sister, Madonna, a demure, warm, funny woman from a hard-working, devout Catholic family of French-Canadian and Germanic descent. It was love at first sight.

After Tony completed his service, the pair decided to go steady while he attended the Catholic Geneva Falls College in Beaver Dam and obtained an engineering degree—highly unusual at the time for a working class, second-generation immigrant. Tony was an industrious man who believed strongly in self-betterment. As Madonna herself put it in 1985: "He wanted to be upwardly mobile and go into educated, prosperous America."

On July 1 1955, Ciccone and Fortin were married. They relocated to Pontiac, near Detroit, and he took work as a defense engineer with Chrysler. Their first child, Anthony, was born in 1956; Martin followed in 1957, and after Madonna (or 'Nonny,' as she was known to the family) came Paula in 1959, Christopher in 1960, and Melanie in 1962.

The early years of Madonna's life were bright and breezy, with much sparring with her older brothers and vying for her parents' attention.

Although she was not the only girl, the fact that she was the oldest made her special. Her mother doted on her, and the young Madonna would often sleep in her parents' bed. But her mother was ill: breast cancer was slowly killing her. In her dying months, Ciccone's children would be farmed out to various relatives while Tony worked and nursed her.

Madonna's mother spent a year in and out of hospital. She rallied for the children, especially her darling Nonny. As Madonna's brother Christopher recalled: "She was really funny so it wasn't awful to go and visit her there. I remember that right before she died she asked for a hamburger because she couldn't eat anything for so long, and I thought that was very funny."

Madonna Ciccone passed away on December 1 1963 at the age of 30, her tired body no longer able to take the strain. She was buried at the Visitation Church in Bay City, Michigan, where she and Tony had been married eight years earlier.

The impact of Madonna's mother's death on her eldest daughter cannot be overstated. It has subsequently—whether implicitly or explicitly—informed the singer's most important work. For a period of time, Madonna became housekeeper and surrogate mother to her younger siblings, supporting a parade of temporary housekeepers drafted in in an attempt to impose order on the family. In 1966, Tony married one of the sternest and most house-proud of these women, Joan Gustafson. The Fortin side of the family had encouraged Tony to partner off with a family friend, but when he took up with Joan they referred to her as "the maid." Tony and Joan went on to have two children of their own, Jennifer and Mario.

Looking back, Madonna described herself as "a very lonely girl searching for something, looking for a mother figure." Her relationship with Joan was always distant at best. "I didn't accept my stepmother when I was growing up," she later told CNN. "In retrospect I think I was really hard on her." (According to her brother Christopher, Madonna would ironically come to embody Joan's strict rules and timetables in later life.) Tony continued his career in the defense engineer, moving to General Dynamics, where he worked with fiber optics.

Madonna grew up in Pontiac in a mixed-race neighborhood that fostered racial tolerance—something that was encouraged by the Ciccone family. It was here that she began to get into music, inspired by the sounds she heard coming from her street. "We were one of the only white families," she later recalled. "All the kids had Motown and black stuff. And they had dances in their back yards, little 45 turntables and a stack of records, and everyone just danced in the driveway and back yard." Racial tolerance is at the center of a lot of her work. Brother Christopher believes that Madonna's kissing of the black saint in the 'Like A Prayer' video was "conceived to highlight her belief in racial equality," and that it was "one of the many proofs that [her parents] succeeded."

Madonna attended various schools in Michigan: first St Frederick's and St Andrew's Elementary Schools and then West Middle School, where she demanded attention by frequently showing her undergarments to boys. The family relocated to a two-story redbrick house complete with creek in the back garden in Oklahoma Avenue, Rochester. As Christopher Ciccone recalls in his 2008 memoir, *Life With My Sister Madonna*, there was only one occasion when Tony disciplined his daughter. After Madonna came home late one night, Joan slapped her, and Madonna slapped her back. She was grounded for a week and "banned from driving her car."

When she arrived at Rochester Adams High School, Madonna worked hard and excelled, even if she was a little unconventional. "I wasn't rebellious in a conventional way," she later told *Vanity Fair*. "I cared about being good at something. I didn't shave under my arms and I didn't wear make-up. But I studied hard and got good grades, rarely smoked pot, though I'm sure I did from time to time. I was a paradox, an outsider and rebel who wanted to please my father and get straight As. I wanted to be somebody."

Madonna also led the cheerleading squad and won the lead roles in school productions of *My Fair Lady* and *The Sound Of Music*. But within a few years she had begun to drift away from cheerleading to the artier, more bohemian end of college. She also lost her virginity at the age of 15 to her 17-year-old high school sweetheart, Russell Long.

It was around this time that Madonna met one of the principal shapers of her early career, Christopher Flynn, a veteran dancer who specialized in modern dance rather than traditional ballet. Flynn became her dance teacher when she took up an evening class in Rochester. A confident, aesthete homosexual 30 years her senior, Flynn was exactly the sort of person Madonna needed, at exactly the right time. He encouraged her dancing and introduced her to the world of downtown Detroit (something that was largely avoided in Rochester because of the proliferation of African Americans). They went to gay clubs and danced, danced, danced. Disco was reaching its zenith, and there was never a better time to be in your late teens.

Flynn later described Madonna as "one of the best students I've had, a very worldly sort of woman, even as a child. We would go to gay bars and she and I would dance our asses off. People would clear away and let her go."

Madonna's brother Christopher joined Flynn's dance class as well. "I've never met anyone like him in my life," he recalled. "He is around five foot eight, a lean man with dark brown hair, dressed in gray jazz pants and a tight leotard with a shirt over it. His voice is high and haughty, and he sounds like a girl." Madonna was acutely aware that she had her first real mentor.

In the fall of 1976, Madonna went to the University Of Michigan at Ann Arbor to study modern dance. She trained to be a dancer—a serious dancer. Detractors through the years who would like to suggest that her success was a matter of luck undervalue not only her tenacity but also her formal dance training. She appeared regularly in university productions, one of which, *Hat Rack*, saw her performing topless save for a black bra. (As we will see many times throughout her career, a good idea can and will always be revisited.)

Under Flynn's tutelage, all boundaries began to disappear. Madonna wanted to push beyond the constraints of a conventional dancing course, so in July 1978 she moved to New York City. Tony was horrified that the first of his children to go to university was also the first to drop out.

It was a huge leap for Madonna, no matter how confident she purported to be. "It was the first time I'd ever taken a plane, the first time I'd ever gotten a taxi cab," she later said. "I came here with $35 in my pocket. It was the bravest thing I'd ever done." And, although she had several friends in New York who were readily on hand to assist her, brave it was. Legend has it that she asked the cab driver to take her straight "to the center of things," where she met a stranger who put her up for a fortnight while she got herself sorted out. She began dance classes and took a succession of jobs to support her dream.

Shortly after arriving in New York, Madonna heard that Pearl Lang was looking for dancers. By now in her sixties, Lang had been a major figure in modern dance. She had been one of Martha Graham's principal dancers four decades previously, and had established her own company in 1953. Now, with Alvin Ailey, she ran the American Dance Center in New York. With her mixture of bravado and cheek, Madonna introduced herself to the dance icon at the Annual American Festival Of Dance in Durham, North Carolina, asking whether there was any room for new talent in Lang's company. Surprised by the brazenness of Madonna's enquiry, Lang said that there might be some understudy work. "I was kind of taken aback," she later said. "I told her I had to see but that we could probably make room. I asked her how she was going to get back to New York. She said: don't worry—I'll manage."

By November 1978, Madonna was dancing for Lang, appearing in a variety of her productions, including *I Never Saw Another Butterfly*, in which she played a Jewish ghetto child, and *Piece For Brass*, in which metal pipes were integral to the dancing. Lang later described Madonna's approach as aggressive, but in a good way. "That's necessary," she said. "If dancers hide they don't come across so well."

To supplement her dancing, Madonna worked as a hat-check girl at the Russian Tea Room on West 57th Street and took more conventional temporary jobs in Burger King and Dunkin' Donuts. To earn further income, she took part in several nude photographic modeling sessions. Unlike many of her peers, who would slip out to the city's perimeter to perform in topless bars to generate income, Madonna posed nude for photographers and for still-life painting, realizing she could make about $100 for a day's work compared with half of that at some grueling burger joint.

It was around this time that Madonna was the victim of a serious sexual assault. Although the attack went unreported at the time, it would shape her outlook (and would later become source material in her 1993 film, *Dangerous Game*). In the immediate aftermath, she began to lose focus, and within a period of weeks had left Lang's dance troupe. But she also felt galvanized to succeed and determined never to be so powerless again.

In 1979, Madonna began dating Dan Gilroy, who had formed a group called The Breakfast Club with his brother, Ed. As a sideline, they had an 'alternative vaudeville' act, Voidville. It was while performing with the Gilroys that Madonna was spotted by Jean van Lieu and Jean Claude Pellerin, two Belgian producers who were in New York scouting for talent for the Paris-based revue of French disco artist Patrick Hernandez.

Van Lieu and Pellerin liked what they had seen and invited Madonna to Paris. They also had the vision to turn Madonna into a singer as well as a dancer—they saw her as an Edith Piaf for the disco generation. In May 1979, Madonna relocated to France. After the relative squalor of New York, she was furnished with accommodation, limousines, and a maid, but she still longed for the cut and thrust of the New York scene; being paraded in front of the French aristocracy did not thrill her. Although nothing really came from this episode, it showed her a way to behave as well as giving her future contacts within the Paris scene. Hernandez later said that Paris put "the bug in her ear that she could sing. Maybe if she had never come, Madonna would have continued taking dance lessons, going to auditions—and never even tried to make it as a singer!"

On returning to the USA in August 1979, Madonna took up once again with the Gilroys. Dan began to teach her the drums with a view to her joining The Breakfast Club, and she would also strum brother Ed's guitar. Of all the steps on the road to superstardom, the time Madonna spent with her first two bands, The Breakfast Club and Emmy, was arguably the most significant. It saw her move away from the dance that she had studied since her teens to concentrate on music—and, importantly, writing her first songs.

The Breakfast Club made punk-infused pop which has yet to be properly documented but which showed Madonna the freedom and possibility of making music for a living. Playing drums and sometimes guitar, Madonna shared the stage with Dan and Ed Gilroy and blond-haired bassist Angie Smit. (When Madonna took on the occasional lead vocal, Dan Gilroy would assume drumming duties.)

Madonna made another career decision that would later return to haunt her when she saw an advert for a film production that needed a 'passionate woman' who could dance and was willing work for nothing. Director

Stephen Jon Lewicki was impressed with Madonna's dedication and offered her the part of Bruna, a punk dominatrix waiting to find a nice boy from out of town ready to fall under her spell, in *A Certain Sacrifice*. After Bruna is raped, the rest of her gang make a sacrifice of her attacker. It was not Madonna's most convincing performance. The project ran out of cash, and would remain on the shelf until 1985—the year Madonna became a megastar.

Of course, 1985 seemed a very long way off when Madonna began cohabiting with the Gilroys in Corana, Queens, in a crumbling, boarded-up synagogue. Old friend Angie Smit was brought in as The Breakfast Club's bassist. Smit looked the part, but Madonna was not happy to share her stage with another woman, so the Gilroys drafted in bassist Mike Monahan, and then—to seal her elevation from drummer to vocalist—percussionist Gary Burke. Burke would later remark that as Madonna's 20 per cent contribution grew to around 80 per cent, the bandleaders, Dan and Ed, became increasingly unhappy.

Madonna, Burke, and Monahan left to form another group. "She was fun, you know," Dan Gilroy later said. "But I knew that, with that kind of drive and devotion to getting ahead, something had to happen. I don't know if she was more talented than the rest of the group. More driven and an incredible attention-getter." The Gilroys persevered, however, and The Breakfast Club would enjoy some success in the mid 80s after signing to Ze Records and entering the US Top Ten with 'Right On Track.'

Madonna took over as lead vocalist when Gary Burke came in on drums. Soon Madonna outgrew the band. She fronted the shortlived Madonna & The Sky and then hooked up again with Stephen Bray, whom she had met back in Detroit while dancing at the Blue Frogge club. At the time he had been playing in a local group called The Cost Of Living, but since then he too had grown tired of the Midwest and moved to New York. The pair began an affair; another band, Emmy, followed.

"I was excited to find that she had written some solid songs," Bray later told VH1. Looking for a name, Burke suggested 'Madonna,' which Bray immediately vetoed. The band was briefly called The Millionaires, then The Modern Dance; eventually Emmy, a nickname that either Burke or Bray had for Madonna, seemed to stick, although they were occasionally billed as Emmy & The Emmys and even Emanon ('no name' backward).

The band played around New York, advertising themselves with posters that read "Punk? Passé. Emmy." Madonna stood out front behind her guitar, playing clipped, choppy new wave. Emmy recorded a demo tape at the end of November 1980; the sound is bright and cheery yet rather unremarkable. 'Love For Tender' finds Madonna sounding part Chrissie Hynde, part Debbie Harry over a ska-influenced beat. She also evokes a female Joe Jackson, emulating the sides he had recently cut for A&M Records. 'No Time (For Love)' follows a similar theme. 'Bells Ringing,' which sounds like a template for Belinda Carlisle's later solo career, is the most successful track, while 'Drowning' is the closest to Madonna's subsequent solo material.

It was around this time that Camille Barbone entered Madonna's life. Barbone and business partner Adam Alter owned the recording studios on West 39th Street where Emmy were rehearsing. She agreed to manage Madonna on the condition that she ditch Emmy—something to which Madonna soon agreed. Although Emmy split up more or less as soon as Camille Barbone arrived on the scene, being in the group had encouraged Madonna to focus on playing live and writing. Dancing on its own hadn't proved successful—and neither, here, had music. But if the two could be put together, maybe something very special could happen ...

Barbone gave Madonna a salary and put her up in an apartment. A live band followed, with John Bonamassa on keyboards, John Kaye on bass, Bob Riley on drums, and Jon Gordon on lead guitar. Riley left the band after a brief affair with Madonna and was replaced by Stephen Bray.

Madonna began to write her own songs, principally with Bray. The music became a hybrid of the club sounds of the time and huge splashes of new wave. She was beginning to build a following through hard work, playing gigs around New York highlighting the demo tape that the group had recorded for Gotham Records at Mediasound Studios in August 1981.

The demo tracks were a vibrant mixture of the early 80s, with all of Madonna's influences paraded unsubtly: Phil Spector overtones in 'I Want You'; ska sounds on 'Love On The Run.' There were, however, few immediate takers for this sound. It stretched the relationship between Madonna and Barbone until Madonna severed ties with her in February 1982.

Madonna became ever more of a face on the New York scene, playing or dancing at Danceteria and the Mudd Club. It was at Danceteria that Madonna approached DJ and A&R man Mark Kamins with a demo of a song that she and Stephen Bray had been working on called 'Everybody.' Kamins—at the time possibly the hippest player on the entire New York scene—was impressed by what he heard and played it there and then.

Kamins and Madonna became lovers. He took her tape to Chris Blackwell, who he worked for as an A&R man at Island Records. Blackwell was an astute judge of commercial potential, but this time he passed. Undeterred, Kamins took the tape to another executive he'd worked for before: Sire Records boss Seymour Stein.

Stein was more interested, and in the summer of 1982 he signed Madonna to a $5,000, two-single deal with Sire, which had made its name as a hugely respected, left-of-center record label. Although bankrolled by the mighty Warner Bros, the label had retained an air of independence borne out by quirky, leftfield acts such as The Ramones, The B-52s, The Pretenders, and, most notably, Talking Heads.

Finally, Madonna had been properly recognized. Although the deal was hardly auspicious, she was on her way.

CHAPTER 2
THE ARRIVAL

When 'Everybody' was finally released as a single in October 1982, the only thing to differentiate it from the raft of similar singles by artists such as Sharon Redd, Evelyn King, or D-Train was that Madonna was white. The sound and feel was distinctly from the street corners, with a splash of Talking Heads-style kookiness—a hangover from Emmy—thrown in.

Although the record made few waves, it was in the main warmly received and led to the release of a second single under Madonna's two-record deal with Sire, 'Burning Up,' in March 1983. Thoroughly impressed with Madonna's desire to succeed and her tunes' canny dance-pop sensibility, and pleased with the modest success of the two singles, Sire president Seymour Stein green-lit an album deal.

The deal underlined the faith Stein had in her. He had, after all, signed her initial record deal while in hospital recovering from an infection. As soon as he heard the demo of 'Everybody,' he later recalled, "I got so excited, I said: I want to sign her right away. I want you to bring her to the hospital. ... I got off the phone, and I looked at myself in the mirror. I was wearing the hospital garb, with the slit up my ass, and I needed a haircut, a shave and a good shower. I got a barber to come cut my hair, and I got my secretary to come with a pair of pajamas and a bathrobe. I wanted her to look at somebody who she thought would be around for a few years to help guide her career—not somebody who was in hospital on the way out. I managed to get it all together by the time she got there."

Stein quickly saw how determined Madonna was to succeed. "To my amazement and disappointment, as anxious as I was to sign her, she was just as anxious to jumpstart her career. If I was lying in a coffin on top of the bed and could get my hand out to sign a contract, she would have been happy. I'm glad I made a presentable appearance, but it was absolutely unnecessary."

If anything, *Madonna* is more a diary of a period of time than a cohesive collection of songs. DJ Mark Kamins had 'discovered' Madonna and helped secure the deal with Sire; in return, it was alleged, she had promised him the job of the producing the album. But she had also guaranteed the gig to her boyfriend and co-writer, Stephen Bray. In the end she chose neither. Working with the small and dedicated A&R team at Sire, led by Michael Rosenblatt, she was open to suggestion and experimentation.

"Madonna is great," Rosenblatt later said. "She will do anything to be a star, and that's exactly what I look for in an artist: total co-operation. With Madonna, I knew I had someone hot and co-operative, so I planned to build her career with singles, rather than just put an album out right away and run the risk of disaster."

As 'Everybody' broke through in the clubs, Madonna took a personal interest in assisting with the promotion, sitting in with Sire dance-promotion man Bobby Shaw during his Friday meetings with New York disc jockeys. It was through these associations that she met the man who would become her new paramour, John 'Jellybean' Benitez. He would prove invaluable in getting her name out into the wider community of tastemakers.

With everything building, an album started to come together. Madonna decided not to work with Kamins, who in reality was more of a figurehead than a hands-on producer, or Bray, who was capable and loyal yet untested, and instead chose the experienced writer-producer Reggie Lucas to oversee the album. "I was really scared," she later said. "I thought I'd been given a golden egg. In my mind I thought: okay, Mark can produce the album and Steve can play the instruments. It was really awful but I didn't trust him enough." (Bray was exceptionally annoyed. Although he would return to the Madonna camp after a suitable cooling-off period, he had initially informed Madonna of her lack of morals and swiftly departed. Ironically, he ended up drumming with Dan and Ed Gilroy in The Breakfast Club.)

Even for a woman who has had her fair share of controversial lovers, Madonna's relationship with Jean-Michel Basquiat was one of her most notorious. The first African-American artist to achieve success in the USA, Basquiat was born in Brooklyn to a Puerto Rican mother and Haitian father.

Encouraged to paint and draw from an early age, he had an unerring belief that he would one day be famous. He began spray-painting graffiti art with his friend Al Diaz in 1977, using the tag 'Samo'—an abbreviation of the phrase 'same old shit.'

Basquiat abandoned the Samo project as soon as it began to gain mention in publications such as the Village Voice. After attending school in New York, he dropped out and lived with friends, scratching a living selling self-designed postcards. He formed a band called Gray, which played all the requisite downtown places, and his local celebrity was such that he appeared in the video for 'Rapture' by Blondie. By the start of the 80s his work was regularly exhibited in New York and was labeled as part of the Neo-expressionist movement.

In late 1982, Basquiat met Madonna. Ed Steinberg, who directed the video for 'Everybody,' recalled that she "came up to me at a party and asked me to introduce her to 'that beautiful black boy in the corner.'" The affair between aspiring singer and artist was heated and intense. Christopher Ciccone, who was taken by his sister to meet Basquiat, later suggested that Basquiat's artistic credibility lent Madonna "the street cred she need[ed]."

The affair was brief. Basquiat's casual use of hard drugs and their attendant rituals alienated Madonna, and by early 1983 the relationship had sputtered out. Although his fame and notoriety grew—he worked with Andy Warhol between 1984 and 1986—it was said that Basquiat never quite got over Madonna. He died five years later of a heroin overdose, his descent into drug addiction triggered by the early death of Warhol. Basquiat occupied a special place in Madonna's heart as well. When they split, he gave her two paintings, one of which still hangs on a marble ledge in her New York apartment to this day.

Recorded at New York's Sigma Sound, with five of its eight songs written by Madonna herself, *Madonna* represents the heat and rush of a city, and indeed marks the last time Madonna would be writing directly at street level. Reggie Lucas brought experience with him. Primarily a guitarist, he had first risen to prominence while playing in Miles Davis's electric band from 1972–76. It was through Davis that he first worked with percussionist James Mtume. Mtume and Lucas formed a writing and production partnership, and by the start of the 80s had won a Grammy for 'Never Knew Love Like This Before,' a massive hit for Stephanie Mills. Lucas was an in-house producer at Warner Bros, Sire Records' parent company, and he certainly knew a thing or two about how records work on the radio. But he did not get on well with Madonna.

It went like this: Madonna would record the basic tracks, and then Lucas—as any experienced producer would do—began to polish and embellish, layering and overdubbing. It was here that he began to incur her wrath. "I thought [he] might be able to push me, having worked with Phyllis Hyman and Roberta Flack," she told the *New Musical Express* in November 1983. "The only problem was that he wanted to make me sound like them."

Try as she might, Madonna could not emulate an African-American diva. In fact, throughout her career, she has always been at her least convincing when giving her most 'soulful' performances—especially here, up against the impressive array of backing singers at Lucas's disposal on this record. The backing vocalists brought in to support Madonna—ex-Chic singer Norma Jean Wright, Gwen Guthrie, and session supremos Brenda White and Chrissy Faith—added weight to Madonna's unconventional and occasionally reedy voice.

In the end, Lucas and Madonna disagreed about the overall sound, and Lucas went off to his next project, leaving Madonna searching for an additional track to complete the album. "I wanted to push her in a pop direction," Lucas later recalled. "She was a little more orientated toward the disco thing, but I thought she had to appeal to the general market."

With Lucas gone, Madonna's current beau, John 'Jellybean' Benitez, came in to help finish off the album. Benitez knew talent when he saw it: "I thought she had a lot of style, and she crossed over a lot of boundaries because everyone in the rock clubs played her—the black clubs, the gay, the straight. Very few records have that appeal." Madonna and Benitez went back to Lucas's production and systematically removed a great deal of the embellishments.

Then, with 'Everybody' scaling the dance charts, Madonna wrote 'Lucky Star' for her friend Mark Kamins. It would be the song to take her to the next level of success. 'Lucky Star' is by far and away the best song she wrote for *Madonna,* and perhaps its most successful appropriation of the black music genre. From the firework-style synthesizer part that opens it to the bubbling, repetitive bassline, it is one of the classic album openers of Madonna's career.

Although it was written for Kamins, 'Lucky Star' can also be heard as a tribute to her mother. Madonna sings that the star is the first thing she sees every night, and that when she is lost, she just turns around "and you're by my side." As the beat gets more intense, the lyric switches to something a little more earthy, with Madonna asking the song's protagonist to "shine your heavenly body tonight." When 'Lucky Star' was issued as the final single from the album in August 1984—it was originally due to be the first, but in the end 'Holiday' took that honor—it gave Madonna her first Top Five hit single.

'Borderline' was the track that showed the possibilities of Madonna's talent beyond dance music. Written solely by Lucas, its radio-friendly pop-chart sound bore similarities to Prince's 'Little Red Corvette,' another record reaching out beyond a conventional audience at the time. Madonna sings with real conviction, and there's a sweetness and heart to the song that shows an appropriate change of character for the pop charts. Madonna really comes alive after four minutes: as she starts to sing around the melody, she produces one of the finest vocals of her career to date, thoroughly undermining the 'Minnie Mouse on helium' criticisms sometimes invoked about her early performances.

Critic J. Randy Taraborelli encapsulates the glory of this record perfectly with the remark, in his *Intimate Biography,* that the combination of Madonna's "not-so-great but affecting voice at the centre of Lucas' full, twinkling instrumentation ... made the track as close to an old Motown production as a hit could get in the dance-music driven 80s."

'Burning Up,' a fine piece of early-80s synth-pop/dance, returns the listener to more conventional territory. Although hardly fantastic, it contains a telling line about how, "unlike the others," Madonna would "do anything" and has "no shame"—her early mission statement, right here. Benitez added a distinctive guitar riff not unlike Adrian Belew's live work with Talking Heads, and the song was released as Madonna's second single in March 1983, with a cover designed by her friend Martin Burgoyne. Although it didn't reach the *Billboard* Top 100, it caused quite a stir on the club charts, peaking at Number Three on the *Billboard* Hot Dance Club Play list. It became something of a dance anthem through the spring of 1983, and stayed on the charts for some 16 weeks.

The album's fourth track, 'I Know It,' is three-and-a half minutes of very little. It sounds like an advert for the latest synthesizer, complete with synth brass and a tinny robotic percussive clatter. It's a dry run for the later 'True Blue'—it swaggers along and is redolent of the girl groups Madonna was so enthralled by, growing up in Detroit. It is amazing to think that, when this record came out, Madonna's immediate frame of reference was Cyndi Lauper. This is the moment she sounds most like her.

What broke the album on the broadest scale was one of the late additions, and the song that opens the second side of the original vinyl LP: 'Holiday,' written by Curtis Hudson and Lisa Stevens. Hudson and Stevens were known as Pure Energy; they'd had a UK hit, 'Bodywork,' under the name Hot Streak. 'Holiday' had originally been offered to Mary Wilson of The Supremes, but Madonna's gleeful interpretation of it is what set her fully on the path to superstardom. Although anything that ends up on a liner note at Madonna level is clearly going to be artist-sanctioned, Gene Sculatti's notes for Madonna's first greatest hits set, *The Immaculate Collection*, contain one of the best encapsulations of the glory of 'Holiday.' The song "simply rocked—gently but insistently—with melodic sweetness," he writes. "It's irresistible pop, and easily one of the most persuasive let's-get-lost songs ever sung."

It was the mix of style and substance that made 'Holiday' stand out. After all, these were the tail-end days of a recession, the new Cold War was at is zenith, and the two key records of the year were telling us to 'Relax' and have a 'Holiday.' The record—and Madonna—coincided with the world struggling out of economic gloom. Madonna acted as a cheerful if slightly naughty cheerleader to pull us all out of it. All of which meant that the lesser tracks on *Madonna*—and let's be frank, 'I Know It,' 'Think Of Me,' and 'Physical Attraction' are no more than moderately generic early-80s, OB-X synthesizer-led pop—were dwarfed by it. 'Holiday' is simply one long chorus, and as UK critic Rikki Rooksby suggests: "You're either on this six-minute carousel or you're getting nauseous watching it go round and round."

It was also with 'Holiday' that Madonna broke cover: after the generic artwork used for 'Everybody' and 'Burning Up,' here she was, front and center, on the cover. This caused some alarm in the South as it became apparent that Madonna was not, in fact, African-American. "It's changing now; just people are more aware of what I'm about and what I can do," she told the *New Musical Express*. "It didn't offend white people, but I think it offended radio programmers in the South. I think that's just reverse racism." As her first charting single, 'Holiday' will always have a special place in Madonna's—and her fans'—heart.

Madonna continues with 'Think Of Me,' a sweet piece of filler, with Madonna once again demanding the attention of a lover. Over a standard 80s synth groove, she points out her importance to him (and therefore the listener, too). There can be no one else but her. The song is topped off by a tenor saxophone solo by the Stanley Clarke and Stevie Wonder veteran Bobby Malach.

Next up is another of Reggie Lucas's compositions, 'Physical Attraction.' The B-side to the 'Burning Up' single, it is nothing remarkable. The breakdown around three minutes in is not dissimilar to anything else that was being released out of New York in 1983, to the point that it already sounded dated by the time most people got to hear it in 1984. The spoken word section in the middle would later provide inspiration for the introduction to 'Into The Groove.' By the time the record dissolves into words that rhyme with 'attraction' after six minutes, the listener is relieved to bid it farewell.

The album ends as it started, with 'Everybody' playing it out to reunite everybody on the dance floor. 'Everybody' already sounded dated—it was, after all, already over a year old. It is, however, really rather sweet, and offers the keynote to Madonna's entire subsequent career. It is only on the dance floor that she will ever find that level of freedom. You dance and sing, get up and do your thing. All the troubles of the world simply melt away. When you listen to 'Everybody' now, its debt to the *Remain In Light*-era Talking Heads—particularly the gentle, burbling synthesizers—is remarkable. (There's also a huge dollop of Kashif's productions for Evelyn King.)

And that was it: just eight tracks to launch Madonna into the world. There had been nine at one stage: 'Ain't No Big Deal' had originally been intended for the album but was dropped. So, and with very little fanfare, Madonna's debut album was released in July 1983. Among the thank-you notes were messages to Mark Kamins, stylist Maripol, "my darling Martin" (dancer Martin Burgoyne), Jellybean Benitez, dancers Erica Bell and Bags Rilez, Michael Rosenblatt, and publicist Liz Rosenberg. Reggie Lucas and Stephen Bray were conspicuous by their absence. Touchingly and simply, the final credit reads: "This album is dedicated to my father."

After some serious discussion about whether the album should be called *Lucky Star*, the title ended up simply as *Madonna*. At the time, it was difficult to discern just how different she would be. Given the album's three producers and the relative lack of light and shade in the material, the whole thing sounds a trifle flat, considering the exuberance of some of the songs. It is the sound of 1982–83, and the sound of an earnest artist making her way in the world. She would never take such a laissez-faire approach to the process again, and from here on would demand complete control over her sessions, choice of musicians, producers, and material. "I didn't realize how crucial it was for me to break out of the disco mould before I'd nearly finished the [first] album," she later admitted. "I wish I could have got a little more variety there."

Madonna drew cautious and possibly even hesitant reviews; it wasn't as if it was the greatest and most innovative album that has ever been released. In 1990, Greg Kot of the *Chicago Tribune* looked back at the album and noted: "Though her voice sounded thin, pinched, girlish, her personality was provocative, sexy, and aggressive—qualities that her early singles hinted at, but which her videos fully exploited." A decade later, in *Uncut* magazine, Gavin Martin wrote: "The sparse grooves and electro effects drew on the New York club culture that bred her but 'Borderline' introduced her calling card—a knack for simple melody and (double) meaning."

The artwork certainly drew some attention. In stark and somewhat over-exposed black-and-white, the shot by Gary Heery of Madonna with one hand against the side of her face and the other tugging on the huge chain around her neck set her immediately—perfectly—in context. She was not your average disco diva, but something more like a street punk. The picture on the inner sleeve—with bare midriff on show—would soon start a trend. "The picture inside the dust sleeve of my first album has me in this Betty Boop pose with my bellybutton showing," Madonna explained to *Time* magazine in 1985. "Then when people reviewed the album, they kept talking about my cute bellybutton. I started thinking about it and I said: yeah, well, I do like my bellybutton. I think there are other un-obvious places on my body that are sexy and the stomach is kind of innocent. I don't have a really flat stomach. I sort of have a little girl's stomach. It's round and the skin is smooth and it's nice. I like it ... "

When Madonna first appeared on the wider public stage, her style had been honed over several years of hard work and magpie-ism. Her look was, in part, inspired by punk—especially the ragamuffin approach of The Slits' vocalist, Viv Albertine—yet her fashion sense was a ragbag of street chic accessorized to the point of excess.

It was while she was living in New York's East Village that Madonna gained the greatest inspiration for her early look. Frequenting flea markets and used stores, she would mismatch her colors, styles, and accessories: lace and lycra; sweat tops and dresses; layering and finding unity in the most wayward of matches. The Puerto Rican influence of the area informed her look and her work; hip-hop, street culture, and graffiti art would all contribute to Madonna's mix. She was partial to breakdancing and would later incorporate it into her 'Borderline' video. Her graffiti tag—'Boy Toy'—became one of her early signifiers.

Well used to dressing for a reaction, Madonna and her friends the Webo Girls (named after a brief Hispanic dance craze that involved a great deal of sexual thrusting) sought to confront with their look, studying the effect they would have on passers-by. Madonna made no secret of her inspiration in a

1985 *Vanity Fair* interview, describing her appearance as "the combination of the dance and the ragamuffin and the new wave and this Puerto Rican street style."

On her early visits to the UK to promote 'Everybody,' Madonna was still finding her feet. "The way we dress is sort of playful-innocent: Bermuda shorts, ankle socks and shoes, crazy hats," she told *Flexipop!* magazine in 1983. "I don't wanna wear something that I'm going to fall out of. I don't feel comfortable like that. But I'm really physical on stage, y'know? I move around a lot."

For moving around, Madonna would appropriate the crop-top and black leggings from her dancing days, then popularized by the aerobics craze and the *Fame/Kids From Fame* phenomenon. In her crop-top, she would flaunt her navel. This was almost revolutionary in the early 80s and caused some alarm from reactionary America.

Madonna's friend Erika Belle styled and designed some of her early outfits, but it was teaming up with French-born, New York-based jewelry designer and retailer Maripol that crystallized Madonna's look. The pair had been friends on the social circuit for some time, while Maripol would soon become art director at Fiorucci in New York.

Maripol styled Madonna for her first two albums. The artwork for *Madonna* embodied the singer's early look with chains, bracelets, and bangles. The bracelets Madonna wore were actually amended electric typewriter drive-bands. The incorporation of Catholic symbolism, crucifixes, and rosaries, would become commonplace in Madonna's varied palette, but came initially at Maripol's suggestion. "For Madonna it was meant to be something very spiritual," she explained in 2007. "I was also raised Catholic, and Madonna and I both rebelled to that. My mother didn't like it. It was a way to [ask] why if I wear it on the ear it makes me a less good catholic girl?"

Maripol's involvement made real all of the work that Madonna had already done. "She came to me and I just styled a bunch of things on her," Maripol continued. "I was already making the rubber jewelry and I was already making the crosses because of my love for the punks. So it was perfect for her ... Erika Bell used to make a lot of her clothes, I would give her clothes from Fiorucci—it was a mix of everything." It was this "mix of everything" that would appeal to millions of fans. For once, they wouldn't have to try too hard to emulate their favorite pop star.

It was during this period that Madonna got her first proper manager, Freddy DeMann, fresh from his success with Michael Jackson. "I remember when she first walked into my office," he recalled in 1991. "I was absolutely smitten with her. She had three problems that day, three pressing problems, and I said: I'll make three calls and take care of your problems. And I did it. The next day she called with five problems. The next day she had eight … Madonna has that ability to grab you by the lapels and soon all you can think about is her."

Madonna was not going to sell on its own. It was all about the promotion: watching the album grow as Madonna marched from one lip-sync to another. She made two visits to Britain, where the UK underground seemed to appreciate her, and played shows miming to tape at London's Camden Palace and Manchester's hipper-than-thou Hacienda Club (run by Factory Records), where her performance was filmed for the British television show *The Tube*.

Madonna was simply not going to let the album fall from the racks. She began a major charm offensive with her record company, making sure that she targeted the key movers—the sales teams as well as the A&R and marketing departments. It was later reported that there was great surprise when she walked into Warner Bros' Los Angeles office. One executive was quoted as saying: "She sounded black and in pops this blond. Everybody was stunned. She charmed the pants off everyone there."

In November 1983, Madonna went home to Michigan for Thanksgiving. It was the first time she'd seen her father for the best part of two years. In January 1984, she made her national television debut and was asked by *American Bandstand*'s veteran host Dick Clark about her ambition. "To rule the world," she said, spontaneous as you like.

Soon after that, Freddy DeMann handed over Madonna's first big royalty check. She peeked at the numbers and said: "At least I don't have to take the subway any more." 'Holiday,' which synthesized everything Madonna had thus far been attempting, was hitting the charts round the world. "My inspiration is simply that I love to dance," she told the *New Musical Express*. "All I wanted to do was make a record that I would want to dance to, and I did. Then I wanted to go one step further and make a record that people would listen to on the radio."

The album was given the classic slow-burn reception. It was the success of the singles that really helped it on its way. 'Holiday' was the first, reaching Number 16 on *Billboard*, before 'Borderline' reached Number Ten in March 1984; her ascent continued with the release of 'Lucky Star,' which reached Number Four after coming out in August.

Madonna was truly on her way. *Madonna* was certified gold by the RIAA by the end of May 1984, and by the turn of the century it had sold five times Platinum. Its success kept on going—as her next album, *Like A Virgin* exploded, many people went back and bought the first album alongside its shiny successor. It was actually repackaged in Europe with a different, color sleeve in August 1985 and renamed *Madonna—The First Album*.

Madonna was finally solvent, yet she kept caution uppermost in her mind. "The first expensive thing I bought was a Roland synthesizer," she later said. "The next big money I got was publishing money for writing songs ... the first extravagant thing I bought that I felt guilty about was a color TV."

Around the time of the album's release, Madonna told the *New Musical Express*: "In America, Warners don't know how to push me as a disco artist or as new wave because of the way I look. I'd rather just start another category. You just have to be patient. I'm not." Within the next year she would indeed establish her very own category—that simply of 'Madonna.' To reiterate what her manager, Freddy DeMann, said: "Madonna has that ability to grab you by the lapels and soon all you can think about is her."

CHAPTER 3
LIKE A VIRGIN

I f ever an album defined an artist and cemented her image in the popular consciousness it was *Like A Virgin*. As the head of steam from her debut album continued to build, it was with *Like A Virgin* that Madonna successfully synthesized all the music she had heard growing up in Detroit and New York. Here, Madonna took Chic's smart disco, the style and glamour of Studio 54, and the prevailing more-is-more attitude of the Ronald Reagan administration and put it all through a punk filter. Although she had enjoyed considerable chart success with her debut album, it was this, her second album, that would change the face of pop in the 80s.

As early as mid 1983, mere weeks after the release of her debut album, Madonna was already clear about what she wanted to do next. "I now know what I want on my next record," she told the *New Musical Express*. "The production won't be so slick, because where Reggie and Mtume come from is a whole different school. I want a sound that's mine. There will be a more crossover approach to it this time. Maybe I should work with a British producer."

She didn't end up with a British producer, but she did get an American obsessed with British acts: Nile Rodgers. "It's funny about the thing with Kamins and Bray," Reggie Lucas later noted, reflecting on the changes of producer on *Madonna*. "The same thing that happened to them pretty much happened to me on her second record when they had Nile Rodgers."

It was something of a stroke of genius for Madonna to work with a 'name' producer for her second album—particularly since, in late 1983, Rodgers was probably the hottest producer in the world. He had been one half of the writing and production team of Chic, the group that seemingly rose without a trace in 1977 to meet the disco explosion head-on. With his partner, Bernard Edwards, he produced the effortless grooves that encapsulated a musical movement that made a virtue out of hedonistic pleasure. People were simply too busy dancing to spot the astute political references and sarcasm of their work. Their first major hit, 'Dance, Dance, Dance (Yowsah, Yowsah, Yowsah),' referenced the 1969 film *They Shoot Horses, Don't They?*, which was about the dance marathons that used to take place in the wake of Wall Street Crash. The marathons would go on for days, with couples dancing for money and some passing out—and in some cases even dying—on the dance floor. The subsequent 'Le Freak' mentioned Studio 54 in its lyrics, went to Number One, and became Atlantic's biggest-selling single of all time.

Chic's greatest moment, 'Good Times,' came out in 1979 on the eve of one of the worst worldwide recessions since the 30s. Rodgers's lyrics paraphrased the Great Depression-era standard 'Happy Days Are Here Again,' and his ironic comment raced to the US Number One spot. Chic then experience their own crash, however, when the Disco Sucks movement reached it popular peak with a Disco Demolition at Chicago's Comiskey Park in July 1979. As the group seemed to have no past apart from disco—unlike fellow travelers Kool & The Gang and Earth Wind & Fire—they seemed to suffer the most commercially, and they never again reached the heights of their late-70s chart success.

Rodgers had had a formidable past and was keen to prove himself outside the realms of the group. He was something of a bohemian self-taught prodigy, sitting in on classes at Juilliard and jamming with Jimi Hendrix at Electric Lady Studios. He'd been a member of the Manhattan Chapter of the Black Panthers before he started playing guitar for a living. He played with both Harlem's Apollo Theater house band and the touring production of Sesame Street. Through these gigs he met Edwards, and while backing the group New York City they hatched plans for their own group.

Madonna's frame of reference had also changed since the recording of her first album. Realizing her own potential, she now saw Prince and Michael Jackson—rather than her New York peers on the post-new-wave scene—as her rivals. Here were two stars who had broken clear of their dance roots and were on their way to global success. Jackson's *Thriller*, in particular, was now well over a year old, and yet was still high in the charts, with countless singles being mined from it. These were the artists Madonna would need to pitch herself against.

Guitarist and songwriter Rodgers was an astute choice to help her achieve that. For his work with Chic alone, he would have been an obvious candidate. His production work with Diana Ross, Sister Sledge, and Madonna's one-time idol, Debbie Harry—that would have been enough, too. But there was more. Rodgers was currently at the absolute peak of his game. He had recently succeeded in turning David Bowie into a mega-platinum superstar for the first time in his illustrious left-of-center career with an album of uptown New York dance grooves entitled *Let's Dance*. Released in April 1983, it gave Bowie his first proper, long-lasting chart hits. In short, Rodgers was hot, and the combination of his disco past and commercial present made Rodgers irresistible to Madonna.

Like A Virgin marked the start of a period during which it was virtually impossible for Madonna to do anything without it being slavishly reported by the world's media. Bringing her personal politics to the global stage, she became the ultimate proof of how hard work, luck, and an ear for what's 'now' can be commodified and marketed to the widest possible audience. But when Rodgers was first asked to produce her, she was just another dance artist who had enjoyed moderate success after years on the New York scene.

Until now, Madonna had wasted nothing and left little to chance. She had taken everything in and pondered how best to mass-market it. Her years of hanging around studios, mixing freely between African-American, Hispanic, and gay scenes, and dancing and singing while stealthily pursuing and building her career meant that she was almost entirely free of the prejudice that had been rife within the music industry. But she did not suffer fools gladly. She was completely focused on making it. She had seen what could happen when she took her eyes off the prize with her first album. She'd told American television that her aim was to rule the world, but she later told *The Face* magazine that she'd been misrepresented: what she really wanted to do was "stand next to God."

Recording for what became *Like A Virgin* began in New York in April 1984. By then, several changes were afoot, with the aim being to take Madonna to the widest possible audience. In Freddy DeMann, Madonna had an astute manager who had guided Michael Jackson on his path to megastardom. He and Jackson had recently parted ways, leaving DeMann free to spend time working with Madonna. And he could certainly recognize her star quality.

Rodgers made a key change to Madonna's sound that would enhance the success of the forthcoming album. When he heard her rough demos, they were very much along the lines of her debut album: heavily sequenced and synthesizer-led. Rodgers felt it important that she play with a live band. But this would not be just any old live band—this was the core of Chic.

Like A Virgin was a phenomenon. It took Madonna's songs and made them sound coherent, full, and—most importantly—muscular. This was music that could stand up to the test, whether it was played in the clubs or on FM radio. Working at the soon-to-be-legendary Power Station studios in Manhattan with young engineer Jason Corsaro, Rodgers marshaled the troops—the same line-up that had played behind Bowie on *Let's Dance*—to make a chart-friendly record.

Madonna had again written several songs alone, and Stephen Bray had returned to assist on three more. Jimmy Bralower added shine to the work with his electronic drum programming, which worked in tandem with Tony Thompson's live work. Madonna was in the studio for every minute of the six weeks it took to make the album.

Drummer Thompson, who helped make the sound so distinctive, remembered making the album with affection. He would eat Chinese food with Madonna in a restaurant around the corner from The Power Station. But his partner of the time—Chic string player Karen Milne, who also appears on the album—was not treated with such affection. "I was hanging out," she said in 2004. "I was there when Tony, Bernard, and Nile would lay down the rhythm tracks. I don't think Madonna liked having other women around. Tony came home one night and said they didn't want anybody else there. The string sessions, however, went fine—even though [Madonna] was inexperienced, she was really clear about what she wanted. She was such a businesswoman. I really respected her a lot—just amazing to watch. She got along great with Nile and Bernard and she liked Tony a lot."

Madonna showed her fire and flint by taking little nonsense from her players, however respected they may have been. "One morning Bernard was an hour late," Edwards's friend, Duran Duran bassist John Taylor, later recalled. "When he arrived, she went off on one, saying that nobody should be late for her sessions. We were gobsmacked when we heard that anyone could do that to Bernard. Where I was coming from, Bernard was a god— to her, he was just the fucking bass player, a hired musician. She had no sense of the history, which was really scary." The mercurial bassist had been struggling somewhat in the shadows of the recent successes achieved by Rodgers, his former partner in Chic. "He's late because he's struggling with his life, but he's one of the greatest talents in the world," Taylor continued. "She should have been fucking grateful that he was going to contribute two hours to her record."

The occasional tensions were masked by an overall camaraderie, however, and a very strong selection of songs. Perhaps the most successful aspect of Rodgers's production of the album was the way he varied the material, not keeping everything at dancing fever pitch. He allowed Madonna to demonstrate her ability with a ballad, and to show that she could handle them just as well as the dance-floor belters that had become her signature style.

Madonna was delighted with the overall result. She felt this was a much more aggressive album than her debut, later noting that she had "chosen all the songs, and I want them all to be hits—no fillers. That's why I've done outside songs as well as six of my own … I wanted every song to be strong." It would of course be two songs that were externally written—'Like A Virgin' and 'Material Girl'—that sealed her success. "I liked them both because they were ironic and provocative at the same time, but so unlike me," she revealed 25 years later. "I am not a materialistic person, and I certainly wasn't a virgin—and, by the way, how can you be *like a virgin*? I liked the play on words. I thought they were clever. They're so geeky, they're cool."

The album begins with the remarkably successful 'Material Girl.' Written by former TK Records soul/disco artist Peter Brown and Robert Rans, it is jaunty and crashing, loud and remarkable, tongue-in-cheek tits-out sass. The coyness and charm in the vocal marks out immediately that this is a new Madonna and a new approach. (The deep male backing voices heard throughout were provided by The Simms Brothers.)

Of course, the song's double meaning was totally lost on those who wished only to accept it literally—something that would give Madonna grief over the years to come. "God forbid irony should be understood," she later said. "When I'm 90, I'll still be the material girl. I guess it's not so bad—Lana Turner was the sweater girl until the day she died."

As the second single from the album, 'Material Girl' made Top Fives across the world. *LA Weekly* later suggested that the song "represents the first time Madonna displayed her knack for telling half a story and letting the listeners argue over her meaning and motive." Madonna has always enjoyed a complex relationship with the song, rarely playing it live.

The album's second track, 'Angel,' has worn very well over time and is possibly the best song here. It was destined to be the third single from the record, reaching the US Top Five and hitting the Number One spot in Australia. It was one of the first songs written for the project, reuniting Madonna and Stephen Bray. It showed how willing they were from the outset to write outside the dance idiom that had sometimes straitjacketed her debut album. With its infectious synth-string introduction and Madonna's double-tracked laugh—a clear echo of Alison Moyet's vocal on the 1983 dance hit 'Situation' by Yaz—its upbeat brio is totally in-keeping with the bright, shiny veneers of the album. Its sound, however, is close and intimate, and very different to the huge clatter and space of the songs either side of it, 'Material Girl' and 'Like A Virgin.' The synthesizer solo and refrain after two minutes add to the zip and polish of the groove, even if *Spin* magazine would later cite it disparagingly as an example of what Nile Rodgers did best: "turning crass product into cash product."

Warner Bros A&R man Michael Ostin chanced upon 'Like A Virgin' when he was listening to a selection of demos by Tom Kelly in LA. After playing Ostin several of their own numbers, Kelly and songwriting partner Billy Steinberg began to talk about a song they had written but had no appropriate artist to sing. By coincidence, Austin was meeting Madonna the next day to discuss her forthcoming album. He played her the song. She thought it was "sick and perverted"—in a good way—and fell instantly in love with it.

Rodgers was initially uncertain about the song, thinking the lyrical hook was not strong enough. Within a matter of days, however, he simply couldn't get the song out of his head—and this was a man who had been present at the birth of many a naggingly insistent hit. As the critic Gene Sculatti later wrote: "From now on, this 'shiny and new,' coolly understated single announced, Madonna records would confound all expectations, including those set by previous Madonna records."

The song caused a furor, of course. "I was surprised with how people reacted to 'Like A Virgin,'" Madonna later said, "because when I did the song, to me, I was singing about how something made me feel a certain way—brand new and fresh—and everyone else interpreted it as 'I don't want to be a virgin any more. Fuck my brains out!' That's not what I sang at all."

On top of all that, it was a fantastic record to dance to. A 12-inch mix was prepared using the prevailing disco-cowbell sound heard on other records of the time, such as Ronni Griffith's superb reading of 'The Best Part Of Breaking Up.'

After that breathtaking opening trio, *Like A Virgin* continues with 'Over and Over.' This one, a hit single in Italy, feels more routine, its repetition putting Madonna back in the clubs of her youth. She never played it again after the Virgin Tour of 1985, but while the song seems crystallized in that time, its mixture of resilience and tenacity made it very personal to her.

'Love Don't Live Here Anymore' was an astute choice of cover version. It was written by Miles Gregory, while the original by Rose Royce was one of 1978's finest ballads. Rodgers himself had tried to emulate the sound on 'A Warm Summer's Night,' from Chic's album *Risqué*. Madonna's take on the song is one that easily splits the crowd. With Rodgers's string arrangement flailing away in the background, Madonna gives it her all, with her fevered repetition of "live here anymore" becoming a bit too overbearing by the song's close. *The Face* magazine was among the dissenters, calling it "an unfortunate sacrilege to the memory of the old Rose Royce song." The song was nonetheless released as a single in Japan in 1986, and retained a special place in Madonna's affections—it is included on her 1995 album of reflective ballads, *Something To Remember*.

Track six, 'Dress You Up,' was the fourth and final single to be drawn from the album. It's bright and campy radio-friendly pop, complete with one of Nile Rodgers's best heavy-rock guitar solos (a possible nod to Eddie Van

Halen's successful cameo on Michael Jackson's 'Beat It'). Written by Andrea LaRusso and Peggy Stanziale, it was the last song to be added to the album. Madonna heard it, liked the fashion metaphors, and thought it perfect for inclusion. In it, she implores her lover to "feel the silky touch of my caresses" before she "create[s] a look that's made for you." The song's marriage of fashion and sex later incurred the wrath of the Parents' Music Resource Center, but it all seems rather innocent in light of some of the other things Madonna would later sing about. It became her sixth consecutive Top Five hit in the USA, and an enduring favorite—one that has featured in several of her live shows, notably on the Who's That Girl World Tour, where she sang it in glasses and a fruit-bowl wig.

Madonna's only solo composition for the album, 'Shoo-Bee-Doo,' is its overlooked gem—a fine ballad that provides some respite after all the noise and size elsewhere. Released as the B-side to 'Dress You Up,' it features one of Madonna's most sensual vocal performances and a throaty, emotional sax solo by Lenny Pickett of The Borneo Horns. The title harks back to the girl groups so beloved of Madonna's youth, and perhaps also hints at the baby talk she and Benitez reportedly used to indulge in.

Like A Virgin gets a little pedestrian toward the end. The mid-tempo Stephen Bray co-write 'Pretender' sounds sluggish, while 'Stay' is a jittery, skittering closer that evokes 'I Know It' from *Madonna*. It is not high art, but it highlights Rodgers's most skillful trick: marrying Madonna with male backing vocalists and ensuring that nobody steals her thunder on record in the way that Norma Jean Wright and Gwen Guthrie did on *Madonna*. The doo-wop play-out after three minutes, with its jolly, mannered scat singing, seems a strange way to end such a tumultuous album. As if with a wink to the camera, Madonna even does a sly David Bowie impersonation.

Although the second side tapers off, veering toward filler, Rodgers had at least managed to make the album sound like a whole work. Noting the success of 'Borderline,' he allowed Madonna to explore her ballad side more, and found that her voice was surprisingly well suited to something a little more down-tempo.

With Madonna's debut—issued to little fanfare the previous year—starting to explode across the world, plans were hatched for a summer 1984 release of her second album. Nile Rodgers received a call from Warner Bros, asking whether *Like A Virgin* should be delayed. "I said: do you want to know the truth? I'd release another single [from *Madonna*], because that shit is happening. We then drop the album after 'Borderline' and 'Lucky Star'—holy shit—biggest record of my life, biggest record of her life."

Warners had initially been apprehensive about abandoning the out-and-out dance approach of the first album but, once they began to live with the new record, they saw its enormous potential. It also gave the company time to ready the lead video for the album's title track—and meant everything was timed perfectly for Madonna to make enormous waves at the 1984 MTV Awards in September.

Madonna's performance at the inaugural MTV Awards was her equivalent of The Beatles appearance on *The Ed Sullivan Show* 20 years previously. It might not have been seen by so many people, but its impact was stunning and immediate. If you weren't aware of her already, well, here she was.

The show was broadcast from New York's Radio City Music Hall on September 14 1984 and featured her performance of the as-yet unreleased title track to her new album. The performance opened with Madonna, bedecked in Maripol accessories, at the top of huge three-tiered wedding cake, dressed in white bustier, stockings, and wedding gown (complete with veil), her groom a storefront mannequin—a none-too-subtle underlining of the fact that this performer needed no man to share her stage.

As the camera pans closer, Madonna's Boy Toy belt—at first glance so provocative, so shocking—appears in full view. Her singing might be somewhat faltering, but her demeanor is one of pure sass and confidence. You can sense the unease in the crowd—surely this was the disco diva who sang about going on holiday? But no one could get between the key relationship here—Madonna and the camera lens. As she moves down the cake, she removes her veil, and then lets down her hair—an exaggerated movie-like cartoon of a bride on her wedding night. And then the writhing on the floor begins.

MTV had, of course, been absolutely central to Madonna's success to date, airing the videos from her first album in heavy rotation. After this performance was aired nationally, it was followed by the promo video for 'Like A Virgin,' shot by Mary Lambert in July. When the single was released in November, it raced to the top of the US charts and remained there for six weeks. Although Madonna would return to the MTV Awards many times subsequently, nothing lasts longer in the memory than her unveiling here as a world superstar; and not only did she have the single, but she had the album to match.

Eventually released in November 1984, *Like A Virgin* would make Madonna a household name. Dedicated to "the virgins of the world," the Rodgers-produced opus yielded four US Top Five singles: the title track (Number One for six weeks), 'Material Girl' (Number Two), 'Angel,' and 'Dress You Up' (both Number Five). Madonna again thanked Maripol and Martin Burgoyne in the liner notes, while extending extra special thanks to "my family for nurturing my strange behavior" and "Freddy DeMann for knowing what to do with it." To John 'Jellybean' Benitez she offered a simple "Goo Goo Ga Ga."

Reviews of the album were largely positive, if tentative. As the taste-making British magazine *The Face* put it: "Her music is developing, refining the early disco-dolly style into a purer pop, but also straying into other areas of black-influenced music. There are some refreshing echoes of Motown on the new LP." *Rolling Stone* put Madonna on the cover in November 1985, but *People* seemed ambivalent, calling the album "a tolerable bit of fluff" and noting: "[While] Ciccone does have a sense of humor ... she is buried under so many layers of self-parody it's hard to tell sometimes." A half-decade later, *LA Weekly*'s Danny (Shredder) Weizmann pointed out: "Second albums are historically dry-up time, especially for phenomena, but by amping up the elements, *Like A Virgin* became not a second album so much as another debut."

Opinion remains split. On allmusic.com, Stephen Thomas Erlewine writes that, beyond its two main singles, "the album vacillates wildly in terms of quality." For *Billboard*, it manages to sustain "a fevered dance-rock momentum." It has been cited by the National Association Of Recording

Merchandisers and the Rock & Roll Hall Of Fame as one of the definitive 200 albums of all time.

Like A Virgin was like an all-you-can-eat buffet—the sound of an artist making it. While the image of Madonna on her debut album was what first introduced her to people, it was he collaboration with Maripol on *Like A Virgin* that was to define her. Maripol styled Madonna and oversaw the cover image, which was shot by Steven Meisel at the St Regis Hotel in Uptown New York. Initially, Sire had wanted Madonna to be styled in the vein of a 'Black Sabbath Madonna.' Maripol disagreed and suggested that the aura of the track 'Like A Virgin' be brought out, especially as it was going to be difficult for even the most sheltered soul to believe that Madonna was still virginal.

On the *Virgin* jacket, Madonna looks out from her bed wearing a customized wedding dress. What caused the greatest commotion was the making explicit of Madonna's old graffiti tag in the form of her Maripol-designed Boy Toy belt, which Madonna is shown seductively encircling between her lace-gloved hands. The connotations cannot be over-emphasized. In six simple letters, the belt confronted and provoked. Although the idea was ostensibly that Madonna was a plaything for men, the more you realized her strength of character, the more you realized it was in fact she who toyed with the boys.

The artwork, shot by Steven Meisel, underlined the importance of the star. Its stunning before-and-after juxtaposition hinted at the Hipgnosis story-jackets of the 70s: here was the buxom, disheveled singer looking anything but virginal, lying on her bed with come-hither eyes. It was irresistible.

It was the back-cover photograph—a sepia shot of Madonna straightening her stockings the morning after the night before—that would win over millions of teenage girls and engage millions more boys. Not every girl would want to wear a wedding dress with a Boy Toy belt, but they all knew how to look uncombed and unkempt. And it was this, coupled with the lyrical thrust of many of the songs, that disgusted parents across the world.

Like A Virgin truly succeeded in elevating Madonna to the superstar league of Prince and Michael Jackson. It was the sound of excitement, a team on the verge of breakthrough, working together to produce something that would be a lasting success—and that was down to the collaboration between Madonna and Nile Rodgers. "Few people knew that the whole Madonna thing was produced by Nile," Atlantic Records executive John DeMairo later recalled. "Whereas now, the whole business is so producer driven—it's like, oh wow, that's Timbaland—if it came out now it would be: Madonna Produced By Nile Rodgers. The whole scene … everything has changed so much."

Like A Virgin remains Madonna's biggest-selling studio album in the USA, with over ten million units sold. It spent three weeks atop the *Billboard* 200 in February 1985, and would remain on the chart for the next two years. Speaking in 2003, Rodgers was realistic about his luck with her second album. "*Like A Virgin* was a fluke," he said. "When I got hired to do that album, her first album had been out a year and had only sold 700,000. That seems cynical—only 700,000. But everybody was concerned. We do *Like A Virgin*, and then out of nowhere, 'Borderline' hits, out of the clear blue sky."

Madonna needed to ramp up her work ethic to ensure that not a moment was wasted on her path to global domination. She needed to prove that she could act, and that she could take this bright, shiny, new sound she'd made out on a nationwide tour. The speed of her success would prove so rapid that, by the following July, she would be on the bill at Live Aid, the world's biggest-ever concert.

CHAPTER 4
INTO THE GROOVE

By early 1985, Madonna seemed like a true multi-media performer. She was everywhere. She had become involved in two movie projects, which seemed to drop simultaneously as *Like A Virgin* climbed the charts.

Madonna had signed to the William Morris agency in 1984 with the hope of getting some acting roles. It was important that she gain a foothold in the film industry, and some significant performances down the bill would get her noticed. Although she auditioned unsuccessfully for a role in *Footloose*, she was offered a part in the Jon Peters production, *Vision Quest*.

Although only a minor entry in the Madonna cannon, *Vision Quest* was significant in that it gave her an entrée into the world of Hollywood pictures, and by singing the film's key song, 'Crazy For You,' she proved she could sing serious, affecting ballads. Taking its name from the Native American practice of taking time in the wilderness to find yourself and come of age, *Vision Quest* follows the story of high school wrestler Louden Swain, played by Matthew Modine, who loses weight to tackle a tough opponent. In the meantime, he falls in love with his father's boarder, Carla (Linda Fiorentino). Love clouds his will to win.

Set in Spokane, Washington, the film is a fairly routine 80s teen drama. Madonna was offered the part of the nightclub singer who performs as the main characters dance together for the first time. Her scenes were filmed on location at Spokane's Big Foot Tavern.

Although there is little substance to the role, it gave Madonna important exposure. She recorded two songs for the soundtrack, both of which were produced by John 'Jellybean' Benitez. While the self-written and moderately generic 'Gambler' was standard soundtrack fare, the other new recording was most certainly not. Written by John Bettis and Jon Lind, 'Crazy For You' became an enormous success, hitting the top of the US singles chart in May 1985 (replacing 'We Are The World'). The film was re-titled *Crazy For*

You in the UK and Australia following the single's success and enjoyed far more success than it would have done had Madonna not appeared in it.

However, if *Vision Quest* was a relatively minor addition to Madonna's canon, her next film, *Desperately Seeking Susan*, took her message around the world. A small, quirky affair, it was originally conceived as a starring vehicle for Rosanna Arquette, but soon became known simply as Madonna's film. Its enjoyable (if wafer-thin) plot and modest budget hardly matter as it captures Madonna at the exact point on her trajectory when she first became a superstar.

Her character, Susan, is a mystifying, hedonistic New Yorker who bears a great deal of similarity to Madonna herself. The part is similar in a sense to the four Beatles' appearances in Alun Owen's script for *A Hard Day's Night*—for years, people believed that *was* them. For many, Susan is, was, and will forever be Madonna.

The *Desperately Seeking* script had been around in Hollywood since the early 80s. It was written by Leora Barish as an update of the screwball comedies of the 40s and 50s, but there are enough shades and nuances in it that it is not simply a comedy. The story concerns a bored New Jersey housewife, Roberta Lee (Arquette), who becomes enchanted by a series of personal ads in a New York newspaper from Susan (Madonna) to her boyfriend Jim (Robert Joy). Roberta goes off to find Susan, assumes her identity, and then all manner of capers ensue. Roberta realizes she is in hot water when one of Susan's ex-boyfriends is revealed to have links to the mob.

The film got the green light in late 1983 and was allocated to director Susan Siedelman, whose debut, *Smithereens*, had recently received positive reviews. Madonna was not the first choice to play Susan: Orion Pictures originally envisaged Diane Keaton as an aging-hippie Roberta, with Goldie Hawn as Susan, but Siedelman knew she wanted someone a little more edgy.

More than 200 actresses read for the Susan role. Jennifer Jason Leigh, Melanie Griffith, Susanne Vega, Kelly McGillis, and Ellen Barkin all considered it, but while Madonna was far less technically competent than these established actresses, Siedelman knew that she would be exactly right for the part of the irreverent, fast-loving urbanite.

"Madonna was someone I knew about from the local club scene,"

Siedelman later recalled. "I'd go to Danceteria and Paradise Garage occasionally, and I'd see her there—I knew who she was, what she looked like." Orion had no idea who Madonna was, but one of the executives' son did, and so Madonna was granted an interview. She arrived without the money for the cab fare, so asked the executives for it. "It was exactly what Susan would have done," Siedelman added. After some additional acting training, Madonna got the role.

Shooting began soon after Madonna's 26th birthday in August 1984 and stretched into the fall. Madonna was the consummate professional, turning up early and showing a great interest in the filmmaking process. "There was so much sitting around, it drove me crazy," Madonna said at the time. "But it's what I'd always wanted to do." There are lots of nice little touches in the film, and as a result it plays as one of the best representations of New York in the early 80s—especially with downtown musical characters such as John Lurie, Arto Lindsay, Adele Bertei, and Rockets Redglare making cameos, and Richard Hell in the substantial role of Bruce Meeker.

The relationship between the two principal stars, however, was not cordial. In *Madonna—The Biography*, Robert Matthew-Walker notes that, on and off the set, Arquette's association with Madonna "raised a few eyebrows." She may have been the established actress with the lead billing, but the filming coincided with Madonna's ascendancy to superstar fame, and Arquette was being eclipsed by the newcomer. She was subsequently quoted as saying: "I thought I was going to be making this small, charming film, not some rock video." She later added: "As soon as Madonna came into the picture the script was changed to suit her ... A disco dance movie isn't what I signed on to do. However, I couldn't get out of it."

The issue of the film as "rock video" came about after the addition of 'Into The Groove,' a song specially written for the film. Aware of just how popular Madonna was becoming, director Susan Siedelman had asked her if she'd be able to come up with a song that could play over its end credits— the idea being that the song could then act as a worldwide advert for the film. Madonna and co-writer Stephen Bray worked quickly, with the singer returning to the out-and-out dance idiom of her early songs—finding freedom and redemption on the dance floor. The lyrics played upon Susan's character, further emphasizing her importance to the film, and were woven into the film's narrative.

Madonna's inspiration came from a dream about a date. "When I was writing it," she later said, "I was sitting in a fourth-floor walk-up on Avenue B, and there was this gorgeous Puerto Rican boy sitting across from me that I wanted to go out on a date with, and I just wanted to get it over with." Considering the enjoyment that might lie ahead, Madonna wrote the lyric quickly and improvised the words to the middle-eight on the spot in the studio. It was easy for her to do, as her best records link back to music and the dance floor, which she loves and craves so earnestly.

Hearing the breezy, synthesized drum-and-keyboard introduction and the playful, assured double-tracked vocal, Siedelman was delighted. The song and its accompanying video—a selection of scenes from *Susan* edited together by Doug Dowdle of Parallax Productions—made the song, film, and by extension Madonna herself instantly recognizable all over the world.

If 'Like A Virgin' and 'Material Girl' were two big steps toward superstar status, 'Into The Groove' sealed the deal. Although it was not released as a standalone single in the USA, it was *everywhere*. Across the rest of the world it took its position at the summit of numerous singles charts. In the UK, it is still Madonna's biggest-selling single to date, coming in at just shy of one million units. The reason it wasn't issued in North America was simple: it would have detracted from the sales life of 'Angel,' the current single from *Like A Virgin*. Instead it was put on the flip-side of the 12-inch maxi-single of 'Angel,' and on the strength of that it was certified gold by the RIAA.

'Into The Groove' was the perfect record to underline Madonna's newfound superstar status. It encapsulated the world's need to celebrate with a conscience at Live Aid in Philadelphia, and became one of the most memorable performances of the day. In Europe, the song was added to later pressings of the *Like A Virgin* LP.

Desperately Seeking Susan was given a limited release on March 29 1985 before opening countrywide on April 12 with the tagline "A life so outrageous it takes two women to live it." At the LA premiere, in April,

Entertainment Tonight's Jeanne Wolf asked Madonna about the similarities between her and the character of Susan. "She's irresponsible, she is adventurous, she is courageous, and she's very vulnerable," the singer replied. "Is she Madonna?" Wolf asked. Madonna broke into a broad grin. "We have some things in common." Fans mobbed her, and Warner Bros executives were on hand to supply posters, albums, and tour jackets to spread the Madonna word.

The final insult to Rosanna Arquette came when she was recognized by the British Film And Television Academy, winning a Best Actress Award—but in the Supporting Role category. Whichever way you looked at it, *Desperately Seeking Susan* was Madonna's film. Even when she is not on screen, most of the dialogue refers to her character. "Susan wasn't a character, she was Madonna," former lover and producer Mark Kamins later noted. "A wisecracking, smart-ass, gum-chewing, savvy, streetwise chick. She was the original club kid, riding a bicycle around New York, always off to the next place."

Desperately Seeking Susan was a huge success. From a modest outlay of $4.5 million, it took more than $27 million at the box office. It was the fifth highest-grossing film in the USA in 1985, and yet Madonna was perplexed. Most reviews, which were largely favorable, suggested she was simply playing herself. Next time, she would have to become someone very different.

As *Desperately Seeking Susan* introduced Madonna to audiences around the world, The Virgin Tour represented Madonna's first proper full-scale live event: a total of 41 nights in 28 cities across the United States and Canada between April and June 1985. It was an eventful, action-packed tour, marked by Madonna's incredible chart success and by the legions of wannabes in attendance. And it sold out within hours. As singer, dancer, director, and driving force, Madonna put together a show that drew on her years of performance training and inherent knowledge of what would make for a spectacle. Her eagerness to please—and the fact that her fame was spreading at quicksilver speed—meant that it became the most-talked about tour of the year.

"That whole tour was crazy, because I went from playing CBGB and the Mudd Club to playing sports arenas," Madonna said in 2009. "After Seattle, all of the shows were moved to arenas. I've never done a bus tour," she added, as a reminder of exactly how successful she'd been. "Everyone says they are really fun."

The tour consisted of only one leg and played solely in North America despite talk of adding dates in Europe and Asia. It started on April 10 at the Paramount Theater in Seattle and ended just over two months later in New York. The 17,622 tickets for three dates at Manhattan's Radio City Music Hall sold out in 34 minutes, hence the additional closing shows at that most prestigious of traditional 'rock' arenas, Madison Square Garden.

This was the high point of the initial phase of Madonnamania, with wannabes lining the concert halls to get a glimpse of their idol. Madonna began to understand the extent of her celebrity when she looked into the crowd and saw herself: "Girls had flap skirts on and tights cut off below their knees. And lace gloves and rosaries and bows in their hair and big hoop earrings. I was like: this is insane!"

The cinematic release of *Desperately Seeking Susan* and the chart success of 'Crazy For You' at the same time as the tour gave the sense of a commercial juggernaut hitting hard. The ticket sales broke records—the press seemed to report exaggerated statistics from every box office as the Madonna phenomena grew. The tour was also a triumph of merchandising. Madonna linked up with Maripol to sell a range of memorabilia, and the concession stalls sold Madonna merchandise faster than it could be replenished. At the April 23 gig at Bill Graham's Civic Auditorium in San Francisco, it was reported that T-shirts were selling at a rate of one every six seconds.

Commentators sneered at the mass-market saturation of it all. *New Republic* wrote that "the predominantly female 13 and 14-year-olds who flocked to Madonna's Virgin Tour rock concerts went home loaded down with overpriced T-shirts, posters, and promo magazines—all, of course, featuring their punked-out heroine."

The tour was commemorated with a 20-page tour book featuring full-color photographs by Steven Meisel and Herb Ritts. Of those 20 pages, four had text—like the show, it was all about the look rather than studying too hard. Madonna's look was quickly and widely copied beyond the concert hall. Here was something the millions of Madonna wannabes could use to emphasize their femininity as well as their bravado and cool. It was street-chic and street-cheap, and easily emulated. Diamante was everywhere, while the bracelets, crucifixes, and Boy Toy belts were in huge demand. This spilled over to Maripol's New York store, Maripolotan, where the novelties were constantly replenished. There was even a lookalike contest in Macy's Department Store, which Maripol judged alongside Andy Warhol.

Madonna's live band marked the introduction of one of her key musical foils: keyboard player Pat Leonard. A 'serious musician' who had most recently directed The Jacksons' Victory Tour, he had initially turned down the opportunity to work with Madonna, having not been overly impressed by the only track he knew, 'Like A Virgin,' but was soon won over by Madonna's tenacity and allure.

Leonard put together a tight group of accomplished players: keyboardist Billy Meyers, drummer Jon Moffett, bassist Bill Lanphier, and guitarists James Harrah and Paul Pesco. Madonna selected the best material for airing live, ending up with a setlist focused on her first two albums, with the addition of the two *Vision Quest* songs, 'Crazy For You' and 'Gambler,' and the hot new 'Into The Groove.' The band-members were stationed either side of the central walkway, where Madonna performed. Every song was accompanied by an energetic dance, either by Madonna on her own or with the support of her backing dancers. 'Like A Virgin,' the show's obvious centerpiece, included a verse from Michael Jackson's 'Billie Jean.' It was part homage, part marking of territory—his level of popularity was clearly in Madonna's sights, and Madonna was his equal.

The opening act was The Beastie Boys—friends of Madonna's from New York who were parading their white bad-boy rap act on wider stages for the first time and beginning to court the controversy with which they would become synonymous. "In the first week she realized we were the perfect group," they later noted, "because the audience hated us so much that by the time she went on stage they went crazy."

The show, a fairly straightforward production, was choreographed and staged by Brad Jeffries and designed by Ian Knight. It had costume changes, a modicum of special effects, and a Vegas-style pizzazz. Madonna's exuberance and desire to delight came across at every instance. With the help of dancers Michael Perea and Lyndon B. Johnson, she created a spectacle, bringing her albums—and, more importantly to the massed throng, her videos—to life with energetic moves, lascivious lolling about, and a bubbling-over sense of fun and adventure. She used the device of bringing a ghetto blaster to center stage, suggesting that the tunes she was playing were similar to those you would hear on the block in New York. The show's marriage of the street-cool and Broadway was instrumental in building her US success. She wasn't elitist, she wasn't all about downtown—she was addressing her show to the lace-adorned teenager at the very back of the biggest arena. She would frequently ask the audience to marry her as she skipped, almost gawkily, from one end of the stage to the other.

Midway through the tour, Madonna played the Cobo arena on May 25 and 26—the same venue she'd seen David Bowie, Elton John, and Bob Marley perform in as a teenager. Each night she played out her Boy Toy character to the nth degree, with punk-styled jackets, bangles, and rosaries. This was the one tour where you saw Madonna looking like everyone first remembers her—that spiky, cheeky, punky caricature. It was surveying the wannabes in the crowd that made Madonna realize that this particular era was over. By the time she appeared at Live Aid just over a month later, her hair was brushed straight and she was wearing a moderately sedate frock coat.

The reception of The Virgin Tour set the tone for the next phase of Madonna's success—popular adoration mixed with either frothing critical delight or sniffy disdain. The response ranged from the scabrous to the just plain wrong. The *New York Times* criticized her vocal performance, while *Billboard* proudly announced: "Cyndi Lauper will be around for a very long time. Madonna will be out of business in six months." *Variety* suggested that Madonna's singing was "like a soundtrack to a more visceral display of herself, her persona, her non-stop dancing, and her surprisingly explicit sexual dare, which included a visual climax—so to speak—to every song." They suggested that despite all this raunch, she managed to look "solicitous and good-hearted—a kind of flirtatious, sugary sex fairy whose outrageous poses were really just a gift for the kids, a fantasy offering to help them grow up."

Time magazine, however, simply watched on in awe: "When the Madonna show detonates at about 9pm ... The strongest impression is of being back in the 60s, listening to The Shirelles." After that, the review continues, "the show turns darker and funkier, with a lot of smoke bombs and jungle-queen strutting in silhouette toward something like a 14-year-old's florid conception of adult sexuality." If the tour achieved anything beyond its enormous box-office success and proof of Madonna's ability as a live performer, it was that Madonna had won over virtually every 14-year-old who was there to watch it.

There was talk of releasing a live album to capitalize on the tour's success, but in the end a VHS videotape of an edited performance from the Detroit show was released to great success in 1985. In footage of the tour, Madonna looks naïve—clunky even—with any remaining subtleties from her promo videos stripped away to provide big, reductive, cartoon-like performances. But with that gaucheness came great charm and a steely professionalism. The Virgin Tour, while not being of the highest artistic merit, proved that not only could Madonna play live, she could scale up her shtick to the biggest sports arenas. It was one of the top ten grossing tours of 1985.

July 1985 was possibly the defining month in Madonna's whole long and star-studded career. *Desperately Seeking Susan* had exceeded all expectations at the box office; The Virgin Tour had come to a close in June, having been scaled up from theaters to arenas after its opening dates; 'Angel' was a US Top Three hit; and 'Crazy For You' was on its way up charts around the world, having already hit Number One on *Billboard* in May. To underline her importance, Madonna's notoriety was sealed by the publication of nude photographs (taken years earlier) of her in two of the widest-circulating men's magazines in the world. And she played arguably the most famous concert of all time.

Madonna's past reappeared in a most dramatic fashion. The modeling and photo shoots she had done as a struggling dance student in New York were emblazoned across the front of *Playboy* and *Penthouse*. On July 10, the latest *Playboy*, containing 14 pages of a young Madonna in various stages of undress, shot in 1979 and 1980 by photographers Lee Friedlander and Martin Schreiber, hit newsstands. The sensation they caused was further underlined when, three days later, *Penthouse* published a 17-page spread, including color photographs, shot by Bill Stone—with the words "MADONNA IN THE NUDE" emblazoned on the front cover.

As Christopher Ciccone recalls in his memoir, *Life With My Sister Madonna*, their grandmother burst into tears when she heard the news. He remembers thinking four things on seeing the pictures: firstly, that they were lackluster; secondly, that it was the first time he'd seen his sister completely naked; thirdly, that she used to be very skinny; and finally, that she had a great deal of body hair.

As the pictures spread out across the world, Madonna appeared—with typically remarkable timing—at the Philadelphia leg of Live Aid, the 'global jukebox' organized by Bob Geldof to raise money for famine-stricken Ethiopia, on July 13. At 4:27pm, having been introduced by Bette Midler as "a woman who had pulled herself up by her bra-straps," Madonna made the Live Aid stage her own.

Appearing after Kool & The Gang and before the satellite broadcast switched back to the final section of the Wembley gig in London, Madonna stood in the eye of controversy in her long brocade coat and high-buttoned shirt and stared the world right in the eye. "I ain't taking shit off today," she said. It wasn't the greatest performance she'd ever give, but it didn't need to be. (For the record, she played 'Holiday,' 'Into The Groove,' and the as-yet unreleased 'Love Makes The World Go Round.')

It was a performance of consummate entertainment, and meant that Madonna was able to silence her detractors and produce mass, populist diversion. Michael Francis, a security man for Kiss and Bon Jovi, witnessed the scene from backstage. "Madonna is tiny," he later wrote in his memoir, *Star Man: The Right-Hand Man Of Rock'n'Roll*. "Dressed as if from a thrift store, with heavy make up and an unruly mass of brightly colored hair, she looks like a naughty teenager as she smiles nervously before running on to the stage, but once out there she commands the stage as if it is hers and hers alone." With one performance—and a mixture of hard work and insouciance—Madonna made clear that those pictures were taken a very long time ago.

What really sealed Madonna's superstar celebrity status in 1985 was her marriage to a Hollywood bad boy, and in Sean Penn she had found the sort of bad boy that any self-respecting father would dread. But between Penn and Madonna was a forceful, passionate, all-or-nothing love.

It was a mixture of intense love and mutual contempt from first sight. The pair met on the set of the 'Material Girl' video, which Penn had been invited to visit by director Mary Lambert. Penn was a talented actor from a privileged Hollywood background, and had previously dated actresses Elizabeth McGovern and Susan Sarandon.

Madonna and Penn had their first date on February 13 1985 at the Private Eyes club in New York. It was said that on another of their early meetings, the couple visited Marilyn Monroe's crypt. The pair's schedules meant that they spent a considerable period of time apart. He was filming in Tennessee while she was completing The Virgin Tour. As John Skow noted in *Time* magazine: "The dreary fact is that stars sometimes lead lives of chaste exasperation."

They decided that they would not be apart for long. On August 16 they married in a blaze of publicity at Kurt Unger's Malibu home. Tabloid helicopters buzzed overhead throughout; Penn likened the day to *Apocalypse Now*. Typically testy in his public statements, he nonetheless described Madonna as "the most wonderful woman—I love her." The wedding was crammed with celebrity: Maripol, Andy Warhol, Cher, Carrie Fisher, Christopher Walken, David Letterman, and Rosanna Arquette were among the 200 or so guests.

From the start of their relationship, however, the press had it in for the couple. Penn was soon sentenced to 60 days in prison for assaulting a photographer. Madonna watched helplessly as the reputation she had fought so hard to build was being sheared away by Penn's bully-boy tactics. But her love was strong enough for her not to worry at this juncture. "Sean will fight for privacy," she later said. "He wants to protect me ... as inefficient as his methods may be, he sticks with what he believes in." This relationship was to shape the next half-decade of Madonna's career.

Madonna's tumultuous 1985, topped off with her Live Aid performance, meant that her next set of new recordings would be the most eagerly anticipated yet of her career. And what followed next firmly cemented her reputation. *True Blue* was the first album Madonna made as a superstar. Her debut had been recorded in obscurity and her second captured an artist on the way to becoming established but still taking baby steps, however assured they may have been. There was nothing tentative about *True Blue*.

Made at the height of her first wave of fame, this was Madonna—finally famous, deeply in love—striking the template for the rest of her career. It was here, as critic Lucy O'Brien later wrote, that she "nailed her signature sound—rhythmic, dramatic, danceable, and distinctively melodic." As *Slant* magazine put it: "*True Blue* was the supreme archetype for late-80s and early-90s pop music."

When it came to making her third album, Madonna's earlier successes meant that she could now work with whomever she liked. Instead of opting again for a big name like Nile Rodgers—to produce but also siphon off a considerable percentage—she decided she would now co-produce the record herself.

Recording began at the end of 1985 in Patrick Leonard's tiny basement studio in Los Angeles. Leonard was to play a significant part in the development of Madonna's sound. He had joined her as musical director for the Virgin Tour and added great commercial veneer to the recording, aiming her sound away from the clubs and squarely at mainstream radio.

Leonard and the record's other producer, Breakfast Club veteran Stephen Bray, set about writing and selecting material that would be recorded over the next four months, with sessions fitted in around the soon-to-be-troubled filming of Madonna's next big-screen outing, *Shanghai Surprise*. The producers worked with a small team of musicians, including guitarist Bruce Gaitsch and drummer Jonathan Moffett.

The material was zesty, purposeful, and brief. There would be no aimless covers, just sharp-edged focus. Leonard and Madonna got on well. He had an uncanny ability to bring out the very best in Madonna's songwriting, and was able to see behind her pop carapace and get her to dig deep. As a result, the album was bright and shiny, yet unafraid to go beneath the surface. It was also the sound of a woman unashamedly in love.

True Blue took its title from Sean Penn's view that "true blue" was a "very pure expression of love." It has been described as a 'girlish' album, and in many respects that is an apt assessment—it marks probably the only time Madonna sang directly to her new, largely female audience instead of aiming for a different one. The innocence and joy of the album still sparkles when played today. "She was very much in love," Stephen Bray later said. "If she's in love she'll write love songs. If she's not in love she definitely won't be writing love songs." If there is a criticism of the record, it's that of its nine tracks, the five that were chosen as singles ('Live To Tell,' 'Papa Don't Preach,' 'Open Your Heart,' 'True Blue,' and 'La Isla Bonita') are so strong and over-played that they overshadow the remainder of the material—which, when set against such anthems, seems slight by comparison.

The album was trailed by 'Live To Tell' in April 1986. It was a most interesting choice for lead single, as it deliberately pulled away from the froth of *Like A Virgin* and settled more on the 'Crazy For You' approach. If 'Crazy For You' was a straight love song, however, 'Live To Tell' was definitely not.

A brave and downbeat selection, 'Live To Tell' had been written by Leonard for the Paramount film *Fire With Fire*. He played Madonna the demo and she quickly wrote a lyric. Leonard and Madonna cut a vocal version of the song, yet Paramount was unsure of Leonard's ability to score the entire film, so it was dropped. Madonna thought the song's filmic qualities should still be utilized on the big screen. She took the demo cassette to husband Penn, who decided it could be appropriate for his new film, *At Close Range*. The song was released with Madonna's demo vocal. Pensive and low-key, it signified her newfound maturity. Her unadorned vocal would provide her forthcoming album with one of its spine-tingling interludes.

The release of the single marked the non-ironic intervention of heavyweight pop critics racing to applaud her. In 1989, the single featured in the Top 50 of *The Heart Of Rock & Soul: The 1001 Greatest Singles Ever Made* by US rock scribe Dave Marsh, who called it "a great reworking of one of the major undiscussed themes in contemporary pop music: spiritual abandonment, lack of nurture, and their consequences." For a pop singer, using oblique references to what was at best parental neglect or at worst child abuse was brave. "I thought about my relationship with my parents and the lying that went on," Madonna was to say. "The song is about being strong, and questioning whether you can be that strong, but ultimately surviving."

The video was directed by James Foley, under the pseudonym Peter Percher, and was Madonna's first without a dance routine. The last time we saw her she was prancing unashamedly in the *Desperately Seeking Susan* video-trailer for 'Into The Groove'; here, she is intercut with male-bonding (and sporadically violent) footage of Penn and Christopher Walken from *At Close Range*. The most notable thing about the video is that she sings completely static, hair coiffed into the classic Hollywood 40s style she wears in *Shanghai Surprise*. With long panning shots of her conventional dress, and her beauty mark accentuated, a clear distinction was being made between the controversial artist who had recently had nude photographs splashed across the media and this sober, prim-looking woman intoning a portentous ballad. If before she had sung about being "like a virgin" while looking like a streetwalker, here she was singing of substantial issues with her innocence reclaimed. The shadow cast by the record would prepare her audience for future, weightier records such as 'Like A Prayer.'

Madonna's newfound sobriety chimed with the public. It was a brave choice for the first release of her imperial phase, but it showed how she, at this moment, was the hottest act in the world. Any initial concerns expressed by Warner Bros about releasing a single without an album to promote were quickly allayed when it reached the US top spot in June. The song retains a particular resonance with Madonna, and it was played in concert, most recently in 2006, where she performed it on her Confessions tour, wearing a crown of thorns while appearing to be crucified on a giant, mirrored cross. (There was little surprise when religious leaders interpreted her show in Rome in August of that year as "an act of hostility toward the Roman Catholic Church.")

True Blue was released in June 1986, quickly lodging itself in the US Top Three and providing Madonna with another chart-topper in the UK. This was Madonna all grown up, a maturity compounded as the album was removed from its iconic blue sleeve and you heard the 16-second flourish of baroque strings that leads into the opening 'Papa Don't Preach.' Starting an album with an overture was nothing new—most recently, British art-pop combo ABC had ushered in their transatlantic hit album *The Lexicon Of Love* with an orchestral introduction—but this was one from an artist who had previously been viewed merely as 'pop-dance.'

Scored by Billy Meyers, 'Papa Don't Preach' is a song of familial defiance with pro-life overtones. Although Madonna was clearly older in real life than she was supposed to be in the song—she was a 28-year-old portraying an 18-year-old, a differential sneered at by critics—her role as teenage mother-to-be was played with sincerity and alacrity. Written by little-known US songwriter Brian Elliott (who'd released a solitary album on Warner Bros in 1978) with additional words by Madonna, it is a perfect encapsulation of the wayward assuredness of youth.

Elliott had been producing a new artist called Christina Dent when he took a demo tape to Michael Ostin at Warners. Ostin was impressed with 'Papa Don't Preach,' which had been inspired by Elliott overhearing conversations by teenage students from North Hollywood High outside his studio window. Ostin—who had found 'Like A Virgin'—asked Elliott if he could play the song to Madonna. Elliott reluctantly took the song from Dent, and it became the opening track on *True Blue*.

Madonna and Ostin met in the studio after Madonna had added various lines and phrases to the finished recording. Although Elliott was told that Madonna would not be present, after the playback he heard Madonna's voice asking him if she had "wrecked his song." "We had a spirited discussion at that point," Elliott told Jay Padroff of *Music Connection*. "About certain interpretations of lines, and it was resolved to the musical delight of all concerned."

Opening the album with the statement "Papa, I know you're going to be upset," Madonna at once provided the flip-side to records such as Cyndi Lauper's 'Girls Just Wanna Have Fun,' stating clearly the consequences that might follow after the laughter. "Immediately they're going to say I am advising every young girl to go out and get pregnant," she told Stephen Holden in the *New York Times*. "When I first heard the song I thought it was silly. But then I thought: wait a minute, this song is really about a girl who is making a decision in her life. She has a very close relationship with her father, and wants to maintain that closeness. To me it's a celebration of life."

There is also a degree of ambiguity, as the "baby" in question could also be the lover she's started seeing, much to her father's disgust. The plea for a father's love is extremely central to the record's success, and, by the very fact that she is still addressing him, there is reason to suggest that the child she may bear will have a similar relationship with its own father, the man who has been 'pleasing' her. But the ambiguity of the pleasure she has enjoyed bears the question of whether her paramour will still be so delighted with all forthcoming responsibility. Whatever the outcome, Madonna gives an authoritative performance, getting inside her character perfectly.

The James Foley-directed video that accompanied this US and UK chart-topper is arguably one of Madonna's most iconic. It developed the theme of the record most literally, and again suggested that Madonna would enjoy a successful parallel career as an actor. With her hair brushed forward, she strides around Staten Island suburbia, looking troubled in her Breton top, with authenticity and élan. She is seen in her now-legendary 'Italians Do It Better' T-shirt eyeing up cartoon-book street-punk beefcake (actor Alex McArthur). Danny Aiello played her father with his customary Italo-American gravitas, and the home movies of the little girl growing up in her single parent family add appropriate pathos. The video raises more questions than answers. Is she going to be happy? Will the child bring fulfillment?

Much can be read about the lack of a maternal figure throughout, especially as Madonna looks for approval from the elderly couple on the ferry in the middle sequence. While the man looks on indulgently, the woman's blank expression underlines the absence of a mother. Madonna's stare to camera—as if to say "don't you stop loving me, daddy, I know I'm keeping my baby"—could easily have been directed at her father, Tony, about her new real-life husband. The final shot, however, is one of reconciliation, with a paternal hand outstretched to the central character. To remind fans that this is a pop video after all, the chorus is delivered by Madonna with her newly styled Marilyn Monroe hair, in bustier and pedal-pushers, dancing in flat shoes.

The *New York Times* suggested that with this track, Madonna was "reaching for the fringes of the permissible." It certainly attracted the controversial support of Tipper Gore, chair of the Parents' Music Resource Center, who said: "To me, the song speaks to a serious subject with a sense of urgency and sensitivity in both the lyrics and Madonna's rendition. It also speaks to the fact that there's got to be more support and more communication in families about this problem, and anything that fosters that I applaud." High-profile US feminist attorney Gloria Allred demanded that Madonna "make a public statement noting that kids have other choices, including abortion." As Dave Marsh put it: "For the first time, Madonna looked like a good Catholic girl." Appearances can deceive, however. On her 1987 Who's That Girl World Tour, Madonna started her overt irking of the Catholic Church by dedicating the song in performance to Pope John Paul II.

Although 'Open Your Heart' was one of the more off-the-peg generic tracks on the album, that did not stop it charging to the top of the US chart when it was selected as the album's third single in November 1986. It was fabulous, muscular, anthemic dance music. The song was written by Gardner Cole and Peter Rafelson, and was originally intended for Cyndi Lauper. After Lauper passed on it, The Temptations, then still enjoying their renaissance after 'Treat Her Like A Lady' were also linked to the song. They respectfully declined when they heard that Madonna was interested.

Originally entitled 'Follow Your Heart,' the song was inspired by a health-food restaurant known to Cole in Canoga Park, California. Cole's Manager, Bennett Freed, had been working with Madonna's management and heard she was looking for new material. Madonna and Leonard added a bassline and Madonna changed the song's inflection from straightforward rock to raucous rock-dance. Her abbreviation of the verse and chorus also impressed the writers. The song is notable for being one of the first to introduce Madonna's hard, strident voice—the one that would cement her reputation as a superstar.

While maybe not one of her very finest recordings, 'Open Your Heart' hit the right note with the US public. After the tentative nature of 'Live To Tell' and the relative experimentation of 'Papa Don't Preach,' here was Madonna updating the dance anthem model she had made her own. It went to the US Number One spot on February 7 1986. Madonna was now unassailable. The accompanying video, directed by Jean-Baptiste Mondino, was shot in Echo Park, Los Angeles, and features Madonna—again confronting her tabloid reputation head-on—as an erotic dancer, performing at a peep-show, who befriends a young boy (Felix Howard) trying to get into the grown-up performance.

The promo would go through many changes and adaptations, but was the first to introduce what would become possibly Madonna's single most iconic wardrobe item: her conical bra. It also reinforced her importance and strength as a woman—she is the center, and the men with their notebooks and cameras are little more than sad, impotent onlookers. Although it was nominated for many awards, it wasn't likely to win one for subtlety. It also explodes the myth of the show and subtly deconstructs Madonna's own iconography: when she leaves the theater, she is dressed the same as the boy, in a simple grey, androgynous suit, dancing freely and happily with him. Throughout the seedy spectacle, she was merely a performer after all.

True Blue continues with 'White Heat.' The song is dedicated to Hollywood legend James Cagney, whose death at 86 was announced during sessions for the album, but it was fashioned more as a tribute to Penn. Cagney was an impeccably behaved gentleman off-screen, something that Penn clearly was not—a fact from which that the world's tabloids were extracting a great deal of mileage. The target of Madonna's affections, however, is told explicitly that he would have to play "her way." Although it boasts support vocals from Jackie Jackson (with whom Leonard had worked on The Jacksons' Victory Tour) and AOR singer Richard Marx, it is one of the album's weaker moments, a thoroughly generic call to arms.

'Live To Tell' closes the first half of the album, with 'Where's The Party' opening the original second side. The only song co-written by all three producers, it is possibly the most straightforward track on the album. It takes the classic blue-collar 'living for the weekend' approach that Madonna had embraced, like so many others, in her early days in New York. It's upbeat, jaunty, and similar in feel to the *Madonna* LP, with its heavily keyboard-driven melody and synthesizer bass. Here Madonna becomes everywoman, leading her crowd toward a good time, just as she did on 'Holiday' and 'Into The Groove.' It also possesses one of the best vocal codas of any Madonna track, complete with the sound of backing vocalists goofing off in the studio.

Without missing a beat, we are into the sunniest moment on the album. Co-written with Stephen Bray, the title track is still one of Madonna's most cherished hits. With an explicit nod to both Motown and the classic girl-groups from the Phil Spector stable, it manages to capture the breathlessness and exhilaration of love in a non-clichéd way. The conflation of the passionate and the platonic—Madonna's excitement that her lover is also her "best friend"—takes the album back momentarily to the playground. If this is the same person troubled by familial demons elsewhere on the album, here she is dancing joyfully in the sun. What really makes the record swing is the vocal support by Siedah Garrett and Edie Lehman, who added authentic girl-group pizzazz to Madonna's impassioned vocal.

James Foley completed his trio of videos for the album with the simplistic, iconic, and fun promo for 'True Blue.' After the pensive introspection of 'Live To Tell' and the message-laden 'Papa Don't Preach,' here is the lighter Madonna dabbling with all manner of American iconography. We see Madonna and her three backing vocalists on a cartoon-like set depicting a more innocent time of finger-pops and Cadillacs. Love without complications has momentarily conquered and its message cannot be ignored. And then there's the hand jiving, the unsophisticated miming, and some business with blue scarves. There is no gravitas, just pleasure, and not a little daftness. But it's carried out with great sincerity—as homage, not parody. It proved that for the rest of her career, for every 'Live To Tell' there would be a 'True Blue,' for every 'Like A Prayer' a 'Cherish,' for every 'Frozen' a 'Ray Of Light'—Madonna's two sides, her yin and yang.

Patrick Leonard and Bruce Gaitsch had originally written 'La Isla Bonita' for possible inclusion on *Bad*, Michael Jackson's follow-up to *Thriller*.

Leonard had sent the track over to Madonna while she was at the height of her misery, filming the troubled *Shanghai Surprise* in Hong Kong. She set to it a lyric that encapsulated her love for all things Latin American (disguised as the imaginary San Pedro).

Gaitsch was somewhat taken aback by her choice of title for the song (which translates as 'the beautiful island'), fearing it to be uncommercial, but he still provided a stunning, Spanish-influenced acoustic guitar solo, which adds flavor and helped make it one of Madonna's most loved sides. The song also shrewdly introduced Madonna to the burgeoning Hispanic market. She was set on expanding her audience, and comments about how the song was "a tribute to the beauty and mystery of Latin American people" made this explicit. Selected as the final single release from the album, 'La Isla Bonita' came out in February 1987. It topped the charts in Germany, France, and the UK, while stalling at Number Four on the US *Billboard* Hot 100.

The video reunited Madonna with Mary Lambert, who had so definitively created her image with 'Like A Virgin.' Heavy on Latin American and Catholic symbolism, it features long-haired flamenco players in the street and bongo players on stoops. After a verse of Madonna longing for the old country, her room is transformed into a deep red paradise of many candles, and she into a Spanish lovely in a flamenco dress. It all ends with a street dance and Madonna disappearing into the Los Angeles streets to continue her quest for this imaginary country.

'Jimmy, Jimmy' is another veiled tribute to Sean Penn, its hard and fast beats signposting Madonna's roots. The character with all his lofty dreams is merely "a boy who comes from bad places." The evocation of an earlier musical era is again made explicit by the bridge's reference to Frankie Lymon & The Teenagers' 1956 hit, 'Why Do Fools Fall In Love.' If Madonna is the fool, however, she is quite happy being so—the closing refrain of "Hey, I really love you Jimmy" could barely be more overt. It is akin to a teenage girl writing her boyfriend's name all over her school books—part declaration of love, part lack of confidence, a fear that she may lose what she has found.

'Love Makes The World Go Round,' which Madonna had delivered so defiantly and appropriately at the Philadelphia leg of the Live Aid extravaganza the previous July, had initially been earmarked as the lead single of the album, but the surfeit of accessible songs pushed it down the list. As a result, it seems weak by comparison. Complete with Paulinho da Costa's clattering percussion, its message of unity and fighting against prejudice would have made it a credible anthem had the main thrust of *True Blue* not been so very strong. And that was that. Madonna's last full-length album for the three years.

The album's overall quality is bolstered by the strength of the performances. Madonna herself is focused, strident, and breathy in the all the right places, taking her newfound responsibility as a superstar very seriously. The musicianship is impeccable. It manages to bring together a great standard of players without it seeming like a manufactured session album. And although it was assembled by two production teams, the album has great cohesion.

Some of the reviews were a little distant and standoffish but most critics were positive. As Davitt Sigerson put it in *Rolling Stone*: "Madonna's sturdy, dependable, lovable new album remains faithful to her past while shamelessly rising above it. *True Blue* may generate fewer sales and less attention than *Like A Virgin*, but it sets her up as an artist for the long run. And like every other brainy move from this best of all possible pop madonnaz, it sounds as if it comes from the heart."

In the end it didn't matter what the critics thought: *True Blue* was an enormous worldwide hit. It reached Number One in 12 countries, sold over 18 million copies, and remains Madonna's best-selling album. Packaged in a heavily treated jacket with its iconic Herb Ritts photograph, it portrays Madonna having one last embrace of her youth before waving it goodbye.

When Madonna dramatically changed her look for *True Blue*, she moved on to more traditional, classic styling, leaving the more outré fashions for her stage costumes. Maripol was left with huge amounts of unwanted stock—and a flood of imitators—and went bankrupt. She wouldn't make another piece of jewelry for a decade, but she and Madonna remained good friends. Madonna's new image, along with the title track, made a play to return to the surface-level innocence of the Eisenhower era, a late flowering of simple values of love and harmony, away from the shame and underskirts of *Like A Virgin*.

If Madonna's love for Sean Penn had not been made patently abundant by the end of the album, the final credit in the inner bag made it crystal clear: "This album is dedicated to my husband, the coolest guy in the universe." *True Blue* itself is still thought of with great affection. It is the view from the summit, after the template was struck and before things would become musically more mature and difficult. It may be flawed, but if pop is all about capturing a moment, Madonna had just released the coolest record in the universe.

CHAPTER 5
VIDEO STAR

Madonna's tight artistic control and high standards meant that her videos would come to be seen as pieces of performance art. Fully understanding how to love—and at times worship—the camera, she began to create a separate videography that would complement yet stand quite discrete from her recorded work. By the time of *True Blue*, the promotional videos to accompany Madonna's singles were as eagerly awaited as the records themselves: what would Madonna be wearing, what would the storyline be?

Madonna was right there at the birth of MTV and immediately understood its potency. "If I didn't have a video, I don't think all the kids in the Midwest would know about me," she later noted. "It takes the place of touring. Everybody sees them everywhere. That really has a lot to do with the success of my albums."

It took a while for these clips to hit their stride, however. Returning to her earliest videos is like looking back at gauche old photographs of an early girlfriend. Ed Steinberg's 'Everybody' clip was a standard in-club performance, with Madonna in a brown jerkin, working through her best 80s dance moves, most notably her early wobbly crucifixion pose. She is backlit by four simple spotlights, and the overall feel is a simple, literal description of the song's message: music taking control.

'Burning Up,' directed by the then-ubiquitous Steve Barron, underlined how strident Madonna was amid the symbolism of flowers, statues, lips, and more dancing in her jerkin. Madonna was styled by Maripol for this one, and there are close-ups of her chains and bracelets as she lays in the road ahead of an oncoming car (which then transforms into a speedboat). Dressed in white and writhing around barefoot, Madonna looks momentarily vulnerable. Yet the final frame sees her driving the car, suggesting that any vulnerability could well have been a device used to fool the car's male driver into handing over the keys.

There was no official promo for 'Holiday,' so the 'Lucky Star' clip, directed by Arthur Pierson, was the first to properly define Madonna for her audience. She and her dancers—brother Christopher and Erica Bell—work through the various moves, Madonna in cropped leggings, dancing perfectly, with plenty of head shots, at once impish, showy and coquettish. The final lingering fade of Madonna in her Ray-Bans suggests that she is the 'lucky star' of the title, and that her viewers have indeed been lucky to share the moment with her.

Michelle Ferrone's clip for 'Borderline' marks the first serious attempt at narrative in a Madonna video. After becoming a model, a girl from the streets is estranged from her boyfriend because of her dalliances with a photographer. The rest involves pool playing, cars, and graffiti art—including the none-too-subtle spray-painting of a cross over a male statue's genitalia. It also acknowledges the popularity of breakdancing, which was almost obligatory for most videos of the era. The suggestion of an affair with a photographer seemed to tip a knowing wink to Madonna's ability to seize an opportunity to flirt where the power lay. Her look to the camera at the end says it all: she is moving on up.

In 1984, Madonna was just one of many women vying for airtime amid the slew of female artists breaking through such as Cindy Lauper and the newly reestablished Tina Turner. The promos accompanying *Like A Virgin* established Madonna as the video megastar. 'Like A Virgin' and 'Material Girl' were just the start—every other promo from 1985, such as the film clips for 'Crazy For You' and 'Into The Groove,' simply underlined and reinforced the message.

The reveal during the first chorus of 'Like A Virgin' of Madonna in her wedding dress was pretty much the moment when the world fell in love with her. Director Mary Lambert captured Madonna in Venice, Italy, one of the most romantic and religious cities in the world. The setting was germane. Here, in her full regalia, she played out the simultaneously sluttish and pure sides of her personality, first in her white dress and then in her more conventional attire on a gondola. The imagery, combined with the strength of the record and the power of its production, made her unassailable. With a lion roaming the streets and a lover—the man who has reinstated her chastity—in a lion mask, the suggestion is that Madonna is still in control in a world of predatory males.

For Madonna then to emulate that most untouchable and tragic of icons, Marilyn Monroe, in her next clip for 'Material Girl'—well, she was clearly marking out her territory. Although there is a longer storyline to go with it, the central clip of Madonna as Marilyn, updating 'Diamonds Are A Girl's Best Friend,' was shown everywhere. "She's the biggest star in the universe right now," the assistant gasps to his director at its start. There is delightful ambiguity as the clip at once congratulates and satirizes the 80s obsession for specious materialism. Mary Lambert's promo highlights the dichotomy between an artist's onstage and offscreen personas; away from the set, Madonna/Marilyn is wooed by the film's director (played by Keith Carradine) with a simple, dowdy bunch of flowers and a ride in his truck. That's all a simple girl needs, not material possessions. And then, possibly, a bigger role in his next film ...

Madonna's acting experience in *Desperately Seeking Susan* and growing understanding of filmmaking meant her performances in her subsequent videos improved a hundred-fold. These advances paved the way for the glory of the *True Blue* videos: the stories-in-song of 'Papa Don't Preach' and 'La Isla Bonita,' the spirited delivery of 'True Blue,' the moving yet static 'Live To Tell.'

It was the ornate detail and storyline of Jean-Baptiste Mondino's 'Open Your Heart' clip that heralded this newfound maturity and ushered in the next era of Madonna videos. Bar the direct film clips and straight-to-camera message of 1987's 'Who's That Girl,' the *Like A Prayer* videos would once again set Madonna far ahead of her peers. The success of Madonna's promos and the box-office business of *Desperately Seeking Susan* meant that she could command higher fees and expect huge audiences—so who better to make a film with than her husband?

The Poison Penns, as they were quickly dubbed, thought that co-starring together would be the best way to silence their critics. It would show that they were both talented, and that the harmony they had away from the cameras could be replicated in front of it. It would also be commercial dynamite, given her standing as the most famous pop star in the world and his as a talented firebrand of an actor. They had already appeared together briefly in the David Rabe play *Goose And Tom Tom* at New York's Lincoln Center, but now they would be playing to the biggest possible audiences.

The couple were offered the lead roles in *Shanghai Surprise*, a comedy based on Tony Kendrick's novel *Faraday's Flowers* and produced by Hand Made Films, George Harrison and Denis O'Brien's successful independent film company (itself largely funded by Monty Python money). Sadly, if ever a film encapsulated Madonna's failure as an actor, this was it. Made at a time when the eyes of the world were on her, it is a feeble attempt at a star vehicle—an opportunist attempt to turn her and Penn into a latter-day Spencer Tracy and Katherine Hepburn. It had long niggled Madonna that critics suggested she wasn't really acting in *Desperately Seeking Susan*. Here, as a virginal missionary, Gloria Tatlock, who falls into the path of wiseacre tie-salesman Glendon Wasey (Penn), she was playing completely against type.

Shanghai Surprise could and should have been a marvelous opportunity to capitalize on her international success. Instead, it will forever by remembered as a global advertisement for the notoriety of Mr and Mrs Penn. Shooting began in January 1986 and was bedeviled with setbacks. After a brief spell of calm in Shanghai itself—where the crew were denied the right to film—production moved to the British colony of Hong Kong. It was enormous, worldwide news, but the combination of an inexperienced director, Jim Goddard, inclement weather, and having to pay protection money to criminal gangs was no recipe for harmony.

By the time filming moved to the UK in February 1986, the British media had become openly hostile. A press conference organized by George Harrison at Kensington Roof Gardens did little to ameliorate the situation. It ended with Madonna suggesting that she had "nothing to apologize for"—a statement that was rounded on by the tabloid press.

Shanghai Surprise was released in August 1968 and was greeted with derision and sneers. Time has not been kind—it remains an almost unbearable blend of British character actors huffing and puffing around the comic-book inscrutability of the Chinese and the solid-oak performances of its stars. Madonna complained that all of her scenes were edited to make her seem airheaded, when, in fact, airheadedness is one of her most endearing qualities in the film. Penn meanwhile looks like a psychotic George Michael.

Madonna later described the film as "a truly miserable experience that I learned a lot from and don't regret." It took $2.3 million at the US box office—from a budget of $17 million—and was nominated for six Golden Raspberries. (It won only one: Worst Actress.)

There is a moment of prescience when Tatlock tells Wasey: "I expect our association to be an extremely brief one." Like the film that so publicly captured their romance, Madonna and Penn's relationship was doomed to failure. They finally split in 1989, and in many respects they never fully got over each other.

"From the time we got married I got the feeling that people wanted our marriage to fail," Madonna later said. "They couldn't make up their minds: they wanted me to be pregnant, or they wanted us to get a divorce. That put a lot of strain on our relationship after a while. It's been a character-building experience."

Some years later, Madonna described Penn as "an incredible actor ... I think he's done very well and I'm honored to know him. He's an incredible human being. He's intelligent, he's talented and even though things didn't work out for us in terms of our marriage, I don't regret marrying him for a moment."

Penn's assessment was more brutal. "I admit it, I was a smart-ass," he recalled. "And so was she. It was a relationship made in heaven, two smart-asses going through life together. How romantic."

For Madonna, the year 1987 was set against a backdrop of tension and sadness. Her volatile relationship with Penn was put under immense strain by her support of her friend Martin Burgoyne, who had been diagnosed with AIDS, and who died at the start of the year while Madonna was putting the finishing touches to her next project: the film, album, and tour *Who's That Girl*. Burgoyne's passing brought the loss of her mother and the precariousness of her marriage into sharp focus.

Originally titled *Slammer*, *Who's That Girl* was directed by James Foley and starred Griffin Dunne and Sir John Mills. Released in August 1987, it was intended as a light comedy—an updated version of *Bringing Up Baby*, the 1938 Howard Hawks film. It centers on the upstanding Loudon Trott (Dunne), who is engaged to be married to Ms Worthington (Bibi Besch), a woman he doesn't love. Then along comes the wild Nikki Finn (Madonna), who has been framed by the mafia for murder. Trott has to escort her from prison to a bus terminal; she hijacks him to prove that she didn't commit the crime. Finn was rather optimistically described in the press release as "a feisty, free-spirited femme destined to take her place among the screen's great comic heroines." She didn't.

Who's That Girl premiered in Times Square on August 6 1987 in front of a crowd estimated at 10,000. Madonna told her story of arriving penniless years earlier. Although her star was now at its early zenith, she was always acutely aware of where she had come from. Her brother, Christopher, accompanied her to the premiere, but would later dismiss the film as "another screwball comedy" in his autobiography, noting that Madonna didn't realize it was "awful" until much too late.

But with Madonna, of course, it was still about the music. Feminist critic Camille Paglia later recalled "my stunned admiration as I sat in the theater in 1987 and first experienced the crashing, descending chords of 'Causing A Commotion.' If you want to hear the essence of modernity, listen to these chords, infernal, apocalyptic, and grossly sensual. This is the authentic voice of the fin de siècle." (She found the film itself "dreadful.")

The film's title track continued the Latin theme begun on 'La Isla Bonita' and became another colossal hit when it was released as a single in June 1987. Madonna had called co-writer Pat Leonard during filming and asked him to fill out a backing track for her to combine with lyrics that reflected the experience of her character. The finished song was recorded in a single day, with Madonna cutting her vocals in a solitary take. Leonard and Stephen Bray added guitars and percussion.

"I had some very specific ideas in mind, music that would stand on its own as well as support and enhance what was happening on screen," Madonna later said. "The songs aren't necessarily about Nikki ... But there's a spirit to this music that captures both what the film and the character's about." It was a Number One hit in the USA, Britain, and Canada. Madonna became the first artist to accumulate six Number Ones in the 80s—and the first female solo artist ever to amass so many.

Although never seen as one of her greats, 'Who's That Girl' offered a neat précis of all of her work to date, and was by far and away the best song on the soundtrack. The companion album was released on July 21 1987 and featured three further Madonna tracks (two of which became singles) alongside cuts from Coati Mundi, Scritti Politti, and Club Nouveau. It was another huge international hit.

Stephen Bray was the album's musical director, and with Madonna co-wrote the Number Two hit 'Causing A Commotion,' an out-and-out retread of 'Into The Groove.' As if the familiar bridge isn't enough, the similarities are underlined by the oh-so-blatant line "It's how you play the game / So get into the groove." But no matter—here was a perfect hit to sustain Madonna's popularity as the Who's That Girl World Tour played around the world.

In Europe, the third single to be taken from the album was 'The Look Of Love,' a touching ballad co-written by Madonna and Leonard that features an intricate keyboard riff that would later be sampled by Soulwax. The final new track on the album, 'Can't Stop,' is one of Madonna's best and most overlooked recordings. It bears all the hallmarks of classic 'up' Madonna as she screams and shouts a lover's name, with an affecting choral vocal at the end, and is dated only by the use of vocoders.

Madonna left nothing to chance on the Who's That Girl World Tour. The 37 dates began in June 1987 and ended in September. At the start of the tour her publicist, Liz Rosenberg, announced: "You'll see a different look this year, but it's still Madonna, still bigger than life." The tour raised the benchmark for Madonna's live performances. Circling the globe at the same time as shows by Michael Jackson and Prince, here was a revue with a variety of new elements: moving stairways, projections, gangster routines, and more. It was Madonna's first fully staged extravaganza, and was directed by film and theater choreographer Jeffery Hornaday, with sets designed by Jerome Sirlin and lighting by Peter Morse.

Pat Leonard once again took on the role of musical director, marshaling a band containing a variety of players able to extemporize and improvise around the songs: Jonathan Moffet on drums, Jai Winding on keyboards, James Harrah and David Williams on guitar, Kerry Hatch on bass, and Luis Conte on percussion. The backing singers were Niki Harris, Donna DeLory, and Debra Parson; Harris and DeLory would become firm friends with Madonna and ended up accompany her on a variety of subsequent tours and performances. The dancers were Shabba Doo, Angel Ferreira, and Christopher Finch, with British faux-soul outfit Level 42 picked as the support act.

When Madonna arrived in Japan to start the tour, the response was akin to Beatlemania. The opening night was halted by a freak thunderstorm, with the 35,000 fans remaining rooted to the spot in the stadium. The show was rescheduled, and the euphoria that greeted the performers was remarkable. Having learned a few things from the tentative and sometimes gauche performances on The Virgin Tour, Madonna was at the peak of her game.

Opening with 'Open Your Heart,' she brought the video to life with a 13-year-old Christopher Finch playing the Felix Howard role. Madonna was revealed as a trim, muscular peroxide blond. For 'Papa Don't Preach,' Madonna wore the leather jacket from the video, with the instrumental break intercut with images of key world events that had taken place during her lifetime: the moon landing, space travel, Martin Luther King, the Kennedys; miniskirts, riots, civil rights, war graves; Tommy Smith's black power salute, crash test dummies, atomic bombs; all pretty chaotic stuff. All of this was played out against a backdrop of the Reagan White House, and ended with a plea for Safe Sex—a message writ large across the tour, in light of her friend Martyn Burgoyne's passing.

The shows became a military operation. The costumes and accessories were all reinforced so that quick changes could easily be performed, with four copies of each outfit. Madonna was completely in charge of everything. Rob Seduski, her chief wardrobe coordinator on the tour, described her as "very hands on. She directs the whole thing ... She's always been totally focused and easy to deal with. If you're straight ahead with her, she's fine. I love that she's always combined theatrics with fashion. That is something that she initiated. It's her trademark."

The tour gained critical favor as it reached America on June 27. *Rolling Stone* suggested that Madonna was "simply the first female entertainer who has ever starred in a show of this scope, a fusion of Broadway-style choreography and post-disco song and dance that tops the standards set by previous live concert firebrands like Prince and Michael Jackson." Many commentators simply looked on in awe at the sheer scale of the tour. Brett Milano of the *Chicago Tribune* seemed aghast ahead of the Soldier Field show on July 31. "Instead of a conventional concert," he wrote, "it's designed as a moveable Broadway show—carried by a whopping 25 semi-trucks." Milano then proceeded to quantify the component parts, numbering the seven costume changes, the two video screens, the six dancers, the Pat Leonard-led band of 'studio aces' and the setlist, which he described as "heavy on greatest hits." (In 1987, this form of stadium tour was still in its infancy, and was mainly the preserve of old male rockers.)

The Who's That Girl World Tour gained even greater impetus when it arrived in the UK in August for the start of its European leg. It was the first time Madonna had given a full show in the UK (her 1983 concerts had been performed to backing tracks). The press continued the war of attrition that had begun the previous year during the filming of *Shanghai Surprise*. On August 29, Madonna presented Jacques Chirac with a check for AIDS charities in front of 130,000 people in Paris, France—her biggest audience to date. The tour ended on September 6 in Florence, by which time Madonna had become the top-grossing female entertainer of 1987. (The tour itself grossed over $20 million.)

A long-form video of the tour—*Ciao, Italia!*, recorded in Turin and Florence—was released the following May. Fresh, spirited, and exuberant, it actually goes some way toward capturing the magic of the live performance. The *Who's That Girl* film and its odds-and-ends soundtrack may have been one thing, but here was a full-strength, full quality production, a mix of spectacle and song with Madonna as ever-so-enthusiastic ringmaster.

Although the album and a film were something of a holding measure, they pulled everything together and brought a natural close to five years of solid hard work. Madonna was now a superstar, with the attendant troubled superstar marriage. The end of the tour coincided with Sean Penn's release from prison after serving 33 days of a two-month sentence for assaulting a photographer. Madonna filed for divorce, but then rescinded and attempted to save the relationship. Her efforts would ultimately fail, but no one could question the zeal with which she attempted to keep it together. Now, however, it was time to take stock.

To keep the Madonna brand afloat, some four months after the release of the *Who's That Girl* soundtrack—and a full 18 months since her last full album—she returned to reinforce her disco roots with the mini-album *You Can Dance*. An oh-so 80s phenomenon, the mini-album had its genesis in the club scene, and had been particularly popular among new-wave artists such as The B-52s, Soft Cell, The Cure, and Pet Shop Boys.

What was particularly successful about *You Can Dance* was the way the tracks were mixed into a continuous segue. It was very much a forerunner of today's club mixes. This had been happening in clubs for years, but Madonna once again popularized a breaking wave by capturing it on vinyl.

The record's striking red jacket showed her dressed for action as a matador. Its seven tracks are drawn from each of her albums to date, with the *Madonna* material faring best. The 'Holiday' mix—with additional beats and guitars by John 'Jellybean' Benitez—works effectively, as do the versions of 'Everybody,' 'Burning Up,' and 'Physical Attraction.' *Like A Virgin* and *True Blue* are represented by just one track apiece: 'Over And Over' and 'Where's The Party.'

As seamless beat-matching (as we know it today) was in its infancy, some of the edits—by Benitez, Shep Pettibone, Steve Thompson, and Forrest & Heller—now sound rather jarring and abrupt. The most successful re-rub, and rightfully so, is Pettibone's colossal mix of 'Into The Groove.' If you look past the dated vocal repetition, this mix adds depth and bounce to the original (the shortened version would end up on Madonna's 1991 greatest hits set *The Immaculate Collection*). The major selling point of *You Can Dance*, however, was the previously unreleased *True Blue* out-take 'Spotlight,' itself an update of the 'Holiday' formula.

You Can Dance was released on November 17 1987, and while missing out on the US Top Ten, it still managed to sell a million copies—no mean feat for a mini-album of material that had largely been previously released elsewhere.

Madonna was publicly strangely silent throughout 1988, aside from her role in David Mamet's three-handed play *Speed-The-Plow*. Written as an attack on the cynicism of the money-grabbing film industry, it is dense and wordy, with the action centered on the verbal badinage between a pair of Hollywood producers, Charlie Fox and Bobby Gould. Gould has the dilemma of presenting two ideas to his paymasters: one a spiritual, moral, and frequently opaque tale based on a novel, the other a huge, obvious, action blockbuster. Gould invites the office temp, Karen, back to his apartment to give her opinion on the novel, with the ulterior motive of having sex with her. However, her analysis of the novel touches him. The next day it is ambiguously revealed that she has only adopted her point of view to get ahead in the industry.

Directed by Gregory Mosher, *Speed-The-Plow* premiered at the Royale Theater on Broadway on May 3 1988 and ran until December 31. Mamet regulars Joe Mantega and Ron Silver played Bobby Gould and Charlie Fox respectively. Madonna played Karen from May until September. The low-key, cynical production was just the thing Madonna needed to show that she could play straight and relatively serious.

The role came about after Madonna had dinner in New York with director Mike Nichols, who told her about the play and recommended her for the part. Speaking to *Interview* magazine the following year, Madonna recalled being "driven blindly" to the character of Karen, although the rigidity of the role and the relatively downbeat character ultimately didn't suit her.

"It was just grueling, having to do the same thing every night, playing a character who is so unlike me," she later said. "I didn't have the glamorous or flamboyant part. I was the scapegoat." By the end of the run, she felt "as miserable as the character I played."

The reviews were decidedly mixed. Dennis Cunningham of CBS felt that Madonna's "ineptitude is scandalously thorough … she cannot give meaning to the words she is saying," but the *New York Times* described her performance as "sincere, self-effacing, and tightly controlled."

If nothing else, the play made Madonna something of a fixture on the Manhattan scene once again. She was living in her apartment on Central Park West and in the midst of her very public relationship with Sandra Bernhard, who comforted her through the dying embers of her marriage to Sean Penn. Madonna later said that playing the part of Karen left her feeling defeated and affected her confidence during the summer of 1988. The result of all that, however, was perhaps the finest album of her career.

CHAPTER 6
IN THE MIDNIGHT HOUR

Although it contains moments of unparalleled fluff, *Like A Prayer* is a personal work of great beauty, and one that delves deep into Madonna's soul. It remains her most accomplished and audacious work, and is very much an 'adult' record—and as such was a brave move for a pop singer, so adored by the youth, to have made.

But the world was changing, and Madonna's fans were growing older, too. A lot had happened since her last full album, the positive, upbeat *True Blue*: AIDS had decimated the happy-go-lucky world in which the singer had grown up, and on January 5 1989, Madonna filed for divorce from Sean Penn (citing "irreconcilable differences"), left their Malibu home, and moved to the Hollywood Hills. Although her private life was in turmoil, she could be secure in the knowledge that she had just recorded her best album ever—a big, mature record that, while nodding to her dance floor roots, had its head in weighty ideas and serious-minded subject matter.

So much fed into *Like A Prayer*: her much publicized friendship with Sandra Bernhard, her crumbling marriage to Penn, her grief following the passing of Martin Burgoyne. Madonna was, in many respects, trapped by the celebrity she had so craved, and for which she had worked so hard. Her love life was in a state of flux, her romance with John Kennedy Jr quashed by his mother, Jacqueline Onassis, who felt it was a little too similar to her late husband's dalliance with Marilyn Monroe.

The rigor and boredom of her run in *Speed-The-Plow* had depressed but ultimately enlivened her. She knew that her return to full-length recording would have to be vibrant, challenging, and different. Intense introspection was to follow—this was Madonna playing nobody except for herself, looking back to her childhood, her Catholicism, her loss. In 1985, she had told *The Face* that at some point she would want to "write about growing up and feeling lonely. How you never find the love you need at home." Now she was giving herself the opportunity to do so. "I wrote what I felt," she later said. For once, she wanted everybody to know what the songs meant. While there is ambiguity in the lyrics, the listener is left in little doubt that the album flows from her soul. "I've been dealing with more specific issues that mean a lot to me," she explained carefully at the time of the album's release. "They're about an assimilation of experiences I've had in my life and in relationships. They're about my mother, my father, and bonds with my family about the pain of dying, or growing up and letting go."

Madonna worked slowly and deliberately on the *Like A Prayer* material. Stephen Bray contributed two of the album's best dance tracks—'Express Yourself' and 'Keep It Together'—as well as two songs that were ultimately left unused, 'First Is A Kiss' and 'Love Attack.' But it was her collaborations with Pat Leonard that gave the album its overall bite. In many respects this is his album as much as it is Madonna's. "She was upset and in tears a lot of the time," he later said. "Normally she's a very fast worker, but it took maybe three or four times as long to make the record because she kept breaking down; we called it her divorce album."

For an album with so bleak an outlook, the sessions were generally very focused. They took place mainly at Johnny Yuma in Los Angeles, the studio Madonna and Leonard had built with the income from *True Blue*. The relationship between the two was close and productive. Sometimes he would come into the studio with a fully written melody, such as the one that became 'Oh Father,' for Madonna to add lyrics; other times, Madonna would arrived with a word or phrase and wait for him to "sort of pound out the chords."

Leonard and Bray worked through their friendly rivalry to support Madonna and coax out her ideas. The musicians on the album include the core of her live band—guitarist Bruce Gaitsch, drummer Jonathan Moffett, and keyboard player Jai Winding—as well as English guitarist Chester Kamen and the legendary session drummer Jeff Pocaro. One of the more interesting guest players was bass player Guy Pratt, who had recently become part of the touring line-up of Pink Floyd and had met Leonard while working with Bryan Ferry. In his amusing book, *My Bass And Other Animals*, he recalls knowing that Madonna had arrived when he heard a cry of "TIME IS MONEY AND THE MONEY IS MINE!" The session went well, with Madonna informing drummer Moffat that he should come in when she lifted her blouse, or telling Pratt he would know he was playing well if it made his "dick hard."

"Madonna was different to most of the female singers I'd worked with in that her demands were feasible and delivered in plain English," Pratt notes, "so us musos could usually understand and deliver what she wanted." Madonna thrived in this setup, working with mature, committed professionals. "To me total control means you can lose objectivity," she later explained. "What I like is to be surrounded by really talented, intelligent people I can trust. And ask them for their advice and input. But let's face it: I'm not going to make an album and not show up for the vocals or make a video and have nothing to do with the script."

The 11 tracks on *Like A Prayer* cover a variety of styles and moods. The pace is set quickly and dramatically by the opener, its title track and lead single. It is as impressive as it is bold, and is arguably Madonna's single best song. The subject matter, instrumentation, arrangement, and subtle use of choir all work to excellent, poetic effect. The song finds Madonna kneeling before a God-like figure, asking for forgiveness. The love she feels reminds her of how she feels toward a lover; the call to prayer brings her back to happier times, where God is a mystery, a muse, the intensity of the lyrics matched by the intensity of the instrumentation.

Despite its weighty subject matter, the song came relatively easily. When Leonard first started working on it, it bore a Latin influence, with bongos and congas, but that soon changed. At Madonna's request, Leonard brought in former Disciples singer Andraé Crouch, who turned up with his gospel expertise—and his choir—and quite literally extemporized around the song. (Aware of Madonna's reputation, Crouch had vetted the words to the song before agreeing to sing it. He had an illustrious past, having sung with such legends as Stevie Wonder and Quincy Jones.)

Never before had Madonna sounded so wonderful on record. The moment she ushers in the massed vocalists with the words "Let the choir sing'" is among the most celebratory in popular music. It was a triumph.

The intensity of the middle-eight, the controlled build of it all, and the unforgettable climax of the accompanying promo video add up to one of Madonna's most dramatic records.

It was of course the video, directed by Mary Lambert, that caused the greatest controversy. It is a fantastic piece of work, featuring what appears to be a black Christ, sex on an altar, burning crosses—just another day at the office for Madonna, then. It took the song's theme of spiritual redemption and recast it as one of Madonna's best and most talked-about clips.

The video gave the public its first glimpse of this new Madonna for these new times. She appeared with minimal make up and black flowing hair, looking to all intents and purposes like an Italian Catholic peasant who had just come from a day out in the fields. The artwork for the 12-inch single release was also noteworthy. While the seven-inch carried the soon-to-be-ubiquitous still of Madonna praying, the 12-inch featured a painting by her brother, Christopher, that once again underlined her new gravitas. Madonna is pictured with the letters 'MVLC' (her confirmation name, Madonna Veronica Louise Ciccone) above her, and a fallen 'P' near her heart. She may no longer have been Mrs Penn, but it was clear that there would always be a place next to her heart for her ex-husband.

On January 25 1989, Madonna signed a $5 million deal with Pepsi to make a two-minute commercial in return for sponsorship of her forthcoming tour. Pepsi-Cola had been edging closer to its long-term rivals, Coca-Cola, thanks to its increasing involvement with rock and pop sponsorship. In the 80s, the company had worked with David Bowie, Lionel Richie, and—most notoriously—Michael Jackson.

In 1989, Madonna was the biggest star in the world, and therefore the perfect candidate to increase Pepsi's market share. It was the scale of the deal that was most noteworthy: in return for $5 million, the company would sponsor the tour and make four commercials, simultaneously broadcasting them in 40 countries on the same night. The deal was signed in time for Madonna to unveil her first new single in 18 months, 'Like A Prayer.' It became a tale of two videos.

A teaser ad was prepared for the commercial, featuring a young aborigine crossing the outback to watch Madonna on a satellite channel in a remote cafe. It was intercut with footage of Madonna rehearsing with a grandiose voiceover: "No matter where you are in the world on March 2, get to a TV and watch Pepsi's two-minute Madonna commercial featuring her latest release, 'Like A Prayer' for the very first time."

So, on March 2 1989, an estimated 250 million people tuned in to watch the commercial, a simple, nostalgic tale overseen by Joe Pytka, who had previous directed promo videos for Michael Jackson. Shot at Culver Studios in January, it was sweet and affecting, underlining the need to "make a wish." It opens with a carefree Madonna enjoying a can of Pepsi while watching home movies of herself as a child. At the end, she toasts her eight-year-old self, celebrating the ultimate success of the young Madonna's dreams of superstardom. The message was clear: wish hard enough, and, with an appropriate amount of highly flavored carbonated water inside you, you too could be a superstar.

Once the 'real,' Mary Lambert-directed 'Like A Prayer' promo aired, however, all hell broke loose. With its underlying plea for honesty and salvation, overcoming racism, and telling the truth, the video featured burning crosses; a statue of the black St Martin De Porres (Leon Robinson), who comes to life in a dream, whispers in Madonna's ear, and kisses her; and stigmata appearing in Madonna's palms. As the black man in the video is wrongfully arrested, she is seen singing in front of yet more burning crosses—and that is only the half of it.

The Pepsi commercial was only shown once more after its much-hyped debut. Although they had scrupulously vetted their own clip, the Pepsi executives realized they hadn't actually asked to see the other video for the single—but then, they argued, why would they have needed to? Certainly, the commercial Ptyka delivered fulfilled all the criteria of the Pepsi brand.

Pepsi was threatened by a boycott of its product—and, allegedly, a removal of their drink dispensers from Catholic schools. The company withdrew the clip and canceled plans for three further commercials. Madonna lost the $5 million sponsorship deal she had just received from Pepsi-Cola, but she kept the money and her artistic integrity, while the tour received a new sponsor in the shape of the electronics giant Pioneer.

"When I think of controversy, I never really think people are going to be half as shocked as they are at what I do," she concluded in 1990. "I really couldn't believe how out of control the whole Pepsi thing got." Nonetheless, when 'Like A Prayer' won the Viewers' Choice Best Video trophy at the 1989 MTV Awards, Madonna—never one to underplay the power of understatement—thanked Pepsi-Cola for "causing so much controversy." As Pat Leonard later noted: "She's always willing to deal with whatever reaction people have. Obviously, if you're on a hill dancing with half a dozen burning crosses behind you, someone's going to say something." People did, but it didn't stop the record selling.

Madonna's relationship with religion has been central to her career. Determined to create controversy from the off, she has, at times, appeared to be waging a one-woman war with Rome.

Madonna grew up in a strict Catholic household. There were, as she has said in many subsequent interviews, nuns and priests in her house, and there was a family ritual where all religious artifacts in the household would be covered in purple cloth. Her deeply religious upbringing proved—alongside the death of her mother—to be the driving force throughout the first half of her career. Her reckless religious polarity defined the first decade of her career: she was taunting the Catholic Church like a naughty schoolgirl one minute, embracing it and asking for forgiveness the next. Everything she said or did seemed to have been designed to push boundaries as far as they would go—and yet this was the girl who believed, until she was 12, that the devil himself lived in her basement.

Early in her career, Madonna revealed: "When I was tiny my grandmother used to beg me not to go with boys, to love Jesus and be a good girl. I grew up with two images of women: the Virgin and the whore." The virgin/whore juxtaposition has guided her through her work from the start. All those great early statements—about how losing her virginity was "a career move," or how crucifixes are sexy "because there is a naked man on them"—were meat and drink to feature writers, and so too was her pronouncement that "growing up I thought nuns were very beautiful. In fact if I hadn't grown up to become a star I would have become a nun."

Madonna turned down the calling to be a nun, she said, only because they wouldn't let her use her own name. "Catholicism gives you an inner strength, whether you end up believing it later or not," she told *Time* magazine in 1985. "It's the backbone. I think maybe the essence of Catholicism I haven't rejected, but the theory of it I have. I believe in God."

Madonna's belief in God meant that she constantly wished to question the rituals and ideals of the church. Her strident feminism, for example, was at odds with the church's belief in male supremacy. 'Papa Don't Preach' took a view that chimed with what she later called her "own personal zeitgeist of standing up to male authorities, whether it's the pope or the catholic church or my father and his conservative, patriarchal ways."

'Live To Tell' spoke of hidden things that could only appear at confession, while by the time of 'Like A Prayer,' religious references were everywhere. Now she was singing openly about her relationship with her faith (or lack of). In interviews, Madonna explained the effect the religion had had on her psyche. "Sometimes I'm racked with guilt when I needn't be," she told *Rolling Stone* magazine. "And that, to me, is left over from my Catholic upbringing. Because in Catholicism you are born a sinner and you are a sinner all your life. ... Catholicism is not a soothing religion. It's a painful religion."

The real trouble started with the already controversial 'Like A Prayer' video and its suggestion that all priests are sexually repressed. The Reverend Donald Wildmon, head of the American Family Organization, was outraged that amid all the burning crosses and interracial love, "Madonna, who [in the video] represents Christ, is shown in a scene suggesting that she has sex with the priest, obviously to free him from sexual repression. That is absolutely repugnant to Christians." (For the next year, Wildmon and his association refused to drink Pepsi.)

Madonna took every opportunity to swipe at religion. "You know how religion is," she told *Interview* magazine in 1990. "Guys get to do everything. They get to be altar boys. They get to stay out late. Take their shirts off in the summer. They get to pee standing up. They get to fuck a lot of girls and not worry about getting pregnant."

A year later, Madonna's Blond Ambition World Tour would be littered with religious imagery. Her simulated masturbation from the raised bed set would draw cries of dismay across the world, as would the 'Justify My Love' video, in which the sex scenes are intercut with images of crucifixes. And that was before her *Sex* book came out.

"I do believe religion and eroticism are absolutely related," Madonna told Norman Mailer in 1994. "And I think my original feelings of sexuality and eroticism originated in going to church ... it's very sensual, and it's all about what you're not supposed to do. Everything's forbidden, and everything's behind heavy stuff—the confessional, heavy green drapes and stained-glass windows, the rituals, the kneeling—there's something very erotic about that. After all, it's very sadomasochistic, Catholicism."

The birth of her daughter, Lourdes, in 1996 and her subsequent embracing of the Kabbalah seemed to bring this chapter a close. To many, it seems as though the days when Madonna was constantly at war with the church have long since passed. But it never quite went away: on the Confessions Tour of 2006, she performed 'Live To Tell' wearing a crown of thorns while being crucified on a giant, mirrored cross, leading religious leaders to describe the tour's stop in Rome as "an act of hostility toward the Roman Catholic Church."

Around the same time, one lone voice appeared to call into question the depth and clarity of Madonna's religious viewpoint. In his 2007 memoir *My Bass And Other Animals*, session player Guy Pratt recalls having a discussion with Madonna about "some aspect of morality," to which she replied: "It's a Catholic thing, you wouldn't understand." Pratt then revealed that he, too, was a Catholic (albeit non-practicing). "Yeah," Madonna countered, "but that's English Catholic, that's different." Pratt goes on to detail how he "tried to explain that was she was thinking of was the Church Of England, but she was having none of it." Since then, he adds, he has felt "slightly skeptical whenever I hear her pontificate about whatever religion she's currently embracing."

'Like A Prayer' proved to be the perfect song to launch its parent album. The single went on to sell five million copies and topped the charts in 15

countries, becoming one of Madonna's most successful and well-regarded works. It also chimed a chord at symbolic moments: she sang it in London's Hyde Park at the Live 8 concert in 2005, dressed in white and holding the hand of Birhan Woldu, the child whose fly-ridden face on CBC News in 1984 encapsulated for millions the Ethiopian famine, and performed a pared-down acoustic version during the *Hope For Haiti* telethon in January 2010.

It would be wrong, however, to take 'Like A Prayer' as an indication that the whole album would feel like heavy weather. It might be serious, but it is not downbeat, as proven by the second track, 'Express Yourself,' one of Madonna's most strident, upbeat anthems. Written with Stephen Bray, it captures the singer at her very best—updating the sassy, saucy feel of 'Holiday' with a rallying call for women to feel comfortable calling the shots in a relationship and having a "big strong hand to lift you to higher ground" (a somewhat bittersweet sentiment, perhaps, given what she had been going through personally at the time).

The song begins with Madonna's conspiratorial suggestion that the sisterhood should listen to her as she has something special to say—and she has. It answers back to 'Material Girl,' to date the most problematic song in her repertoire. While audiences were flummoxed by that song's irony, here there is little doubt. "You don't need diamond rings or 18-carat gold," she sings. "Fancy cars that go very fast / They never last no, no." The message is punched home by a big, Motown-influenced horn arrangement and booming bass beats.

As Camille Paglia later noted, "Madonna's command of massive, resonant basslines, which she heard in the funky dance clubs of Detroit and New York, has always impressed me. As an Italian Catholic, she uses them liturgically ... She sensed the buried pagan religiosity in disco." It's true: religion seems to seep through every pore of this album. But while she may have grown serious and deep, Madonna had not forgotten where she came from, and knew what many of her fans still wanted her to be. "If you don't express yourself, if you don't say what you want, then you're not going to get it," she later explained. "And in effect you are chained down by your inability to say what you feel or go after what you want."

Shot at Culver Studios in April 1989, the video for 'Express Yourself,' directed by David Fincher, is much less weighty than its predecessor. Set in a huge factory, it chimed with the wave of popular feminism of the late 80s that Madonna had helped nurture, and which would soon be expressed on the big screen in *Thelma And Louise*. The heavily stylized clip, based on Fritz Lang's 1926 film *Metropolis*, is a nod to the Chippendales generation. Madonna, dressed as Marlene Dietrich, looks on at her exclusively male workforce from her penthouse office as she decides which worker to single out to be her partner. As she strokes her cat, Ernst Stavro Blofeld-style, she views all the men toiling for her, the queen bee. Lots of water splashes around as Madonna makes her choice, leaving the other workers to scrap among themselves—these perfect yet uncivilized men.

Released as a single in May 1989, 'Express Yourself' continued to bolster the success of *Like A Prayer*. Although it reached Number One in only a handful of countries, it lodged high in a range of international Top Fives. The song became a stage favorite, and was performed with gusto at the 1989 MTV Awards show, offering a preview of the style and choreography that would soon be incorporated into the Blond Ambition tour.

The third track on *Like A Prayer* provides some relief from the relentless pace of the album's opening duo. The offbeat lope of 'Love Song' was the result of Madonna's much talked-about collaboration with her 80s megastar equal, Prince. The pair had a brief affair in 1985 after meeting at the American Music Awards in January of that year, a few weeks before Madonna met Sean Penn. As had been the case before with Jean-Michel Basquiat, it seemed inevitable that these two strong-minded and charismatic individuals, operating in roughly the same artistic space, would come together, however briefly. Rumor has it that Madonna was once in line to star opposite Prince in his *Graffiti Bridge*, until she decided that the project was too complex and unsuitable for her career path. 'Love Song' is a remnant of a musical the pair had intended to write together. While enjoyable, it was doomed not to match expectation. Two suns that burned so bright alone here render each other dim.

Madonna would later play down her relationship with Prince. "Ever since I've known Prince I've attached a smell to him, which is lavender, and I don't know why," she later said. "He reeks of it … he's very private and very shy. He's great when you get to know him, charming and funny in his own way. More than anything, he really comes alive when he's working ... I think Prince leads a very isolated life and I don't ... and that is the big difference between us."

'Love Song' is sparse, skeletal, and funky. Madonna speaks French; Prince delves deep for his best falsetto and produces something of a screeching beauty. And then it's over, and we're back to the confessional.

'Till Death Do Us Part' provides a great juxtaposition, highlighting the disintegration of Madonna's marriage with raw, exposed lines such about "turning your back on me at my hour of need." The song has a relentlessly jolly backing and comes complete with a engagingly childlike synthesizer riff and a Hawaiian-style guitar-solo, perhaps intended to distance the singer from the subject matter. This is further underlined by the fact that Madonna sings it in the third person, as if she is simply a singer of songs, playing another character. It ends with a breakdown over a wah-wah guitar before she intones the song's title over silence. "It's very much drawn from my life," she later admitted, "factually speaking about a relationship that is powerful and painful." The smashing of a bottle at the ends confirms that this was no joy ride.

Until the birth of her own daughter in 1996, Madonna's life and career seemed to be shaped by her mother's early death, best summed up by her oft-quoted line about becoming an over-achiever "to get approval from the world." Reflections on her family are the undeniable center of *Like A Prayer*, and 'Promise To Try' is clearly and openly about Madonna Fortin Ciccone, her mother. Here Madonna is at her most personal—almost unbearably so. The song is arranged simply for voice, piano, and a double string quartet. Madonna tells her inner child to cherish the memory of her mother, realizing that it is almost too late now, nearly 30 years after her mother's death. The words are delivered without any embellishment; the subtle orchestration and rawness of emotion are enough to floor the listener. Such introspection could easily have been rendered gauche and mawkish in lesser hands, yet here Madonna is straightforward, candid, and ultimately sympathetic. The song lays bare Madonna's inability to get truly close in a relationship for fear that the person she attaches herself to will eventually go. By the end of the song, however, she is telling herself that, while she will never forget her mother, she has to move on. "I can't kiss her goodbye," she sings, "but I promise to try."

Like A Prayer was the first Madonna album to be released after the CD format became fully established and so, after that emotional low point, we launch straight into a euphoric, upbeat number. 'Cherish' continues Madonna's long line of infectious and throwaway yet perfect, high-grade pop. It was written with Leonard and is, indeed, something to cherish, despite Madonna's later dismissal of it as "retarded" in a 2009 interview with *Rolling Stone*.

Written in the style of a giddy, girl-group ballad, 'Cherish' offers some necessary light relief. It might not share the strident feminism of 'Express Yourself,' but the lyrics—about Madonna's need for "two hearts that bleed in burning love"—are once again straight from the heart—with a wink and a twinkle in her eye, of course. There is also a clear nod to the beautiful 1966 hit of the same by The Association, which opens with the line "Cherish is the word I use to describe."

'Cherish' was released as the album's third single in August 1989, its Herb Ritts-directed video complemented the song perfectly, helping it to Number Two on *Billboard* and Number Three in the UK. Shot at Paradise Cove Beach in Malibu that July, the video shows Madonna splashing in waves and looking fresh and sweet: Madonna the lover, the friend, the companion, smiling in rapture, waiting for her merman (played by another of her paramours, dancer Tony Ward, who would later make a rather more fulsome appearance in the 'Justify My Love' promo). Unsure whether to be a one-woman *From Here To Eternity* or a very soppy home-movie, the clip is, either way, light and affecting, suggesting that after all the fuss, Madonna was just a sweet girl in the prime of her life having fun.

Track seven on the album offers something else again. With its pink elephants, lemonade, and call to the land of make believe, 'Dear Jessie' was Madonna's first attempt at something deliberately whimsical. Written ostensibly for Pat Leonard's three-year-old daughter, it demonstrates another remarkably separate facet of the new Madonna: after the religious discourse, the feminist anthem, and the affecting love song, now it's time for the tricksy children's ballad. The song can also be seen as another paean to Madonna's inner child, too—a retreat to a place of happiness and calm in times of crisis. It has a merry-go-round tempo change and heavily treated, Beatles-esque strings on the play out. It's also tremendous fun. With its animated video, 'Dear Jessie' was released as a single and kept the album in the hearts and charts of the world over Christmas 1989. By then, *Like A Prayer* was on its way to becoming something of a greatest hits. 'Dear Jessie' was another huge success, portraying Madonna as a kindly, child-loving soul, a long way from the corsets and crosses of yore.

The focus and intensity of the album's troubled heart demonstrate that all the emotions are real. There is not a hint of flippancy in these songs. After her mother has been dealt with, it's time for Madonna to explore her relationship with her father, and so, following the joyous crash of 'Dear Jessie,' the strings swell in for the deliberately ambiguous 'Oh Father.' The song chronicles a childhood full of love and hate, of a child craving recognition and receiving apathy and cruelty in return. Now that she has grown up, she no longer needs her dad, but she cannot live without him.

Recorded in a tiny New York studio during her run in *Speed-The-Plow*, 'Oh Father' deals not just with Madonna's father but with all the other authority figures in her life as she makes it clear that they "can't hurt me now." The lyrics may leave some listeners feeling rather sorry for her father, and by the end of the song it seems that she does, too. "You didn't mean to be rude," she sings. "Somebody hurt you too." There are clear parallels with Madonna's feelings toward religion—another relationship she will never truly be able to free herself from—which would be further emphasized when she performed the song at an altar on the Blond Ambition World Tour.

If anyone had any doubt about the song's true subject matter, the accompanying video rammed the message home with all the subtlety of a sledgehammer. Shot in black-and-white by David Fincher, it shows a girl gamboling playfully in the snow as a priest gives the last rites to her mother. The father sobs as the sheet is placed over his wife's head; the child looks on in wide-eyed puzzlement, not understanding what is happening. As the father and daughter argue, the clip ends with Madonna looking on at the child dancing, more or less, on her mother's grave. Described by Madonna as her tribute to Simon & Garfunkel, it was an ambitious choice of single, and ended up breaking her run of 17 consecutive Top Ten hits, its subject matter a tad too portentous for the pop mainstream. It reached Number 20—her lowest placing since 1984—but still served as another huge advertisement for the album.

After 'Oh Father,' more light relief comes in the shape of an almost entirely contradictory plea for family, 'Keep It Together.' Written with Bray, it has a classic go-go-inflected groove, and marks the first time that the dance-floor sound of 1983 truly surfaces on the album. The song is a rallying cry for unity and togetherness in a family, suggesting that growing up in those middle class suburbs can't always have been so awful; the middle-eight, with its "wouldn't change it for another chance," makes this explicit. Madonna would later describe 'Keep It Together' as her tribute to Sly & The Family Stone—she incorporated parts of 'Family Affair' into it on the Blond Ambition tour—but there is also a generous to nod to her former producer Nile Rodgers's anthem for Sister Sledge, 'We Are Family.' Released as the final single from the album in early 1990, it reinstated Madonna into the Top Ten after the 'Oh Father' intermission.

Possibly the least well-known track on the album, 'Spanish Eyes,' returns to the sweet Latino influenced setting of 'La Isla Bonita' with mariachi trumpets and a sultry rhythm. Described by the *Atlanta Journal Constitution* as "a cross between Ben E. King's 'Spanish Harlem' and something by Billy Joel," it's a pleasing diversion, but a minor work in comparison with much of the rest of the album.

Further underlining the grown-up feel of the record, *Like A Prayer* ends with a Beatles-like throwaway. As if the intensity could not be maintained, it collapses in on itself. 'Act Of Contrition' is essentially the album's title track spun backward, with Madonna intoning a version of The Lord's Prayer over the top. Beneath this most personal and solemn vow, however, is an absolute cacophony of sound, with Madonna seemingly unsure what she really wants right until the very end. "I reserve, I resolve, I have reservations, I have a reservation," she says, before screaming: "What do you mean it's not in the computer?" With that, she brings her most accomplished album to a close on a question mark.

Final mixing of *Like A Prayer* took place at the start of 1989. Guy Pratt recalls popping by the studio to find it "full of lava lights, candles, and incense, all very vibey." For Madonna, the album was a reflection on how she had changed. "My first couple of albums I would say came from the little girl in me, who is interested only in having people like me, in being entertaining and charming and frivolous and sweet," she said. "And this new one is the adult side of me, which is concerned with being brutally honest."

The album was released with what was, for Madonna, a daring cover—her face wasn't on it. But her crotch was, decked in old-school denim, the universal symbol of rebellion, but also the uniform of the rock establishment. Madonna was a grown-up artist, and grown-up artists didn't need their faces on their album covers. (It was also saturated in patchouli, that most mystical and hippie-like of scents.)

While her previous albums had contained a variety of dedications to boyfriends and husbands, here there is just one brief line: "This is for my mother, who taught me how to pray." To further emphasize the symbolism of it all, promotional votive candles were produced, signifying the important religious overtones of the work.

The reviews were rightly rapturous: here was a remarkable collection of tunes and sentiment. In the UK, *Q* magazine felt that "the tribulations of the last couple of years may have personally matured her, but with this album she has completed the remarkable act of growing up publicly." *Rolling Stone* called *Like A Prayer* "proof that not only Madonna should be taken seriously as an artist, but that hers is one of the most compelling voices of the 80s." For the *Chicago Tribune*, it was Madonna's "most accomplished and mature record," and one on which her voice "softened and deepened, dropping from the shrill chirp of the early days into a darker, more melodic mid-range," while the *Atlanta Journal Constitution* offered a perfect encapsulation of everything with the *Onion*-like headline "Ex-Boy Toy Turns Herself Into Adult On *Like A Prayer*."

Madonna's change of direction had worked incredibly well. Released on March 21 1989, *Like A Prayer* topped the charts the world over. It went on to sell over 11 million copies worldwide and has been certified Quadruple Platinum in the USA alone. It is a deep record, with an incredibly moving heart, heralding a new gravitas. Soon, other pop artists were growing up, too: George Michael released *Listen Without Prejudice* and lost a swathe of his audience; Prince denounced his record company and become a symbol; U2 realized that the only way to continue was to go a bit stupid and make *Achtung Baby*. The success of *Like A Prayer* had an indirect hand in all of this. As Madonna herself concluded: "The overall emotional content of the album is drawn from what I was going through when I was growing up—and I'm still growing up."

It was now the end of the 80s, the world was turning, and Madonna had been able to adapt and grow with the times. Her place in the world of entertainment was assured, and in the space of less than ten years she had become the single most important female pop music artist in the world (and undoubtedly one of the top five acts overall). The array of accolades as fans and pundits looked back to review the era was almost overwhelming. She topped *Billboard Magazine*'s Music Of The 80s poll in three categories: Pop Artist Of The Decade, Dance Artist Of The Decade, and Dance Single Of The Decade for her infectious 1985 anthem 'Into The Groove.' She was named Mega-Artist Of The Decade by MTV—and this at a time when Michael Jackson was at his zenith. And, in line with her earlier wish to "stand next to God," she topped a poll of 16 to 26-year-olds asked to name their ultimate heroine by the UK's Channel 4, leaving British Prime Minister Margaret Thatcher in second place and Mother Teresa third.

CHAPTER 7
I'M BREATHLESS

The critical and commercial reception of *Like A Prayer* made it clear that Madonna was now working on a different level than back when she was merely a pop superstar. She now had the 'serious' critics on her side, and the crossover potential not only to sell millions but also to create some lasting cultural impact. As a result, the Blond Ambition World Tour became a celebratory affair at the very crest of the first wave of Madonna's enormous commercial success.

The Virgin and Who's That Girl tours were enormous undertakings but operated along fairly linear stadium-concert lines. Madonna's new show would be themed: the band—the central plank of any stadium concert—would be confined to the margins to allow the singer and her dancers full reign to create a spectacle that referenced Fritz Lang's *Metropolis*, Busby Berkeley, and Stanley Kubrick's *A Clockwork Orange*.

Madonna began gathering ideas and concepts for the tour in September 1989. She was in complete control, taking a direct hand in all the hiring and firing. Brother Christopher took the role of artistic director, while the choreography was by Vince Patterson.

Rehearsals began in January 1990 on a Disney soundstage in Los Angeles. Madonna was to leave nothing to chance: in all, she would be accompanied on the tour by around a thousand people. Musically, this would be her first tour without Pat Leonard. Jai Winding took over as Musical Director and played keyboards, supported by Kevin Kendrick and Mike McKnight; Darryl Jones, soon to play with The Rolling Stones, was on bass. Carlos Rios and David Williams played guitar, with Jonathan Moffett on drums and Luis Conte on percussion. Niki Harris and Donna DeLory would once again sing and dance behind Madonna. Much of the spectacle came from her fleet of dancers, who would share center stage with Madonna again in the tour documentary *Truth Or Dare*.

Madonna gave an excited explanation of the scale of her concept to

Glenn O'Brien of *Interview* magazine. "I've created five different worlds, and the set is all based on hydraulics," she said. "One is going down and another is coming up. The world changes completely. I think of it more as a musical than as a rock concert." There was the "very hard and metallic" set for the "heavy-duty dance music," and another she described as "the temple ruins ... all these columns, trays of votive candles, a cross."

"I do 'Like A Virgin' on a bed," she continued, "but we changed the arrangement, so it sounds Indian. Then I'm being punished for masturbation on this bed, which is, as you know, what happens." After a more serious interlude, she would play three songs from *Dick Tracy* on "this art deco 50s-musical set" and the rest on "our *Clockwork Orange* cabaret set, a very sparse set with a backdrop of an orgy of naked people. The paintings are like Tamara de Lempicka—Cubist-like nudes—no pornography, no genitals. You just see people having fun."

The most talked about aspect of the show, however, was Madonna's chest. Over Christmas 1989, she flew to Paris to be fitted by Jean Paul Gaultier for her costume, a micro-boned corset and arguably the single most iconic item of clothing she would ever wear: an enormous conical bra that emphasized her weapons of mass seduction, accentuating her power, her womanhood, and her ambiguous flirtation with caricature.

With set, dancers, and band in place—and a documentary film crew on hand to capture every moment of backstage activity—the Blond Ambition World Tour began in Japan on April 13 and took in 57 shows in Europe, the Far East, and North America.

The 'Like A Virgin' sequence set out to shock and, as the tour traveled the world, shock it did. Based on an idea by Christopher Ciccone, it saw Madonna lying on a bed like an Egyptian queen, writhing and grinding, surrounded by two pretty male dancers in conical bras of their own; by the end of the song, after dry humping the bed, she would be simulating frantic masturbation. As one critic put it: "There were those male dancers adorned with breasts that flopped like so many pairs of flaccid phalli while her own set looked like armor-plated projectiles."

The Blond Ambition World Tour was huge news wherever it rolled. Madonna was threatened with arrest on the grounds of public indecency at the Montreal Skydome in May. The pressure got to her. By the time the show reached North America in June, she had had to cancel some shows because of a throat infection. In Rome, Madonna was threatened with excommunication unless she toned down her show. She refused and instead held a press conference at Rome Ciampino Airport to announce her right to freedom of expression. In the UK, the BBC came in for criticism when it broadcast one of her Wembley shows—peppered with expletives—live on air. Representatives from Radio One had traveled to Italy to assess the show's suitability for broadcast and allegedly warned Madonna against bad language. The company subsequently issued a statement to say that "we were astonished that our warning had quite the opposite effect."

These controversies aside, the Blond Ambition tour set the standard for rock performances for the rest of the decade. Madonna had drilled her team to perfection, and the energy that emanated from the stage was, at times, overwhelming. A triumph of pacing, well-chosen material, and, above all, fun made it the must-see tour of the year. All the elements were brought together by the time of the stunning encore of *Like A Prayer*'s 'Keep It Together,' which was accompanied by elaborate dance routine involving chairs and bowler hats.

The tour was a huge commercial and critical success. It was awarded the *Rolling Stone* Critics Award for Best Tour—something that would usually be reserved for the likes of Bruce Springsteen—and was named Most Creative Stage Production at the prestigious Pollstar Concert Industry Awards. The performance at the Stade De L'Ouest in Nice was broadcast live to 4.3 million households on HBO in the USA; issued on LaserDisc the following year, it earned Madonna her first ever Grammy.

The Blond Ambition tour was a triumph of the sort that Madonna might never match. As a large-scale touring operation, its central core was tight and controlled, with Madonna very much the matriarch. "The look of the tour was stunning," Luc Sante of *The New Republic* wrote. "The Jean Paul Gaultier outfits were … redolent of Brunhilde and *Attack Of The Amazons* and the homey sinister allure of the 50s bondage accoutrements immortalized in those little books published by Irving Claw."

According to the *New York Times*, Madonna had "insisted that pleasure and sexuality are positive, liberating forces, not to be constrained by anyone's unexamined stereotypes. And with the whole world watching, she has only gotten bolder." Not everyone enjoyed the show, however. For *Variety*, her "stabs at humor" were inane, while "her vocals on 'Express Yourself' sounded so much like the studio version one wondered how much was live and how much was Memorex."

Madonna's next film project, *Dick Tracy*, was a clear signal that she wanted to enter the Hollywood mainstream. After the notable failure of both *Shanghai Surprise* and *Who's That Girl*, it was time for her to get her act together, lest the opportunity to make it in Hollywood desert her once and for all.

Before *Dick Tracy* got underway, however, she had a small role to play in *The Bloodhounds Of Broadway*. An ensemble piece based on Damon Runyon's compendium of stories, it was directed by Howard Brookner, who would sadly die of AIDS before its release. Madonna plays Hortense Hathaway, a chorus girl and the love interest for Feet Samuels (played by Randy Quaid). The film also features Matt Dillon, Rutger Hauer, and Jennifer Grey, with whom Madonna duets on 'I Surrender Dear.' It was largely ignored, and is so episodic that it is alleged that when one cinema showed it with a reel missing, no one realized.

Nobody would be able to ignore *Dick Tracy*. The cartoon detective was something of an American icon, created in October 1931 by Chester Gould. This was to be a huge film, and one that united three legends of the post-67 'New Hollywood': Warren Beatty, Al Pacino, and, in a send-up of his usual serious persona, Dustin Hoffman as Mumbles. Envisioned by Beatty as an oversized human cartoon with gangsters wearing face-distorting prosthetics, *Dick Tracy* resonated with the recent revival of the *Batman* franchise. The world was turning, communism was failing, and big comic book gestures looking back to a simplified America where evil was curtailed by invincible heroes was big news on the world stage.

Taking the part of sultry nightclub singer Breathless Mahoney was a shrewd career move for Madonna, but she wasn't the first choice for the part. It was offered first to Sean Young, who allegedly bailed out after Beatty began to make unwanted advances toward her; Michelle Pfeiffer, Kim Basinger, and Kathleen Turner were all in contention. But Madonna had set her sights on it—and also on Beatty, one of the most notorious womanizers in Hollywood.

For Beatty, *Dick Tracy* provided an opportunity to write, direct, and produce an update of both the old comic strip and the subsequent television series. Famous as much for bedding women as for making movies, he had not made a film since the 1987 debacle *Ishtar*, a bewildering haze with which he singlehandedly wiped away any goodwill or gravitas he'd earned from the Oscar-winning *Reds*.

Beatty had been aware of Madonna since *Desperately Seeking Susan*. He became captivated with her, and she wooed him for the part in *Dick Tracy*. Their relationship—on and off screen—became the stuff of tabloid legend. It was expedient, to say the least, and often unpredictable. She was reported to have tipped a plate of food in his lap when she heard him talk about Julie Christie, one of the most notable of his many ex-girlfriends.

Dick Tracy started shooting at the end of February 1989, just as 'Like A Prayer' was gearing up for release. Madonna had to dye her hair bottle-blond for the film—right after she had made such a bold statement by returning her natural color. "It took me so long to grow my hair out, and I really wanted to have dark hair," she later said. "Women with blond hair are perceived as much more sexual and much more impulsive ... Fun loving, but not as layered, not as deep, not serious." She took Screen Actors Guild wages for the role—reportedly $1,440 per week—although she also shrewdly negotiated for a share of the profits.

The film is good fun. Beatty gets opportunities throughout to gently send up his reputation, as does Pacino, whose character 'Big Boy' Caprice tips a wink at his more serious gangster roles of old. Madonna plays sultry well. Alongside numerous 'dick' gags, she has an array of peachy exchanges with Beatty:

TRACY: No grief for Lips?
MAHONEY: I'm wearing black underwear.

TRACY: You know, it's legal for me to take you down to the station and sweat it out of you under the lights.

MAHONEY: I sweat a lot better in the dark.

Dick Tracy went on general release in June 1990 and was met with a certain wariness by the press. Madonna had, after all, hardly set the bar sky-high with her recent film work. "We all know what *Dick Tracy* will be like," claimed the UK's *Sunday Correspondent.* "Riddled with meretricious gimmickry and goodie vs baddie clichés—just as everyone knows that, after *Shanghai Surprise,* no one will be lining up to see Madonna for her thespian attributes." On *Good Morning America,* however, film critic Joel Siegel praised Madonna's "best work ever—she redefines the phrase 'blond bombshell' for a whole new generation."

Madonna seemed to be everywhere to promote the film. In April, she had appeared on *The Arsenio Hall Show* to perform the lead single from the soundtrack, 'Hanky Panky,' and talk extensively about spanking. The film was released to coincide with her 1990 Blond Ambition World Tour and took $23 million at the US box office in its first three days. It became the highest grossing film of Beatty's entire career, and was Madonna's first box-office hit for five years.

I'm Breathless: Music From And Inspired By The Film Dick Tracy was released on May 22, and is the soufflé-light yin to the portentous yang of *Like A Prayer.* It contains an interesting mix of Madonna originals and soundtrack songs written by Stephen Sondheim. Three of the songs appear directly in the film: 'Sooner Or Later,' 'What Can You Lose,' and 'More.' (A fourth, 'Now I'm Following You,' is a vocal version of an Andy Paley instrumental used in the film.) 'Sooner Or Later' won Sondheim the Academy Award for Best Original Song in 1990. It features in what is probably Breathless Mahoney's most spectacular scene in the film, wherein she lies down on the top of the piano to sing.

Elsewhere on the album, 'I'm Going Bananas' is an amusing homage to Carmen Miranda, while 'Cry Baby' is fluffy and altogether rather stupid. 'What Can You Lose,' a duet with Mandy Patinkin, is another Sondheim *tour de force*, with piano by Bill Schneider. It might be stagey and theatrical, but Madonna never disappoints on the big occasions and here acquits herself with élan.

The best song on *I'm Breathless* is the Madonna–Pat Leonard co-write 'Something To Remember,' which features session legend Jeff Pocaro on drums, Leonard on piano, and Guy Pratt, who so enlivened the *Like A Prayer* sessions, on bass. The jazz-trio format works especially well behind Madonna, so much so that she would return to the simple, effective track as the title song of her 1995 ballads collection.

'Now I'm Following You' comes in two parts: a straight, retro Ginger Rogers–Fred Astaire number, with vocals by Beatty, and a clumsy, percussion-heavy 90s dance mix. The song borrows heavily from Malcolm McLaren & The Bootzilla Orchestra's recent *Waltz Darling*, which combined classical and opera with dance grooves. *Waltz Darling* also features a track called 'Deep In Vogue,' which became a huge US club hit and gave Madonna and new collaborator Shep Pettibone an idea.

Pettibone had been mixing Madonna's records for some time, and had now risen to prominence as the chosen one to be her latest co-writer and producer. What the pair of them came up with for the final track on *I'm Breathless* would end up overshadowing the entire release.

A musical sketch from the *Like A Prayer* sessions, 'Vogue' was originally intended for use as the B-side to 'Keep It Together.' Warner Bros felt the song was far too strong for that purpose, however, and suggested instead that it would be the ideal lead track for the *Dick Tracy* project despite the fact that it was not used in the film and sounded so stylistically different to the rest of *I'm Breathless*—and no wonder, for it is one of Madonna's finest records. "The record company went bananas, her manager went bananas," Pettibone, who co-wrote the song, later recalled. "Everybody said this is a major smash record—we're not going to lose it as a B-side."

Madonna's lyrics compare the faltering, predominantly gay dance craze of 'vogueing'—mimicking the poses struck in *Vogue* magazine—to the style of high-period Hollywood glamour. By the time of the record's release, however, vogueing was somewhat over. In truth, it had never really taken off. The song takes in a variety of Madonna themes: trying to escape heartache, the pain of life, longing to be something better, and, of course, the joy of dance. It recalls Chic's 'Le Freak' in the way that it lets people in on the secret of where the best sounds are, and closes with a rap detailing various Hollywood styles: "Ladies with an attitude / Fellas who were in the mood." It's a one-in-a-million pop moment.

With backing vocals by Niki Harris, Donna DeLory, and N'dea Davenport, and programming by Pettibone, 'Vogue' was a very modern-sounding dance record. It soon surpassed 'Like A Prayer' as Madonna's biggest-selling worldwide hit and one of the best-loved singles of her career; its parent album, *I'm Breathless*, went to Number Two on the US *Billboard* chart and was soon certified double platinum.

To complement 'Vogue,' David Fincher created a classic, sepia-hued video, a throwback to the golden age of Hollywood. Shot at Burbank Studios in February 1990, it has a glorious Art Deco feel, with many scenes intended to recreate the work of Hollywood photographer Horst P. Horst. Choreographed by Karole Armitage, the video received its world premiere on MTV on March 29 1990, with Madonna looking feminine and beautiful in it. The song itself went straight into the Blond Ambition repertoire and added a real lift to the proceedings.

On September 6 Madonna returned to the MTV video awards to reenact her tour performance—except here, everyone was dressed in pre-revolutionary French costume, with Madonna center stage as an undergarment-exposing Marie Antoinette in huge wig and court dress, seemingly unconcerned by having her breasts fondled by her dancers.

The *Dick Tracy* experience had been largely positive for Madonna. For once she hadn't been savaged by her critics, and the film kept her profile high as her Blond Ambition tour crossed the world. With the success and plaudits she had received, it seemed like a good time for Madonna to do what had been repeatedly asked of her since 1986: give in and release a greatest hits collection. This being Madonna, however, it would come with a twist.

The Immaculate Collection signaled the end of Madonna's imperial phase—after this, things would never be the same again. For now, she had such an elegant sufficiency of material that she could fill a double album and a long-running CD and still not include all her hits.

Madonna's first 'greatest hits' compilation took a different approach to her first decade, with each of the songs given a shiny new remix or, in some cases, a radical dance reworking. Assembled by Shep Pettibone, Goh Hotoda, and Michael Hutchinson, these mixes are discreet and gimmick free, and as a result they stand up perfectly alongside the originals.

The Immaculate Collection—its title another witty nod to Madonna's religion—comprises 15 oldies and two new tracks. There are no massive sidesteps, nothing out of the ordinary. These are pure pop nuggets, diamonds sparkling. The liner notes encapsulate the chutzpah involved in this remarkable cash cow. "In the years since [her arrival], the ensuing hoopla has further fogged the issue of Madonna's music," industry veteran Gene Sculatti writes. "It's easy to forget that before her hit singles became Events, they were great records, the best of which hit pop's cosmic G-spot, got a groove, and literally shook the world."

Sculatti's notes conclude with a note that highlights the barely concealed glee of everyone involved in the project. "Like no other singer (or writer or producer) in recent memory, she continues to demonstrate an uncompromising commitment ... to never stay put," he writes. "The experience of honoring that commitment has made the 'Material Girl' 'rich.' It has also enriched popular music as a whole—pushing it to new limits, pulling apart preconceptions about what it can say and do."

Alongside The Beatles' 'Red' and 'Blue' sets, The Rolling Stones' *Hot Rocks*, and The Isley Brothers' *Forever Gold*, *The Immaculate Collection* remains one of the finest compilation albums of all time. It reached Number Two on the *Billboard* chart and is rumored to have sold 30 million copies worldwide, making it the biggest-selling compilation ever issued by a solo artist.

The album was released in a blaze of worldwide publicity. On December 7 the UK's highbrow arts show *Omnibus* screened *Madonna—Behind The American Dream*, a look behind the scenes of the Blond Ambition World Tour that acted as both a trailer for *Truth Or Dare* and an extended advertisement for *The Immaculate Collection* itself.

The album was delivered in the shortlived QSound format, intended to provide the illusion of a three-dimensional, quadraphonic mix despite actually being stereo. Of greatest interest were the two new tracks recorded specially for the album. Whereas 'Rescue Me,' is a dramatic slice of operatic pop that some would say had forgotten to pack a tune, 'Justify My Love' served as the curtain raiser for the next stage of Madonna's career.

A sensuous, percussion-led slice of lust-pop, 'Justify My Love' simply oozed controversy. It was written by Ingrid Chavez (who was initially not credited), with additional material by Lenny Kravitz and Madonna, and produced by Kravitz and Andre Betts. With Kravitz's backing vocals high in the mix, a breathy Madonna pleads with her lover to justify her love. It still sounds modern now, two decades later.

It was the accompanying promo video that really sparked controversy. Directed by Jean-Baptiste Mondino, it shows Madonna living out her fantasies in a random hotel. Sadomasochism, voyeurism, masturbation, and lesbianism all pepper the proceedings. We first see Madonna shambling up a corridor, carrying a suitcase, looking either heavily drugged or on the verge of collapse. After meeting a lover she takes off her coat to reveal only black lace underwear, stockings, and high heels.

The whole thing blurs sex and religion. Scenes of kissing, caressing, and painted mustaches are intercut with images of a dancer, a crucifix, and Jesus in the sacrificial position. The video ends with Madonna rushing back down the corridor, looking deliriously happy. For Camille Paglia, writing in the *New York Times*, 'Justify My Love' was "truly avant-garde, at a time when that word has lost its meaning in the flabby art world. It represents a sophisticated European sexuality of a kind we have not seen since the great foreign films of the 50s and 60s."

Not everyone was so delighted. The *New York Daily News* sneered that, if you took out "the black lingerie, sex scenes, and flesh," you'd be left with "ten seconds of ill-focused dancing." MTV—always Madonna's staunchest defender—had no option but to ban the video, with one source quoted as saying that this one "is just not for us … I can't believe Madonna ever thought we would air it."

Madonna's response was curt. "Why is it that people are willing to go to a movie and watch someone get blown to bits for no reason but nobody wants to see two girls kissing and two men snuggling?" she asked. She thought she could get away with it—that people would cave in and show the video—but not this time.

In this instance, however, something far more interesting happened. Warner Bros successfully released 'Justify My Love' as one of the first video singles, and when it was screened in short, late-night bursts, the shows broadcast around it enjoyed enormous ratings. "Madonna can turn catastrophes into triumphs," Seymour Stein told *Vanity Fair*. "When I saw the 'Justify My Love' video … I knew there would be problems. But it's turned out to be the biggest-selling video of its type."

An alternate mix of 'Justify My Love,' dubbed 'The Beast Within,' was reported to contain Satanic messages, and also drew criticism from Rabbi Abraham Cooper of the Simon Wiesenthal Center, Los Angeles, who claimed that the lyrics were anti-Semitic. Madonna's response was unequivocal. "People can say I'm an exhibitionist, but no one can ever accuse me of being a racist," she said. "I am not going to defend myself against such ridiculous accusations. My message is pro-tolerance and anti-hate."

'Justify My Love' provided Madonna with another US Number One hit. Her dalliance with explicit sex and eroticism could have ended here, but she enjoyed the furor that surrounded the video. Support from heavyweight critics such as Camille Paglia—who called Madonna "the future of feminism" in the *New York Times*—spurred her on to take matters even further, leading her down the wayward path that was to preoccupy the next five years of her career.

When *Truth Or Dare* opened in May 1991, Madonna was arguably the biggest pop star in the world. The build up to its release was spectacular, as if to prove the strength and size of the Madonna juggernaut. In March 1991, she attended the 63rd Academy Awards at the Dorothy Chandler Pavilion, Los Angeles. She was accompanied by Michael Jackson, and the pair were treated like hallowed royalty, sitting at the front, the camera panning for every reaction and nuance.

Introduced by host Billy Crystal as "the NC-17 portion of our show," Madonna performed 'Sooner Or Later' from *Dick Tracy* dressed like a cross between Jean Harlow and Marilyn Monroe, peeling off her gloves and delivering the first verse with her back to the audience, caressing her backside, shrugging off her stole. And yet this was just the tip of the iceberg of publicity into which *Truth Or Dare* collided.

One of the greatest popular music concert documentary dramas ever, *Truth Or Dare* laid bare Madonna's carapace of strength and inner vulnerability. She is the absolute dead center of the film: it is hard to take your eyes off her as she is in almost every frame. Capturing her at perhaps the most interesting point in her career, shortly after she had released a work that gained tremendous critical respect without losing mass appeal or sales, this bold, saucy film is full of incidental moments that add delight and texture to superstardom and gives rare insight into what it's like to be at the very apex of pop success.

The job of directing *Truth Or Dare* fell to 26-year-old Alek Keshishian after David Fincher, with whom Madonna had made several promo videos, pulled out of the project. Keshishian was something of a child prodigy, having previously directed Harvard's Experimental Theater, with whom he put on a pop-opera version of Emily Bronte's *Wuthering Heights*. Madonna became aware of him after granting the use of one of her songs in the musical and invited him to join her in Japan to film some backstage material.

Keshishian made it clear that he was uninterested in making an "unrevealing puff piece pandering to the celebrity." He famously told Madonna: "I'll film you without make-up, I'll film you when you're being a complete bitch, I'll film you in the morning before your sleeping pill's worn off." He wasn't scared of being fired, and as a result produced a work of some—albeit heavily authorized—authenticity.

The film begins on the last night of the Blond Ambition World Tour in Nice, France, in August 1990, before flashing back and taking the viewer with Madonna and her troupe through Japan, North America, and Europe. The backstage scenes were shot in monochrome, creating a neat contrast with the glossy in-concert performances. We see Madonna acting like a mother to her entourage; Japan in the rainy season; color sequences of 'Express Yourself' and 'Vogue' being brought to life; Madonna in her iconic Gautier bustier; Niki Harris and Donna DeLory; Warren Beatty hiding in the shadows; Madonna's unease with showbiz 'friends'; her vulnerability, and then her rage, directed here at the Canadian Mounties who threaten to arrest her in Montreal. We even see vogueing eunuchs.

"I am an artist and this is how I choose to express myself," Madonna says in the film. *Truth Or Dare* is most touching when she returns to Detroit. After all this time, and all this success, she still wants the approval of her family. She bemoans the way her brother Marty acts toward her—how stardom changes the people close to you. "There's no place like home," she says at the start of the gig, and later introduces her father to the stage before getting everyone to sing 'Happy Birthday' to him.

Backstage, Madonna speaks to her father and stepmother, Joan—for so long the bane of her life. She talks about the show—"it's a journey"—like a 12-year-old explaining her art to mom and dad. One of the most talked-about sequences comes when she visits her mother's grave and then lies down on it, with 'Promise To Try' playing in the background.

Madonna seems happiest when she's with her dancers. When a make-up artist named Sharon is raped, Madonna's reaction is simply to laugh. She seems more concerned with the warring factions between her dancers. In Europe, we see her fighting for "freedom of speech, expression, and thought" during her battle with the Catholic Church in Rome. Sandra Bernhard appears later on, and here Madonna is caught off guard, revealing that, after her mother's death, she had recurring dreams about being strangled, to the point where she took to father Tony's bed every night. Then, perhaps having realized that she has let too much honesty come through, she adds: "I went straight to sleep after he fucked me."

Truth Or Dare highlights the ennui of being a superstar. An embarrassing after-show party in Los Angeles causes Madonna to wonder: "Who do I want to meet next? I think I've met everybody." In the end she decides she wants to meet Antonio Banderas, but is instantly deflated when she learns that he is married.

The 'spin the bottle,' truth-or-dare sequence comes late in the film, and it's here that we famously see Madonna fellate the empty bottle. Less well-remembered from the same sequence is the part where she is asked the name of the love of her life. "Sean," she replies, and for once we seem to see a chink in her armor, the vulnerable four-year-old climbing into bed between her parents. Elsewhere, she seems remote and rather unlovable, no more so than when an old school friend, Moira McFarland, asks her to be godmother to her new baby. (Madonna brushes the offer aside.)

The film closes with scenes of various people talking to Madonna on the bed in her hotel suite, cut against footage of the fantastically staged 'Keep It Together' sequence. Commentators were quick to pick up on the conversation at the end with dancers Niki and Donna, in which Madonna plays down her singing and dancing but admits that she is "interested in pushing people's buttons."

Warren Beatty is, at best, a spectral presence. He tends to duck away from the camera, but does utter one key phrase that at once captures the all-encompassing reach of Madonna's multi-platform, multimedia world: "Madonna doesn't want to live her life off camera, let alone talk." The film succeeds in capturing the isolation of a superstar. Who is the real Madonna? What is fake? It's almost impossible to tell, and counterproductive to try. But what the film is, certainly, is great entertainment.

Truth Or Dare remains charming and shocking in equal measure. It is always compelling, and its use of alternate color and black-and-white sequences—potentially rather wearing—works well over the course of the film. Known outside North America as *In Bed With Madonna*, the film had its premiere at the Cannes Film Festival in May 1991. Madonna showed her Gaultier bra and the world's press slavishly reported it. The film itself was well received, and the Madonna brand rolled on for yet another year.

Although *Truth Or Dare* is edited to suggest that Madonna and her troupe were one happy family, this was not exactly the case. In 1992, a year after the film's release, three dancers—Gabriel Trupin, Kevin Stea, and Oliver Crumes—filed a suit against Madonna at Los Angeles Superior Court. They claimed that they had been misled about how footage of them would be used in the film, and that their privacy had been invaded. Madonna was furious, allegedly telling Crumes, after a chance meeting: "If you want money, why don't you sell that Cartier watch I bought for you?"

The case was settled out of court but left Madonna ever more suspicious of those around her. It undoubtedly played out to her the idea that, as she puts it in the film, she had "unconsciously chosen people who are emotionally crippled in some way." And yet it mattered little: *Truth Or Dare* went on to gross $29 million. It still ranks among the very highest grossing documentaries of all time and will probably be the Madonna artifact that is still shown a thousand years from now.

After the Blond Ambition tour, Madonna had one piece of innocent business to complete before she returned to being a figure of controversy. The feel-good comedy *A League Of Their Own* provided her with a much-needed success at the box office, and brought with it her first positive film notices since the release of *Desperately Seeking Susan* seven years earlier.

Directed by Penny Marshall, the film is a fictionalized account of the All American Girls' Professional Baseball League, established in 1943 by confectionary magnate P.K. Wrigley in an attempt to keep the sport alive during the Second World War. It folded in 1954, but there was a wave of nostalgia for it during the early 90s, with a documentary broadcast on PBS.

Madonna is part of a strong ensemble cast that also features Tom Hanks, Geena Davis, and Rosie O'Donnell. She plays center-fielder Mae 'All The Way' Mordabito, a good-time girl fond of both men and drink whose best friend is Doris Murphy (O'Donnell). It's a real blowzy performance, all Mae West, for which Madonna drew on her schooldays and time spent living cheaply in New York. Told her dress is too tight by her teammates as she prepares for a night out, she replies: "I don't plan on wearing it that long." She later emerges smirking from confession with a most flustered priest behind her, and teaches fellow player Shirley Baker (Ann Cusack) to read by showing her erotic literature. "Hi, my name's Mae," she says, "and that's more than a name—that's an attitude."

The O'Donnell–Madonna double-act provides further wry moments. "What if, at a key moment in the game, my, my uniform bursts open and, uh, oops, my bosoms come flying out?" Madonna asks. "That might draw a crowd, right?" "You think there are men in this country who ain't seen your bosoms?" O'Donnell replies.

A new Madonna track, 'This Used To Be My Playground,' plays out over the closing credits. It was recorded at the tail end of the *Erotica* sessions. Shep Pettibone came up with the music to which Madonna added a poignant lyric that conflates nostalgia and loss. The result was a mournful number in the manner of 'Rain' or 'Live To Tell' with a string arrangement by Jeremy Lubbock.

Released as a single to support the film, 'Playground' reached the top of the *Billboard* chart in August 1992 but was not included on the soundtrack album and did not appear on any official Madonna album until the release of 1995's *Something To Remember*. *A League Of Their Own* itself made $107 million at the US box office from a $40 million budget. It showcased what Madonna does best in film—taking her part in a strong cast and playing a notable supporting character. What she did next could not have been more different.

CHAPTER 8
THE MAVERICK

P op star, film star, media doyen: it was now time to add label boss to Madonna's impressive and rapidly growing business empire. Madonna established Maverick in April 1992. Her break into the management and record company side of things was inevitable given the amount of power she held in the early 90s, but it wasn't her first venture into business. She had already launched a clothing line, Wazoo; Boy Toy Inc, which dealt with her music and record royalties; the video production companies Slutco and Siren Films; Webo Girl music publishing; and Music Tours Inc.

The idea of artists starting their own imprints was hardly new. Ever since The Beatles launched Apple, their very own brand of "Western Communism," in 1968, every major artist seemed at one point or another to want their own label. But Madonna was clear that Maverick—a 60/40 partnership in her favor with the Warner Music Group—would not simply be a vanity label. She wanted an aggressive and impressive A&R policy to showcase the best in left-field international talent.

Maverick was born in 1992 with Film and Music divisions as well as television, book publishing, and—most lucratively for Madonna—merchandising wings. The company was named for a 19th century Texas rancher, Samuel A. Maverick, which seemed about right: she was going to do things her way. "I want a real record label with real artists," she said. "I don't want to be Prince and have everybody be a clone of me. That's not having a label, that's having a harem. They only function for as long as he's interested in them. I want artists who are going to have a life of their own and who have a point of view."

Much was made about the numbers. "Although Time Warner executives would not confirm figures that have been widely circulated," the *New York Times* reported, "Madonna's renegotiated recording contract is said to give this singer a $5 million advance for each of her next seven albums and a 20 per cent royalty rate." This put Madonna on a par with Michael Jackson, whose recording contract was the highest in the industry at the time.

She was clear in her intent. "My goal, of course, is to have hits with the new company," she said. "I'm not one of these dumb artists who is just given a label to shut her up. I asked for a record company. So I'm not going to be invisible or simply phone in my partnership. There's no honor or satisfaction in palming the work off to someone else."

Madonna wanted to work with her approved clique of artists, writers, and photographers—to "incorporate them into my little factory of ideas"— and brought in business executives she knew and trusted. Freddy DeMann, who had proved invaluable as her manager, became the new company's president, industry investor Ronnie Dashev helped raised funds, and 20-year-old wunderkind Guy Oseary headed the A&R division. Seymour Stein also played a significant role in A&R initially as Maverick's releases would be a joint venture between his Sire Records and its parent company, Warner Bros.

The business and media world was suitably impressed with the deal— how could they not be? "The news that Madonna has just clinched a deal making her the highest-paid performer in the history of the pop industry only confirms what we already knew, which is that she is now the biggest star on the planet," the London *Times* announced. "The days when one could mention Michael Jackson or Prince in the same breath are long gone."

Maverick's first major venture was the two-pronged assault of *Erotica*, her first proper studio album since *Like A Prayer*, and *Sex*, her first foray into book publishing. No phase of Madonna's multi-faceted career has ever managed to polarize opinion quite so much. Even now, it seems hard to believe that a celebrity of her stature would issue something so deep, so dark and personal to the widest audience possible.

The two projects were released on the same day in October 1992, and it remains almost impossible to separate them. The controversy surrounding *Sex*—and Madonna's strange desire for her alter ego, Mistress Dita, to take center stage—certainly detracted from the glory of the album.

Even from a 21st century perspective, this phase of Madonna's career seems quite unbelievable. She had been testing the boundaries right from the start, so it was not uncommon for her to come up with something controversial. But to deliver a book of lewd and often plainly horrible photographs of herself in a catalogue of un-erotic, graphic sexual poses that overshadowed a really rather good album still seems foolhardy.

It was as if, now that she had exorcised her personal and religious demons with *Like A Prayer*, Madonna felt it was time to challenge hypocrisy, rattle the cages of the moral majority, and exploit the double standards of society. Her method was simple: shock, shock, and more shock. She was after all the most famous performer in the world, and for now at least had an unparalleled platform.

Shortly after releasing *The Immaculate Collection*, Madonna told *Vanity Fair*: "My drive in life is from this horrible fear of being mediocre. And that's always pushing me, pushing me. Because even though I've become Somebody, I still have to prove that I'm *Somebody*. My struggle has never ended and it probably never will." What she planned to do next would be anything but mediocre.

Although she had appeared only intermittently in the public eye, Madonna had been typically industrious in the period between the release of *Truth Or Dare* during the summer of 1991 and the publication of *Sex* the following October. She had set up Maverick, filmed *A League Of Their Own* and *Body Of Evidence*, and appeared as Marie in Woody Allen's film *Shadows And Fog*. ("He doesn't give you a lot of nurturing," she later said of the director. "He hands you your lines and you do it.") She had also been closely linked to Jennifer Lynch's debut picture, *Boxing Helena*.

Even now, *Sex* evokes a level of extreme incredulity. How could a star this far into her career publish something that most would be racing to cover up? The world had already seen the skeletons in Madonna's closet when, seven years earlier, she had been left deeply embarrassed by the publication—over which she had no control—of nude photographs in *Penthouse* and *Playboy*. Now she was very much in control.

The idea for the book began with the suggestion by Simon & Shuster editor Judith Regan that Madonna create a book of erotica. Madonna decided to undertake the project herself, as part of her new Maverick enterprise. It would be a bold way to launch her new company. Although brother Christopher suggested that Madonna take a more limited edition approach and get photographer Helmut Newton involved, she aimed for what she knew best: the mass market.

The *Sex* photographs were shot by Madonna's old friend and collaborator Steven Meisel, principally in Miami and New York, during the summer of 1992. Also involved were art director Fabien Barron, who had worked for *Vogue* and was part of the relaunch of *Interview* magazine in 1990, and writer Glenn O'Brien, who helped Madonna to establish an alter ego, Mistress Dita.

Running to 128 large-format pages, *Sex* was published on October 21 1992 with a retail price of just under $50 and an initial print run of 1.5 million copies. The design was extremely complex, with the book's ring-bound aluminum jacket sealed in a Mylar bag to add to the mystique. (Also included was a CD containing an early version of 'Erotica,' titled 'Erotic,' that makes explicit the song's Middle Eastern influence.)

So what of the book itself? After violating the Mylar packaging, the reader is presented with a series of pictures accompanied by excruciating soft-porn text. "This is a book about sex," Madonna writes at the start. "Sex is not love. Love is not sex." She goes on to explain that any similarity between the book and real characters and events is not just coincidental but ridiculous. "Nothing in this book is true. I made it all up."

Sex moves through a variety of scenarios and bad prose. A doctor asks if it's possible to experience pleasure and pain at the same time ("Sure!" Dita replies. "That's what ass-fucking is all about!"). Elsewhere, being tied up is compared with being strapped into a baby seat. What caused the greatest controversy, however, was Madonna's assertion that women who stay in abusive relationships "must be digging it"—as if it's some form of lifestyle choice.

Still surprising is the list of heavyweight friends Madonna was able to coax along on her sexual journey, among them Isabella Rossellini, Big Daddy Kane, Vanilla Ice, Naomi Campbell, and Ingrid Casares. The brutal starkness of the material and its blank photography still startle. Madonna often looks gorgeous, but by the end you really have seen enough. You can almost sense the initial conversations—the ticking of boxes set to offend. There's a series of shots taken in a New York Dungeon, the Vault; sadomasochism; a rape scene in a school gymnasium; lesbianism; Madonna seemingly about to have sex with a black couple. "I'm dealing with sexual liberation of the mind," she said by way of explanation. "This book is based on fantasies in an ideal world—a world without abusive people, a world without AIDS, a dream world."

Sex was launched at a party in downtown Manhattan on October 15; celebrities in attendance included David Lee Roth, Rosie O'Donnell, and Spike Lee, for whose *Girl 6* Madonna had recently filmed a cameo. She was rumored to be planning to turn up in the nude but in the end came dressed as Little Bo Peep.

No advance copies of *Sex* (or *Erotica*) were circulated—a surefire way of stoking critical ire. In an interview with the UK's *Independent* newspaper a few days before its release, Madonna's publicist, Liz Rosenberg, described the book in carefully chosen terms: it was, she said, "beautifully done" and "very, very funny." The rest of the media got ready to pounce. For the *Washington Post*, *Sex* was "an oversized, overpriced coffee-table book of hardcore sexual fantasies sure to separate the wannabes from the wannabe-faraways. ... Is *Sex* boring? Actually, yes."

This was probably the key argument: in a pre-internet world, pornographers and fashion photographers alike had mastered the art of filling 128 pages with high-quality images. Here they were bald, unappealing, unattractive, and frequently dull. For some critics, *Sex* appeared to revile the sort of characters Madonna was supposed to be celebrating by "presenting portraits of sexual freaks instead of highlighting the sensuality of the images." Writing in the UK's *Observer* newspaper, Martin Amis concluded: "There is the feeling that *Sex* is no more than the desperate confection of an aging scandal-addict, whom with this book, merely confirms she is exhausting her capacity to shock."

Critical opprobrium is good for business, however. The book sold out on the day of its publication, and Madonna was ready for the criticism. "I called my book *Sex* because it was a very provocative title and I knew people would buy it because of that," she said. "I knew people would want to buy it and look at the pictures, and yet they denounced it at the same time, so I thought, that's a statement of our society in itself. People want to know about it, but if you ask them about it, they'll say it's bad. I was trying to make a point with it all."

Taking into account reprints, *Sex* went on to become the biggest-selling coffee-table book of all time, and yet the resulting furor had a lasting effect on its author. As biographer Andrew Morton would later note, this time Madonna had no one to blame but herself. "She was learning that the handmaiden of absolute authority is total responsibility."

"I divide my career [into] before and after the *Sex* book," Madonna later told *Spin*. "Up until then, I really was just being a creative person working and doing things that inspired me and I thought would inspire other people. After that, I suddenly had a whole different point of view about life in general. Ever since that book, I think there are the people that look at me and go: oh man, she just went off the deep end, she went too far. I can't deal with her, she disgusts me. And then I think there are other people who, even if they didn't like the *Sex* book, go: oh well, she survived that and she goes on and she continues to do what she wants to do—in spite of the fact that the press beat the shit out of me. Very few people came to my rescue. It was an incredibly eye-opening experience."

The speed of the sell-out and the size of the backlash played ostensibly into Madonna's hands. "I made my point completely and people know I made my point," she told the *New Musical Express*, "and that's why they are so pissed off at me."

Released the very same day, *Erotica* features a strong selection of material, opening the next phase of Madonna's musical career by going off in perhaps the only direction Madonna could have chosen after the crowning glory of *Like A Prayer* and *The Immaculate Collection*. Running to 75 minutes, it is effectively a double album. Shep Pettibone was the principal producer of ten of the 14 tracks, with the remainder overseen by 'Justify My Love' producer Andre Betts.

The album returns to the urban groove of Madonna's debut of a decade earlier. Whereas *Like A Prayer* had a resolutely West Coast sound, Madonna wanted *Erotica* to sound if it had been recorded in "an alley up in Harlem." Recording began in the fall of 1991 and continued throughout 1992 at Mastermix and Soundworks studios. Madonna, Pettibone, and drum programmer Tony Shimkin recorded more than 20 demos. Most of the material ended up on the album—including a number of demo vocals—but several tracks, such as 'Jitterbug,' remain unreleased to this today (others, such as 'Up Down Suite,' ended up as B-sides).

"All the writing was done at home, in my apartment in Manhattan, and 90 per cent of the production was done there also," Pettibone later explained. "It turned out to be a very easy way of working. She'd come over at two in the afternoon; we'd work until eight or nine. She doesn't bring piles of records into the studio. Not at all. In fact, I only did that once—I said: check out this record, but she turned round and said: why would I want to listen to that? I wouldn't want my records to sound like someone else's."

Ostensibly a concept album about eroticism and sexuality, *Erotica* was the first release on Madonna's Maverick imprint. In contrast to the organic sound of *Like A Prayer*, *Erotica* is heavily programmed, with a club-oriented sound. Emerging from the sound of crackling vinyl—the liner notes make clear that "all surface noise on the song has been included intentionally"—the title track continues along the trajectory established by 'Justify My Love.' Originally entitled 'You Thrill Me,' the song is bereft of any noticeable melody, but swings and grooves in a great fashion.

We are introduced early on to Madonna's alter ego: "My name is Dita," she says. "I'll be your mistress tonight / I'd like to put you in a trance." The model of control and domination runs throughout as Madonna/Dita prepares to "teach you how to fuck." The sparse grooves are embellished by a sample of 'Jungle Boogie' by the legendary New Jersey funksters Kool & The Gang—several years before the song became cool again as part of the *Pulp Fiction* soundtrack—and an uncredited lift from the 1962 recording 'El Yom 'Ulliqa 'Ala Khashaba' by the Lebanese singer Faruz.

'Erotica' was released as a single ahead of the album on October 13 and made the Top Three in both the USA and the UK. (While still relatively successful, it was the first lead single from a new Madonna album to fail to reach the US Number One spot since her debut.) The accompanying video, by *Sex* art director Fabien Barron, is a composite of images used in the book, with the main focus on shots of Madonna and Ingrid Casares kissing. One-and-a-half minutes in, Madonna and another woman are seen performing fellatio on a popsicle, with the position of Madonna's finger making it look like a crucifix.

A lush if uninterested take on Peggy Lee's 'Fever' seemed a peculiar choice for the second track, yet, with its club-inspired video, it become an international success when released as the fourth single from the album in March 1993. Madonna actually met Peggy Lee during the recording sessions after seeing the aging jazz legend perform at the New York Hilton. She recorded her version of 'Fever' on August 16 1992, her 34th birthday, after improvising the vocal over the unreleased 'Goodbye To Innocence.' The video, directed by Stephane Sednaoui, captures Madonna and a male dancer gyrating at high speed. Madonna alternates between a red wig and dress and a gold Jean-Paul Gaultier outfit—with her hair and skin painted gold, too.

'Bye Bye Baby' has a loping, swing-beat groove, with Madonna's heavily processed vocals distancing her from the song. "This is not a love song," she repeats throughout—until it all grinds to a halt and she says: "You fucked it up." It was eventually released in the Far East and Australia as the sixth and final single from the album with a composite promo video made up of performances from The Girlie Show.

The fourth track on the album, 'Deeper And Deeper,' is an undeniable classic and perhaps Madonna's best dance-anthem of the 90s. With its huge, stabbing horns and swelling strings, it alludes to all the records that were in the air when Madonna arrived in New York in the late 70s, conveying all the requisite drama. And when the record references 'Vogue,' Madonna becomes post-modernity itself. This is a superior piece of dance music, with Donna Delory and Niki Harris's backing vocals at the end adding a real girl-group authenticity to proceedings.

'Deeper And Deeper' was the second single to be taken from the album, reaching Number Seven on the *Billboard* Hot 100 and burning up the club listings. Bobby Woods's promo video is a great piece of cinéma vérité showing Madonna and friends in full dance-floor mode. Shot at the

Roxbury club in Los Angeles, it pays tribute to Andy Warhol and features Madonna's longtime friend Debi Mazar, director Sofia Coppola, and German actor Udo Kier.

Erotica's André Betts-produced tracks are smoother and jazzier, with bass by Doug Wimbush and piano by James 'Sleepy Keys' Preston. 'Where Life Begins,' however, is little short of a smutty mess, with the woman who made *Like A Prayer* now reduced to singing: "Colonel Sanders says it best / Finger licking good? / Can you make a fire without using wood?"

'Bad Girl' is one of several *tours de force* on the album, with Madonna admonishing herself—or at least Dita—for her recent behavior. It was originally in line to be the second single from the album, complete with raunchy video, but its release was delayed until February 1993, the feeling being that the controversy already surrounded the album needed to be toned down. By then, most people had had enough of Madonna's sensationalism, and 'Bad Girl' stalled at Number 36 on the US chart. The single's sleeve, which shows Madonna holding her breast while smoking in bed, suggested that this was simply more pornography, although David Fincher's little-seen video, starring Christopher Walken as Madonna's guardian angel, is a classic.

Track seven, 'Waiting,' seems to nod toward the dense, skunk-infused grooves of Manchester's Happy Mondays, whose recent album *Pills 'N' Thrills And Bellyaches* had been a critical success in the USA. Betts and Preston lay endless jazz piano over a furiously mechanical swing beat, while Madonna, in her Dita drone, fills the song with zest. There's a great nursery rhyme-style breakdown three-and-a-half minutes in, while the 12-inch mix features a rap by Everlast.

The next two tracks are fairly forgettable. 'Thief Of Hearts' begins with a broken bottle sound similar to the one used on *Like A Prayer*'s 'Till Death Do Us Part.' Sampled beats gather pace, and what melody there is gets squashed between enormous drum fills. The six-minute 'Words' is a 'Vogue' retread with a little Eastern spice on top. A minor work, it closes with the sound of a typewriter—a nod, perhaps, to 'Wordy Rappinghood' by Madonna's former Sire label-mates, The Tom Tom Club.

Track ten, 'Rain,' is significant: something to remember. It follows the line of Madonna's best power ballads: it's conventional and linear, and comes as a great relief. It is a pleasure to hear an unambiguous lyric and melody ten tracks into the album. The words are a little basic, but they're still poignant. The accompanying video was one of the trickiest shoots of Madonna's career as it required her to be covered in water for five days solid. Mark Romanek shot the clip in black-and-white and then hand-colored everything blue. The result is stunning and sweet, and a good fit for one of Madonna's super-ballads. It was released as the fifth single from the album, in a remixed version, in July 1993.

'Why's It So Hard'—Madonna clearly unable to resist the innuendo—is the crux of the album. Here she makes an impassioned plea for man to love fellow man regardless of color, creed, or sexuality, and the sentiment and heartfelt vocal are just enough for the song to escape its swing-beat straightjacket. Then comes 'In This Life,' which recalls the stark, sparse, emotional intimacy of 'Promise To Try.' With sympathetic strings by the New York Philharmonic Orchestra and piano by James Preston, it has what *Q* magazine described as "the touching delicacy of a Randy Newman ballad." Written about friends Madonna had lost to AIDS—principally Martin Burgoyne and her original mentor, Christopher Flynn—it is one of her most touching songs, and would prove pivotal to the forthcoming Girlie Show tour.

The uncensored version of the album then leads into 'Did You Do It,' a rap version of 'Waiting' delivered by André Betts, Mark Goodman, and Dave Murphy. It's a simple piece of hip-hop braggadocio, with lines about "dropping off a load," being "about to explode," and whether or not any of them "did it"—to Madonna, of course. It's not bad for what it is, but should really have been a B-side at best.

Both versions of the album end with the atmospheric and trippy 'Secret Garden,' Madonna's final collaboration with Andre Betts, on which she returns for one last time to her Dita persona over block piano chords and layered extemporization. For all her sexual questioning, here it seems that she is still looking for some old fashioned romance, leaving listeners with the revelation that she is looking for "a heart that will not harden."

Erotica was housed in a jacket designed by Fabien Baron and Siung Fat Tjia at Baron & Baron, with six panels of *Sex*-style photographs by Steven Meisel. It came in two editions: a 'dirty' one with 'Did You Do It' included, and a 'clean' one without. Madonna concluded her list of acknowledgements by thanking "Shep and Dre for bringing out the be(a)st in me. Words cannot express. I'm unworthy."

For all its faults, *Erotica* is a major work, and one that represents the continuation of Madonna's musical maturity, but the reviews were understandably mixed. *Q* magazine spoke for many with its reference to "simultaneous brilliance and baloney from the same team and all within the broad dance idiom. Madonna mixed up? The signs are that, once she's popped her kit back on and realized we like her for herself, it'll all turn out nicely."

The album had shipped two million units by January 1993, with sales rising to around five million worldwide by the end of 2009. Given how well her previous albums had sold, it seems that—in this instance at least—sex didn't sell. By now, however, record sales had become almost incidental to Madonna. She was everywhere—you didn't need to own a Madonna record to know what she sounded like. In late 1993, Dr Kay Turner put together a book called *I Dream Of Madonna*, detailing 50 dreams different women had had about her. If people were dreaming about her, then her work as a superstar was done.

It remains a great shame that *Sex* obscured the greatness of this album. Had it simply been called *Bad Girl*, with a greater focus on its inherent maturity, it might have been seen as a companion to *Like A Prayer*. (Imagining how double albums would be so much better with a bit of pruning is an age-old pastime, but you cannot help but think of how great *Erotica* could have been had 'Fever,' 'Thief Of Hearts,' 'Words,' and 'Did You Do It' been omitted.)

"The biggest disappointment of my career is the fact that *Erotica* was overlooked because of the whole thing with the *Sex* book," Madonna later said. "It just got lost in all that. I think there are some brilliant songs on it and people didn't give it a chance. That disappointed me, but I'm not disappointed in the record itself."

Sex—and, by association, *Erotica*—was supposed to be amusing. Madonna's discourses on S&M, lesbianism, and victimization were meant to be taken with a pinch of salt. But the trouble by this point in Madonna's career was that her audience had stopped laughing with her, simply because they didn't know whether they should. Nothing seemed to be accidental or simply for fun—it was measured, quantified, and considered. Audiences were beginning to laugh not with her but at her, which became more than apparent with her next film project.

Had the timing been different, *Body Of Evidence* might have been better received. But by the time it came out, in April 1993, most people had quite simply seen enough of Madonna's body. Her breasts were no longer enough to hold the viewer's attention through a frequently risible 101-minute film.

Body Of Evidence was intended as an update of *film noir*, the critically-lauded genre that had received a smutty jolt in the arm with *Basic Instinct*. Madonna plays Rebecca Carlson, a femme fatale whose penchant for vigorous sex soon extinguishes millionaire Andrew Marsh (Michael Forest). She stands to gain financially—as long as she can avoid a murder charge. Willem Dafoe plays Frank Dulaney, the attorney who becomes her sex stooge.

The director, Ulrich Edel, had a suitably arty pedigree: his *Christiane F* is a sewer-level trawl through the underbelly of heroin addiction in Berlin, and his *Last Exit To Brooklyn* a convincing interpretation of the Hubert Selby novel. But *Body Of Evidence* is a bewildering, directionless romp that seems to misfire from the off.

Madonna delivers most of her lines in a cod-Brooklyn accent, and we get to see plenty of her body, but little credibility can be found in the picture. The script is woeful. "You're young and beautiful and involved with a wealthy older man," Dulaney says at the start, although Madonna, now 33, looks a trifle too mature to be playing the ingénue. The pair's exchanges before and during sex had audiences sniggering.

"Have you ever seen animals make love, Frank?" she asks at one point. "It's violent, it's intense, but they never really hurt each other."

"We're not animals," he replies.

"Yes we are," she says.

The main sex scene is excruciating. "There's nothing wrong with admitting that you want me, Frank," Carlson says over billowing curtains and *Betty Blue*-inspired music. After much ripping of shirts and sucking of nipples, she tells him she wants to do things "my way" and proceeds to pour burning wax over him.

Eventually, after sodomy in an underground car park and much pathos in the courtroom, Carlson is acquitted. "Thanks, you almost convinced me," she tells Dulaney. She gets her comeuppance in the end when she's shot and falls through a window—no doubt to cheers from many of those who had stuck it out until the end.

Body Of Evidence was simply reviled—there is no other word for it. For Roger Ebert of the *Chicago Sun Times*, it confirmed Madonna as "the queen of movies that were bad ideas right from the beginning." He gave the film one star. The *Detroit News* reported that only 52 people attended a screening in a 237-seat theater in Peoria, Illinois—and that most of them giggled their way through it. The film won two not-so-coveted Golden Raspberry awards: Worst Screenplay and Worst Actress.

Away from the spotlight, Madonna worked hard to ensure that her growing Maverick enterprise retained a personal face. She was involved at some level with every aspect of the company's projects. Although *Sex* and *Erotica* had their share of detractors, they set Maverick off on an even financial keel. But it was the label's other signings that proved this was not just a vanity project for its multimillionaire CEO.

The bases of art and commerce were covered early on. For megabucks, the label signed Seattle-based Candlebox, whose debut album would sell four million copies in the USA alone; for credibility, it brought in Meshell Ndegeocello, whose *Plantation Lullabies* was nominated for a variety of Grammy awards and was later cited as "the birth of neo-soul." It was Guy Oseary's signing of Alanis Morissette, however, that really cemented Maverick as a credible, multimillion-dollar venture.

Morissette had been a teen star in her native Canada with two albums to her name but had grown increasingly frustrated and came to the USA looking for a new deal. After meeting songwriter Glen Ballard, she set to work on an album that would change the course of popular music in the 90s and inspire another wave of female performers—just as Madonna had done in the previous decade.

When Morissette signed to Maverick in 1995, the label anticipated sales of around 250,000 copies of her *Jagged Little Pill*, but her confessional style struck an enormous chord with the record-buying public. The album sold upward of 16 million copies in the USA alone, and more than 33 million copies worldwide.

Madonna was delighted. "She reminds me of when I first started out: slightly awkward but extremely self-possessed and straightforward," she said. "Anything's possible, and the sky's the limit." No Madonna album had sold as many copies since *Like A Virgin*—in fact, Madonna's first two Maverick albums, *Erotica* and *Bedtime Stories*, would sell only around six million copies in total in the USA. Although Morissette would never be so popular again, her work as an ambassador for Maverick had been signposted to the world's artistic community. Here was an organization that nurtured talent and was certainly not simply a hobby for Madonna.

Maverick was unsuccessful in its attempts to ensnare bands such as Hole and Rage Against The Machine but did bring in The Prodigy, one of the coolest acts on the planet at the time. The band had been impressed by Oseary and DeMann—and also by the fact that Madonna would be their new boss. Other future signings included Erasure, William Orbit, Michelle Branch, and Muse.

The company's film wing fared less well. The Maverick Picture Company put out both *Dangerous Game* and *Canadian Bacon*, but neither fared particularly well at the box office. The company regrouped in 2001 as Maverick Films and enjoyed a modicum of success with *Agent Cody Banks* and Madonna's own *I'm Going To Tell You A Secret*.

In 1998, Freddy DeMann was bought out of the label, with Guy Oseary replacing him as CEO. The label had by then established a reputation for releasing film soundtracks, including *The Wedding Singer*, *The Matrix*, and the *Austin Powers* series. Quentin Tarantino had his own imprint within the organization, A Band Apart, which was home to the soundtracks for *Jackie Brown* and the *Kill Bill* films.

Madonna's involvement in Maverick ended in 2004, when she filed a lawsuit against Warner Music, claiming that it had mismanaged Maverick's resources. In return, Warners alleged that Maverick had hemorrhaged money on its own. The case was resolved by Warners purchasing Madonna's share and by her subsequent banishment from her own label. "It was an effective way of settling the lawsuit," Maverick's lawyer, Bert Fields, said at the time. "It's clean and equitable, and it doesn't have anything to do with her record contract." Oseary, who remained a firm friend of Madonna's, was retained as the company's CEO.

Although Maverick is still a subsidiary of Warner Bros, it effectively ceased to exist after 2006. After Madonna's departure, the film wing became Imprint, with Madonna retaining her own film production company, Semtex. For Madonna, the most important thing was that Maverick had not been a flash in the pan, and had been able to sustain some very credible talent in her 12-year tenure at its helm.

CHAPTER 9
DANGEROUS GAMES

After the mixed critical response to her recent work on screen, on record, and in print, all eyes were on whether Madonna could once again raise the stakes on stage for her fourth major tour.

Trailed as a mixture of rock concert, fashion show, carnival performance, cabaret act, and burlesque night, The Girlie Show was audacious. It took its name from Edward Hopper's 1941 painting of a nude dancer, chiffon wrap trailing behind her, on a vaudeville stage. Realizing that she was no longer as popular as she had been in the past, Madonna set about assembling a trimmed-down extravaganza, with 39 shows in five continents. This time, after the 57-date excess of the Blond Ambition World Tour, she wanted to keep things brief.

Rehearsals started in July at Sony Studios in Culver City. In preparation, Madonna and her brother Christopher—the show's director—watched Bollywood musicals, Thai dancing, and the Burt Lancaster film *Trapeze*. Such was Madonna's status that she was able to hire the venerable Gene Kelly, one of the Hollywood legends name-checked on 'Vogue,' to choreograph the 'Rain' sequence. As if to underline her status, she fired him after a week, unhappy with his work.

As far as the music was concerned, tour veteran Jai Winding took charge of a band that included Michael Beardon and Mike McKnight on keyboards, Paul Pesco on guitar, Victor Baley on bass, Omar Hakim on drums, and Luis Conte on percussion. Regular foils Niki Harris and Donna DeLory continued on backing vocals, accompanied by a troupe of eight other dancers.

The Girlie Show opened on September 25 1993 at London's Wembley Stadium and ended on December 19 in Tokyo. Dolce and Gabana designed the costumes—this was high concept art at its finest—with Jeffrey Hornaday again responsible for staging the production.

The performance itself was elaborate and circus-like, with Pierrot, the sad clown from the *commedia dell'arte*, keeping an eye on proceedings throughout. There were three main sections to the show, which began with a continuation of themes from *Erotica* and the Hopper painting. After dancer Carrie Ann Inaba slid, topless, down a long pole in the center of the stage, Madonna rose through the floor wearing a mask, surrounded by male dancers dressed as boxers, to deliver 'Erotica.' Next up was 'Fever,' for which a vulnerable-looking Madonna removed her mask and crop top. At the end of the song she disappeared into flames, perhaps making a figurative descent into hell for her recent public sins. 'Vogue' was pure circus, with a variety of Eastern dance moves; 'Rain' was rather more unsettling, with Madonna, Harris, and DeLory all dressed in black cowls. 'Rain' segued into the legendary Temptations hit 'Just My Imagination' before a surreal and rather mawkish *Singing In The Rain* interlude.

Things livened up considerably for the second part of the show, with Madonna returning to the stage on a mirror-ball for a storming 'Express Yourself' that used as its basis the 1980 Lipps Inc hit 'Funky Town.' 'Why's It So Hard,' with its message of "love your sister, love your brother," quickly descended into an orgy. While watching Madonna being groped by her boy and girl dancers might have been the money shot for some concertgoers who wanted to see a bit of spice, it was in reality simply a piece of old-fashioned vaudeville. This Studio 54-esque section of the show came to a close with 'In This Life,' with Madonna alone on stage and completely shorn of artifice. She would frequently introduce the song, written about friends who had died of AIDS, with the claim that the disease was "the greatest tragedy of the 20th century."

After another somewhat pointless interlude set to the 'The Beast Within,' The Girlie Show moved in to its third and final part, set in a *Cabaret*-influenced Weimar Germany. Madonna sang 'Like A Virgin' as Marlene Dietrich, flanked by Harris and DeLory; all three would act like leery men, groping the dancers and swearing. Superb readings of 'La Isla Bonita' and 'Holiday'—performed here in military style—cut through the sleight of hand, while 'Justify My Love' was delivered as a kind of gavotte.

The high production values were set aside for a simpler closing sequence, with 'Everybody' wheeled out again in tribute to Madonna's first decade as a performer. As if to further illustrate her love for Sly & The Family Stone, she sang part of 'Everybody Is A Star' at the start and then 'Dance To The Music' while introducing her band and dancers. At the end of the show, Pierrot was returned to the stage to be unmasked, with the big reveal that it had been Madonna all along, watching proceedings with detachment—a metaphor for her relationship with the controversy surrounding her career.

Because of the furor over *Sex* and *Erotica*, The Girlie Show barely grazed the USA, stopping in just three cities, all on the East Coast. One of them was in Auburn Hills, in metropolitan Detroit—the home of Chrysler, Madonna's father's workplace for so many years.

The tour also stopped in Canada and Puerto Rico where, in front of 26,000 fans, Madonna rubbed the country's flag against her crotch—an act for which she was later condemned by the country's House of Representatives. At her second show in Buenos Aires she sang 'Don't Cry For Me Argentina' to an ecstatic crowd. The tour then moved to Australia, where several performances were filmed for later broadcast.

Despite its flaws, The Girlie Show was a remarkably audacious and entertaining enterprise—remarkable in part because of the way Madonna had been able to expand what was essentially a small-scale revue into huge areas. It was, however, yet another example of how, the more famous she grew, the more studied and stylized her performances became, the joie de vivre of her early work all but extinguished.

Time magazine described the tour as "at once a movie retrospective, a Zeigfield Revue, a living video, an R-rated take-off on Cirque Du Soleil ... once the Harlow harlot and now a perky mannequin, [Madonna] is the greatest show-off on earth." As far as Jon Pareles of the *New York Times* was concerned, "most of the two-hour show is devoted to repositioning Madonna from trend-spotter to part-time nostalgia merchant, and from titillating novelty act to all-around entertainer."

The Girlie Show was important in that it reestablished Madonna as a top live draw, refocusing attention on her music and performance as opposed to the various controversies that had surrounded her since the turn of the decade. The tour ended on December 19 in Tokyo, by which time it had brought in over $70 million. It would be Madonna's last live show of the 20th century. Once the standard long-form video tie-in had issued, she would enter a new, more sensible, more serious phase of her career. (Never one to miss an opportunity for a double-entendre, she called the video *The Girlie Show—Live Down Under*.)

Midway through the tour, in October 1993, Madonna's latest film project went on release. After *Body Of Evidence*, Madonna knew that she would have to make a proper, mature film if she was to silence her critics. But *Dangerous Game* was another strange choice. As one of the first Maverick Picture Company projects, Madonna was the film's co-producer, and her choice of director, Abel Ferrara, was controversial if not entirely unpredictable. Ferrara had made his name with the 70s 'video nasty' *Driller Killer* and had recently shot the critically lauded *The King Of New York* with Christopher Walken and the notorious *Bad Lieutenant* with Harvey Keitel.

Layered with multiple meanings and much meandering, *Dangerous Game* was originally called *Snake Eyes*. Madonna plays a popular television actress, Sarah Jennings, desperate to break out of type by working with a serious film director, Eddie Israel (Harvey Keitel, white-hot from his appearance in Quentin Tarantino's *Reservoir Dogs*). Madonna's performance in the film is actually half-decent. Ferrara might have been mired in controversy but he knew how to cajole a top-line performance. It's just a shame that hardly anybody saw it.

Madonna was unhappy with how the film turned out and would later bemoan the fact that she didn't have the power in the film industry that she had in the music industry. "It had such a different texture and meaning and outcome for me," she said. "When I went to see a screening of it, I cried, because I really did think I did a good job as an actress. I don't think it should be called *Dangerous Game*. It should be called *The Bad Director*."

Dangerous Game was one of only two films made by the Maverick Picture Company (the other being the comedy *Canadian Bacon*). A serious, downbeat little movie, it was misinterpreted as just another slice of sleaze in the vein of *Sex* and *Body Of Evidence*. It did not fare well at the box office, but it did gain the respect of Madonna's brother, Christopher. "This is the best movie she has ever made," he told her. "I think she can act, this time, I mean it." Allmovie.com agreed, noting that she seems "less mannered, more off-guard, and more affecting than she ever has before or since." This new approach would carry over into her new album, *Bedtime Stories*.

Bedtime Stories marked the first and possibly last time since her debut that no one really cared what sort of album Madonna was going to release, because no one really cared about Madonna. All credit to her, then, that she released a low-key record divested of all the drama of *Like A Prayer* and all the furor that surrounded *Erotica*.

Bedtime Stories is rather muted by comparison to its immediate predecessors. It is discreet and understated, a direct attempt to reconnect with her audience. The 90s seemed to be a caring, touchy-feely decade, a long way from the brash disconnection and personal politics of the 80s. As her *Erotica* alter-ego Dita, Madonna seemed strangely out of step with the times—like a lot of the art she herself enjoyed, she was there to be admired yet difficult to love.

And then came *Bedtime Stories*, a strange, light-blue kind of record. Madonna had initially intended to work with Shep Pettibone again after their fruitful collaboration on *Erotica* but in the end opted to seek out the cream of the current crop of producers to give her album a more contemporary sound. She eventually settled on four names: Dave 'Jam' Hall, who had made his name with Mary J. Blige; Dallas Austin, hot from producing TLC; Babyface, who had worked with Boyz II Men and Bobby Brown; and British producer Nellee Hooper, fresh from overseeing recordings by Massive Attack and Björk.

"She knows how to man a project," manager Freddy DeMann said at the time. "She knows how to surround herself with the biggest and the best, and I think that's been one of her greatest achievements. She's not like a lot of people who feel they have to do it all themselves. She wants assistance, but only from the most qualified people."

Madonna ended up re-recording a lot of the remainder of the album to fit stylistically with Hooper's production. "I wanted a lot more of an R&B feel to this record," she explained. "The idea going in was to juxtapose my singing style with a hardcore hip-hop sensibility and have the finished product still sound like a Madonna record. I began the process by meeting with the hip-hop producers whose work I most admired. It was important, if I were to use a variety of collaborators, that the end product sound cohesive and thematically whole. I wasn't interested in the variety pack approach." This was the era of the processed beat and the sample—five of the album's 11 tracks contain snatches of other songs.

Bedtime Stories was recorded between February and August 1994 in nine different studios, a far cry from the one-room production of *Like A Prayer*. After sessions in Los Angeles, Atlanta, and London, the secret of the album's success came with the final mix at Sterling Sound, New York, overseen by Madonna, Jon Gass, and Alvin Speights (with Hooper contributing mixes of 'Forbidden Love' and 'Sanctuary').

Taking a break from the recording sessions, Madonna agreed to appear on David Letterman's *Late Show* on CBS on March 31 1994. Dressed head to toe in black, she appeared refreshed and somewhat riled from the outset.

She arrived on set to the Paul Shaffer house band's rendition of 'Holiday,' her unease with the situation clearly signaled by her opening line about only being there because the New York Knicks weren't playing that evening. When Letterman taunts her to kiss a member of the audience, she asks: "Why are you so obsessed with my sex life?" And then the swearing begins.

"You are a sick fuck, I don't know why I get so much shit," Madonna continues. The usually unflappable Letterman laughs nervously. "You realize this is being broadcast, don't you?" he asks. When he tries to move on, Madonna asks if he has smelled the underpants she gave him earlier. The conversation then turns to oxymorons—"'untrue rumor' [is] like 'funny David Letterman'"—and the chaos escalates to the point where the host seems desperate to cut the interview short.

The show inevitably got enormous ratings—and provided critics with another opportunity to attack Madonna. "She has nothing to sell but shock," Ray Kerrison of the *New York Post* wrote. "Sadly, since she cannot soar with the eagles, she forages with the rodents." Madonna countered by suggesting that no matter how much Letterman and his team suggested otherwise, she had been set up with the material.

In some respects this was perhaps the final act of the 'controversial' Madonna. "This was a time in my life when I was extremely angry," she recalled four years later. "Angry with the way I was brought up. Angry with how sexist this society that we live in is ... just everything ... I lashed out and that night was one of those times. And I am not particularly proud of it."

Around the same time, Madonna provided the main theme for *Truth Or Dare* director Alek Keshishian's debut feature, *With Honors*, which stars Brendan Fraser as a student who loses the only copy of his thesis and Joe Pesci as the man who finds it and offers it back one page at a time in return for food and accommodation.

'I'll Remember' is an adult ballad that signposted a new, mature direction. Working again with Pat Leonard, Madonna seemed to be drawing a clear line in the sand after her wayward recent behavior, delivering an impassioned vocal over heavily sequenced keyboards. The song's sobriety and melody were important—this was the sort of record an artist in her later thirties should be making.

"I think most of the time, when my records come out, people are so distracted by so much fanfare and controversy that nobody pays attention to the music," Madonna said at the time. "I can't tell you how painful the idea of singing 'Like A Virgin' or 'Material Girl' is to me now. I didn't write either of those songs, and I wasn't digging very deep then. I also feel more connection emotionally to the music I'm writing now, so it's more of a pleasure to do it."

'I'll Remember' was a huge international success, giving Madonna another Number Two hit on the *Billboard* Hot 100. She sings straight to the camera in the promo video, wearing a close black bob and a large crystal necklace. There are no body parts on show. There is a direct line from this record to the next four years in Madonna's career, during which she would play her role a little straighter and, as her old paramour Prince might have said, act her age, not her shoe size.

The tone of the single informed *Bedtime Stories*. Although the album is rather muted, there's an overall sense of optimism, with Madonna able to reflect on the tumultuous period that had recently passed before her. She sounds happy and expansive, if somewhat exhausted. "I've been in an incredibly reflective state of mind," she told *Q* magazine. "I've done a lot of soul-searching and I just felt in a romantic mood when I was writing for it."

The album opens with 'Survival,' a mellow, loping groove produced by and written with Dallas Austin. Madonna cuts straight to the chase with its opening lines, making it clear that she won't be ducking any issues. "I'll never be an angel," she sings. "I'll never be a saint." She's been busy surviving, she says, and whether it's heaven or hell, she'll be "living to tell." This reference to one of her most famous tracks was like a sly nod to history in a James Bond film, as if to indicate that that is another installment in a long-running franchise. (Further underlining that continuity, the track also features tour stalwarts Niki Harris and Donna Delory on backing vocals.)

Putting 'Survival' at the start of the album immediately set its course. These are new times: if you don't like it, it's not for you. Both this track and 'Human Nature' address the controversy of the preceding years. "The other songs could be about anybody," Madonna said in 2004, "but in these two it's quite obvious that I'm addressing the public."

The album's second track, 'Secret,' was produced by Dallas Austin and chosen as the lead single from the album. It was originally entitled 'Something's Coming Over Me'—a title more in keeping with *Erotica*—and was one of the tracks Madonna worked on initially with Shep Pettibone, who eventually had his co-writing credit reinstated in time for the 2001 hits compilation *GHV2*.

'Secret' was released as a single on September 28, its acoustic guitar, subdued synthetics, and warm, direct vocal offering a perfect example of what listeners could expect from the rest of the album. It reached Number Three on the *Billboard* Hot 100, and Madonna was sufficiently impressed with it that she sanctioned a plethora of different mixes, many of which were later collected on a promotional mini-album. 'Secret' was also one of the first releases that she promoted on the internet, then very much an underground phenomena. An exclusive 30-second sound file was made available for fans to download and discuss on a message board. This was truly ahead of its time. The accompanying message might look like pure web nostalgia today—it opens with "Hello cyberheads"—but it was 1994, after all.

Directed by photographer Melodie McDaniel, the 'Secret' video was filmed at the legendary Lenox Lounge jazz club in Harlem, which had once counted Malcolm X, Langston Hughes, and James Baldwin among its clientele. Shot on September 9 1994, it shows Madonna singing the song from the stage with what appears to be a jazz band, then leaving the club and heading home. Her performance is intercut with shots of the Harlem milieu, including transvestites and street gangs, complete with rippling naked torsos. To remind the viewer who it is they are watching, the middle section captures Madonna lying at another woman's feet and being drizzled with holy water. The video ends with the singer back at her apartment, in the arms of her lover. By the end, we are not totally sure what secret she has been keeping.

The third track on *Bedtime Stories*, 'I'd Rather Be Your Lover,' features Maverick signing Meshell Ndegeocello on bass and is the first of the Dave 'Jam' Hall productions on the album. Breathlessly contemporary, it includes a sample from Blue Note guitarist Lou Donaldson's version of The Isley Brothers 'It's Your Thing.' The rap at the end was originally going to be performed by Tupac Shakur, but he was on criminal charges at the time, so Ndegeocello stepped in instead.

The Dallas Austin-produced 'Don't Stop' is another dance-floor anthem in the tradition of 'Everybody,' 'Into The Groove,' and 'Vogue,' yet its torpid pace renders it somewhat anemic. Madonna seems to be singing from cue cards rather than letting the music soothe her soul. It's not that the song is bad, it's just rather too understated to support such celebratory lyrics. For once, her heart doesn't seem to be in it.

Nellee Hooper produced 'Inside Of Me,' which continues the mid-paced shuffle but has a rather more insidious groove. It's like an updated 'Erotica,' but with a melody, and takes the inner hurt of a lover scorned as its subject matter. "In the public eye, I act like I don't care," she sings, "[but] when there's no one watching me, I'm crying."

'Human Nature' is the album's keynote. Produced by Dave 'Jam' Hall and based around a sample from 'What You Need' by hip-hop group Main

Source, it is driven G-funk synths and louche beats. Although Madonna was keen to present a new, mature image, the mood and message remain the same—completely unrepentant. "Express yourself / Don't repress yourself," she begins, and there is little doubt as to what she is referring when she asks: "Did I say something wrong? Oops, I didn't know I couldn't talk about sex (I musta been crazy)."

The video, directed by Jean-Baptiste Mondino, was filmed at Raleigh Studios in Hollywood on May 6–7 1995. Inspired by comic artist Eric Stanton, it continues in the brightly lit, heavily stylized manner of his previous work with the singer, 'Open Your Heart' and 'Justify My Love.' Madonna appears with her hair in cornrows wearing a full-body rubber cat-suit—a look most likely appropriated from her most recent inspiration, the Icelandic singer Björk. The video opens with four dancers clamped onto her with their faces hidden, their hands roaming freely around her body. The metaphors are as unsubtle as ever: as Madonna sings about the need to express yourself, the dancers prize her legs apart. (She later appears chained to a Perspex chair, wearing a wild wig, apparently parodying some of the pictures from the *Sex* book.)

For the chorus, Madonna and her five dancers gyrate spectacularly in small square boxes. Madonna then strips down to rubber bra and panties to dance between ropes held by the others; for a moment she can be seen in the center of a pentagram. Like the descent into flames during The Girlie Show, it's another indication of where she thinks she'll be going after her recent behavior, although she's still adamant that she's "not apologizing." The video ends with her staring straight into the camera to confirm that she has "absolutely no regrets" before pretending to box.

'Human Nature' was the fourth and final single to be taken from the album. It was released in June 1995 with a photograph by Bettina Rheims on the cover showing Madonna lying on the floor with her eyes closed. Warner Bros had dearly wanted to release 'Don't Stop,' the album's obligatory dance-floor track. Madonna won out, but 'Human Nature' failed to make the US Top 40. It did reach Number Eight in the UK, however, and was an enormous club hit elsewhere. At least five different remixes of it appeared, the most notable of them by British dance duo Orbital.

The seventh track on *Bedtime Stories*, 'Forbidden Love,' marks the first appearance of writer-producer Kenneth Brian Edmonds, rechristened Babyface by none other than Bootsy Collins. It's another languorous groove, and one that Madonna was pleased enough with that she also included it on her *Something To Remember* collection a year later. Next up, with Tommy Martin's luscious Spanish guitar and Dave Hall's subtle string arrangement, 'Love Tried To Welcome Me' is one of the best Madonna tracks you've never really listened to. It has an orchestra feel reminiscent of Chicago's 'If You Leave Me Now' and a sweet, subtle vocal, making it the album's standout ballad.

Apart from the wailing siren in the background, 'Sanctuary' is another return to the phased whispers of 'Erotica.' It uses a sample from Herbie Hancock's 'Watermelon Man,' while Madonna quotes from 'Voices' by the poet Walt Whitman in the middle section. Based on a track by Anne Preven of the LA band Ednaswap, it's probably the best example of the blissed-out trip-hop vibe Madonna had been aiming for. Madonna met with Preven to discuss the restructuring of the song, but it soon became clear that Madonna was not especially interested in Preven's suggestions.

The electronic pulse of 'Bedtime Story' finally ratchets the album up a gear. Written by Björk, Nellee Hooper, and Marius de Vries, it's the only track on the album that Madonna did not have a hand in composing. She was greatly impressed by Björk, who had made a huge international breakthrough with her first solo record, 1993's *Debut*, and was so smitten by 'Bedtime Story' that she retained the Icelandic singer's vocal phrasing. The heavily sequenced track sounds not unlike the British dance trio Underworld, but even with its electronic throb it still seems bereft of the beats with which Madonna's previous albums had been so richly laden.

Madonna chose 'Bedtime Story' as the third single from the album. Despite topping the *Billboard* Dance Club chart, however, it rose no higher than Number 42 on the Hot 100. A total of 15 different mixes of the song were made available. To promote the single, Madonna hosted a Bedtime Story Pajama Party at New York's Webster Hall, where she read David Kirk's children's book, *Miss Spider's Tea Party*, to an invited audience. The event was broadcast on MTV, and Madonna spoke at length to Kurt Loder about her forthcoming pitch for *Evita*. The record was a sizable hit in the UK, where Madonna performed it in front of a backlit wind-tunnel at the 1995 BRIT Awards.

The accompanying promo video was directed by Mark Romanek, who first worked with Madonna on 'Rain.' Inspired by surrealist painters such as Leonora Carrington and Remedois Varo, it draws on the record's trance-like ambience and emphasizes the otherworldliness of the lyric. It is weird, to put it mildly. "Me flying through the hallways with my hair trailing behind me, the birds flying out of my open robe—all of those images are an homage to female surrealist painters," Madonna told *Aperture* magazine. "There's a little bit of Frida Kahlo in there, too." The imagery of the video—which can now be seen in New York's Museum Of Modern Art—and the feel and groove of the song were a direct precursor to Madonna's 1998 album and single *Ray Of Light*.

The longevity of *Bedtime Stories* can be largely attributed to the gorgeous, wholesome closing track, 'Take A Bow.' Released as the album's second single, it provided Madonna with her first US Number One since 'This Used To Be My Playground.' It wasn't just a flash in the pan, either: in an era of Montell Jordan and TLC, Madonna held on to the top spot for a full seven weeks—her longest ever run at the top of the US charts.

'Take A Bow' is by far and away the best thing on *Bedtime Stories*. It also sounds unlike anything else on the album, with Babyface's vocal acting as a fine counterpoint to Madonna's. It's a surprisingly beautiful record, and one that came at a time when most people had almost forgotten that Madonna could make beautiful records, its Far Eastern influences just the right side of kitsch.

The video for the song was shot over three days in November 1994 in Antequera, Spain. It was directed by Michael Haussman and starred bullfighter Emilio Munoz, with Madonna as his spurned lover. It came in for considerable criticism from animal rights groups because to its subject matter, but Madonna was unrepentant. (The bulls used in the filming were put out to grass afterward, and no animals were hurt.) The video is desperately theatrical, with various shots designed to capture the pathos of the situation between the champion toreador and his lover. There's also an interlude with Madonna writhing on a bed in high-quality undergarments.

Madonna sent a copy of the 'Take A Bow' clip to Alan Parker to convince him that she was suitable to play the lead role in *Evita*, while MTV was on hand to record a seven-minute making-of documentary: *Madonna— No Bull!* 'Take A Bow' was very good to Madonna, but she has never performed it in on tour. (She did sing it, with Babyface, at the American Music Awards in January 1995, and offered a lip-synced version at the same year's San Remo festival.)

Bedtime Stories was prepared for release in the fall of 1994. The cover was designed by Fabien Baron and Patrick Li at Baron & Baron Advertising and photographed by Patrick Demarchelier, who captured Madonna's new look, described by *Q* magazine as "30s Hollywood meets early-70s flash: Jean Harlow and Angie Bowie." Although initial pressings were mistakenly printed the right way up, the correct version shows Madonna upside down, meeting the camera from her bed with a classic Hollywood gaze. Her heavily made-up lips are parted to reveal brilliant white teeth; she has a ring through her nose. She looks alluring and provocative but not overly sexual. Inside are five further pictures of Madonna on a bed: laughing, praying, passed out. She opens her personal credits by saying that making the album "was a true test of my sanity and stability" before listing the people who helped her hold on to it. The end of the list makes clear how much she was enjoying her new role as CEO with its closing message to "everyone at Maverick— MAVERICK RULES!"

Reviews of the album were mixed but the overall feeling was one of tentative approval. It was a muted, understated record, and the reviews seemed to follow suit. "More than any previous Madonna album, the latest finds her telling us the truth about her life," Jim Farber of *Entertainment Weekly* wrote. "Madonna's lyrics mingle sex and romance in more personal ways than before." For *USA Today*, S&M now meant "silky and mellow."

Bedtime Stories was just a little too smooth for some. "Rather than signify some bold new direction for Madonna, *Bedtime Stories* hardly takes any risks at all," Steve Dollar of the *Atlanta Journal Constitution* wrote. "If it's not sensational, then it is comforting. Songs such as 'Forbidden Love,' 'Sanctuary,' and 'Inside Of Me' offer a kind of deluxe smooch music, with musings on the glory of love, the discontents of romance and the pursuit of pleasure." For Mat Snow of *Q* magazine, it was as if "the whole body of her voice has been electronically filtered out to leave only its outline." Retrospective reviews have been kinder, however; on allmusic.com, Stephen Thomas Erlewine suggests that *Bedtime Stories* contains some of Madonna's "most humane and open music; it's even seductive."

There was no tour for *Bedtime Stories*, but Madonna was around to promote the album. On February 13 1995 she returned to *The Late Show With David Letterman*—the scene of a debacle a year earlier—to talk up *Bedtime Stories* and highlight the forthcoming release of 'Bedtime Story' as a single. She brought Letterman some long-stemmed roses and a box of chocolates as a peace offering. She told him she was a changed woman before turning to the camera to announce: "I'm not going to say fuck anymore."

Bedtime Stories was a sizable international success, selling roughly as strongly as *Erotica*. It reached Number Three on the US chart and by November 2005 had been certified triple platinum. The album was nominated for a Grammy for Best Pop Vocal Album but lost out to Joni Mitchell's *Turbulent Indigo*. Only a few songs from the album have featured in subsequent live sets. Madonna wanted to tour the album but was unable to do so because of her commitment to *Evita*, which was finally looking like becoming a reality. "I want to go on tour, believe me," she told MTV. "I'm dying to perform the music from this record, but I've been waiting five years for this role and I'm not going to screw it up."

Things may have calmed down somewhat, but life as a superstar was still eventful, and fame brought with it some considerable downsides. It was at the end of the promotion for *Bedtime Stories* that Robert Dewey Hoskins, a fan who had been stalking Madonna, was shot and wounded as he scaled the wall of her home in Los Angeles. From here on, Madonna would keep 24-7 security.

When Madonna departs this planet, *Bedtime Stories* will be the album that people come back to and rediscover. She achieved another personal first with this album, but not one that would go on to be written about: she had succeeded in becoming Just Another Artist. Here was a pleasant, well made, and almost thoroughly unremarkable record.

After the relatively warm critical reception for *Bedtime Stories*, Madonna wished to capitalize on the renewed focus on her music. *Something To Remember*—a stopgap release issued just as she was preparing to work on *Evita*—reminded her audience that she was still very much about the music.

Released in November 1995, the album acted as a curtain-closer to five years of unprecedented tumult. It also underlined her greatness by gathering together a few rarities, non-album singles, greatest hits, and miscellaneous tracks that showcased her sweeter side. It was, in effect, a second best-of collection—a Madonna for the sensual rather than overly sexual. Only two tracks featured here also appear on *The Immaculate Collection*: 'Live To Tell' and 'Crazy For You.'

The artwork came from her much-loved photo shoot with Mario Testino for Versace. This was a sober, sensible Madonna, eyes closed, pensive—a serious artist with the ballads to match. Inside was a note from Madonna lamenting the fact that "so much controversy has swirled around my career this past decade that very little attention gets paid to my music. The songs are all but forgotten." She goes on to say that although she has few regrets, she has "learned to appreciate the idea of doing things in a simpler way. ... So, without a lot of fanfare, without any distractions, I present you this collection of ballads. Some are old, some are new. All of them are from my heart."

The first of the new songs is 'I Want You,' a collaboration between Madonna and the British trip-hop group Massive Attack, whom she met via *Bedtime Stories* co-producer Nellee Hooper. The track was originally included on the Motown tribute album *Inner City Blues: The Music Of Marvin Gaye*, but legal wrangling had prevented it from being released as a single.

Madonna was back on more conventional ground with the other two new tracks, 'You'll See' and 'One More Chance,' which she co-wrote with David Foster. Both were chart hits, while 'Oh Father,' from *Like A Prayer*, was released as the third single from the album. 'La Isla Bonita' was included on the Japanese version of the album, while 'Veras'—the Spanish language version of 'You'll See'—appeared on the Latin American edition. 'One More Chance' is particularly affecting, and perfectly positioned to assuage any doubts about the singer's forthcoming portrayal of Eva Peron.

Something To Remember certainly chimed well with the public. It reached Number Six on the US chart and achieved triple-platinum status. It was also Madonna's final release on Maverick via Sire, her home for the past 13 years—a period that had seen her create some of the best-known hits of the age and grow to became a superstar, the like of which had never been seen before. Now, however, it was time for Madonna to cut her ties with the past and look toward a new chapter of her life and career: a substantial film role and motherhood.

With her 40th birthday on the horizon, speculation about when she would find a father for her child had reached fever pitch. Ever since she married Sean Penn in 1985, the media had been waiting to put its 'Madonna And Child' headlines to use. A man was needed to sit in the "daddy chair"— a phrase Madonna and her brother Christopher hit upon in the 90s. In his autobiography, *Life With My Sister Madonna*, he recalled asking: "Who's sitting in the daddy chair today?" He notes that his sister required the ideal daddy-chair candidate "to be smart and good looking" but had "no strictures about race or religion."

Although she had been cagey on the subject when she was with Penn, by the early 90s Madonna had begun to speak more openly about her need for children. In 1991, while promoting *Truth Or Dare*, she said: "I long for children. I wish that I was married and in a situation where having a child would be possible. People say: well, have one on your own. I say wait a minute—I'm not interested in raising a cripple. I want a father there. I want someone I can depend on."

Carlos Manuel Leon was someone that Madonna could depend on. (He was also a good-looking Latino, not unlike the men she had fantasized about in 'Into The Groove' a decade earlier.) Born in New York to Cuban parents, he was eight years her junior and worked as a personal trainer. He had also done some acting and dancing work and harbored ambitions to be a professional cyclist. The pair met on September 8 1994 while jogging in Central Park.

Shortly after that, Carlos was introduced to Christopher, who later described him as "a fish out of water in Madonna's rarified world," but conceded that Leon was "far from stupid." The relationship soon grew serious. Madonna's friends described Leon as "sweet." Publicist Liz Rosenberg called him "lovable." As author Douglas Thompson later sneered: "They could have been talking about a pet."

At a press conference to promote her appearance at the 1995 Brit Awards, Madonna was asked about her love life and then, in a roundabout way, about her pregnancy. Asked whether she would choose to disclose her past to any potential offspring, she replied: "I want them to know me completely."

This was a theme to which she would return often. Later, when the popular press goaded her about the possible effect of her life choices on her daughter, she returned to her most infamous work. "I will explain that the *Sex* book is a work of art," she said, "underlining the importance of irony and provocation in an artist's life."

Madonna fell pregnant in late 1995. From this point onward, things would truly change.

PART 2
RAY OF LIGHT
by Eddi Fiegel

CHAPTER 10
DON'T CRY FOR ME

"I see this role as being my destiny," Madonna said, when asked about her latest film role as Eva 'Evita' Perón, the iconic Argentinean First Lady who had inspired Andrew Lloyd Webber and Tim Rice's hit musical. It was a part which resonated more powerfully with Madonna than any she had played before and perhaps any she has tackled since. But looking at the parallels in the two women's lives, it's not too hard to see why.

Evita Perón had started life as Eva Duarte, an illegitimate young girl from an impoverished background in rural Argentina whose family had been ostracized by the wealthy and privileged society her married father once belonged to. After moving to Buenos Aires and finding fame, first as an actress and then as the wife of the ambitious military leader Juan Perón, she became not only the most powerful woman in Argentina but also one of the most glamorous women in the world. This was the tale of a highly intelligent brunette who came to the city and found international success as a blond; someone who polarized opinion and was seen as "either a saint or the incarnation of Satan."

The role seemed perfect for Madonna in every sense. She had always been captivated by the movies—even more than wanting to be a pop star, she had wanted to be an icon of the silver screen, just like her idols: Greta Garbo and Monroe, Grace Kelly and Jean Harlow. But despite making numerous films, she had yet to gain respect in Hollywood. Until now.

Lloyd Webber and Rice first found success with *Evita* on stage in London and New York in the late 70s, but although various film directors expressed interest in taking the production to the big screen, it took nearly 15 years for the project to finally come to fruition. A catalogue of high-profile names had been associated with the film along the way, including Mike Nichols, Francis

Coppola, and Alan Pakula. The maverick British director Ken Russell, who had famously brought The Who's rock opera *Tommy* to celluloid, was involved at one point—he even started shooting with a cast that included Liza Minnelli as Evita and, true to Russell's reputation for the fantastically camp, Boy George as The Pope.

By 1988 the project had been assigned to Oliver Stone, who got as far as scouting for locations in Argentina. What was not confirmed was who would play the title role. If the list of directors associated with the project seemed long, the list of actresses vying for the lead amounted to a global search on the scale of the hunt for Scarlett O'Hara in the 30s for *Gone With The Wind*. Madonna had expressed interest early on but was only one of an extraordinary array of actresses and singers considered for the part, among them Glenn Close, Barbara Streisand, Ann-Margret, Olivia Newton John, Bette Midler, Gloria Estefan, and Stone's apparent favorite, Meryl Streep.

Streep was a classically trained singer as well as an Oscar-winning actress, but Madonna too was a strong contender. She had numerous meetings with Stone and the producers, but Stone had a notorious ego, and tension soon grew between the pop diva and the wayward director. Streep consequently became the key contender, and in the summer of 1989 recorded demo versions of the *Evita* songs. The tape was then sent to Rice and Lloyd Webber, who had final approval on casting; by the time they decided they were unconvinced by the demo, Stone had moved on to *The Doors*.

Several other directors came in and out of the picture over the next few years until, in 1994, the British director Alan Parker was finally confirmed to adapt the original stage musical for the screen. Parker had been keen to film *Evita* since the 70s but the timing had never been right. He had excellent credentials, having previously directed the children's gangster caper *Bugsy Malone* (starring a teenage Jodie Foster), *Fame: The Musical*, Pink Floyd's *The Wall*, and *The Commitments*. But, frustratingly for Madonna, he also had a preferred choice for the leading role: Michelle Pfeiffer, another award-winning actress who could also sing, and had done so to great success in *The Fabulous Baker Boys*.

It was here that fate would intervene on Madonna's behalf. The producers and director took so long to start work on the film that by the time they were ready, Pfeiffer was no longer available, having only just given birth to her second child. This, finally, was Madonna's chance. She continued to lobby the heads of the film studios involved but knew that the man she really needed to convince was Parker. Having never met him before, she decided to write him a letter to explain why she believed she was perfect for the role, and how only she could understand Perón's "passion and her pain."

"I wanted to let him know exactly how I felt," she recalled. "So I wrote him a letter—an impassioned plea, more exactly. I don't remember how long it was or what I said exactly, but I do know I felt as if I was completely possessed while doing it." She sent with it a copy of the promo video for 'Take A Bow,' hoping that the clip, in which she appears in 40s dress alongside Latin American and Catholic iconography, might serve as a kind of unofficial audition.

The package—and the letter in particular—clearly had the desired effect. Madonna may not have remembered how long her letter was but Parker later recalled there being no less than eight handwritten pages. He was suitably impressed not just with the fact that she had taken time out to write such a personal, heartfelt letter but also with her evident desire for the part. "She said that no other person could play the part," he recalled. "That she'd sing, dance and act her heart out. And she did."

Although she was initially triumphant at having landed the role she had wanted so much, it soon became clear to Madonna that *Evita* would be anything but easy. Many of the songs in the musical—particularly the stand-out hit, 'Don't Cry For Me Argentina'—required an extensive vocal range and were notoriously difficult to sing, even for singers experienced in musical theatre. She therefore agreed to undertake several months of training with famed voice teacher Joan Lader, a hallowed figure in the singing world who had previously taught Roberta Flack, Dianne Reeves, and Patti Lupone (who had herself starred as Evita on Broadway).

At Lader's Manhattan apartment, Madonna learned how to sing from her diaphragm as opposed to her throat—a common mistake among many untrained pop and rock singers—as well as how to make her diction clearer and how to project in a more specific and structured style. Madonna was delighted with the results. "I suddenly discovered that I had been using only half of my voice," she told Robert Hilburn of the *Los Angeles Times*. "Until then, I had pretty much accepted that I had a very limited range, which is fine. Anita O'Day and Edith Piaf had very limited ranges too, and I am a big fan. So I figured I'd make do with the best I had."

Some months later, work on *Evita* finally started. Before filming began, the entire score was to be recorded in the studio, so that the actors could lip-sync to the soundtrack later on. In theory, working in a recording studio should have given Madonna the opportunity to ease into the project in a familiar, comfortable environment, but the first day proved to be much more of a challenge than she had envisaged. Alan Parker would later describe it as "Black Monday."

In contrast to the standard pop-rock practice of having the vocalist record in a relatively small, intimate space while listening to a pre-recorded backing track on headphones; here, in the manner customary for recordings of stage musicals, Madonna was expected to sing live in a vast studio accompanied by a full orchestra. Despite the voice lessons, she was daunted by the idea of singing with 84 classical musicians ready to hear her every mistake. To make matters worse, the song scheduled to be recorded on that first Monday was 'Don't Cry For Me Argentina'—not only *Evita*'s most famous song but also its most demanding.

If that wasn't enough, Andrew Lloyd Webber—who Madonna felt from the start doubted her singing abilities—was present at the recording. The combination of nerves and this unfamiliar, uncomfortable setup did not make for a successful day's work. After hours of tense, failed attempts, the session ended with Madonna in tears and an emergency meeting called between director, writer, and star.

The tears did not last long. Madonna made it clear that she would not be happy to continue on this basis, resulting in a major change in plan. From here on, she would record her vocals at another, more contemporary studio, with the orchestra parts recorded separately elsewhere. In addition, she would record only in the afternoons and on every second day so as to give her time to rest her voice.

Four months and 400 hours of sessions later, the soundtrack was finally complete, and filming could commence. But if the sound recording had proved difficult, filming would be even more of a challenge. "It was difficult on every level," Madonna told CNN's Larry King. "We were filming in Argentina and we were making a movie about a person who was a very controversial political figure. So there were mob scenes about people who didn't want us to make the movie—and mob scenes about people who wanted us to make the movie. And then, you know, the heat and the thousands of extras ..."

Events in Argentina were lively from the start. Madonna arrived in Buenos Aires in January 1996, one month before filming was due to begin. She had decided to spend some time researching her character, and although she had read biographies and watched documentaries, in order to really get under the skin of her character and get behind the myths, she wanted to get more detail from diplomats, politicians, and filmmakers who had known Eva Perón.

She checked into the luxury Four Seasons Buenos Aires, a French chateau-style *grande dame* of a hotel whose opulent high ceilings, floor-to-ceiling windows, and expansive balconies emitted a sense of faded, old-world grandeur. She was given the hotel's best suite—and would have been delighted had it not been for the scores of fans outside unceasingly chanting "Eva" and "Madonna" and singing the words to her songs. "This is very flattering during the day but not so great at night when I'll be trying to sleep," she wrote in a diary entry later reproduced in *Vanity Fair*.

The day after arriving in the country, Madonna was due to interview an Argentine diplomat who had known Eva Perón when she was young—a relatively straightforward engagement, one might think, but not, as it turned out, for Madonna. "Unfortunately, about 500 screaming fans made my departure next to impossible," she wrote. "The police are not terribly organized down here, and I didn't have enough security, so the three feet I walked from the building to the car were very scary. Somehow I got pulled down to the ground for about three seconds. I managed to crawl into the car and shut the door, only to find that one of my shoes was missing and the heel was broken on the other. They were Versace. Don't worry. When everyone was in the car we sped away, only to discover that a young girl was holding on to the roof of the car for dear life. So we stopped and pulled her off as she kicked and screamed and cried that she loved me. I wanted to give her the business card of my shrink, but my driver drove away too fast."

A few more scenes of this nature followed, culminating in the arrest one day of Madonna's personal assistant, the late Caresse Norman. Madonna had sent Norman out as a decoy so she could slip out unnoticed from the hotel's other entrance and go to Recoleta, the cemetery where Evita was buried. But when fans discovered the ploy, Norman was dragged out of the car and subsequently arrested for various misdemeanors including that of not carrying her passport. Madonna's patience had by this time just about reached its limit. She told her producers that she would quit the film unless they arranged to send extra security immediately.

Aside from the chaos of having to brave thousands of fans without adequate protection, Madonna could not help noticing the less-than-welcoming graffiti in the streets, shouting slogans like: "Evita Lives, Get Out Madonna." Rumors had apparently begun to circulate that the Argentinean people's beloved Evita was not going to be portrayed favorably in the film; even the country's President was said to have called the entire project "a disgrace." To make matters worse, the fact that many of the film crew were British did not seem to help, given the relatively fresh memory of the 1982 Falklands conflict.

There was, however, the occasional enjoyable diversion. Many of the Perón supporters Madonna interviewed were gentlemen of the old school. They were consequently rarely less than gallant, and she found both their information and support comforting. "Some of the old men all but foamed at the mouth when they talked about the old days," she recalled. "It was like we were back in 1942. They still seemed smitten with her. I kept being told how much I looked like her or moved like her. I got a lot of reassurance from all of that."

Madonna also found time to go for drinks with the world-famous tenor Plácido Domingo, who had turned down the role of Juan Perón but by this time regretted it. "Latin men were put on earth to charm women," she wrote in her diary. "And torture them!"

Madonna's susceptibility to Latin charm was meanwhile to provide another cause for rumor and gossip. The narrator/Che Guevara role in *Evita* was to be played by Spanish heartthrob, Antonio Banderas, whom Madonna famously said she found "very sexy" in *Truth Or Dare*. Before filming had even begun, rumors began to circulate in the press that Banderas's girlfriend of the time, Hollywood actress Melanie Griffiths, was nervous about Madonna sharing a film set with her boyfriend, and that she would therefore be accompanying Banderas to Argentina for the duration of the shoot. Madonna found the situation enormously irritating, stating immediately that she was not interested in Banderas, and that her remark in *Truth Or Dare* was no more than a throwaway line. Eventually she spoke directly to Griffiths, and the tensions for the most part dissipated.

Madonna got along very well with the rest of the cast and crew, including her other co-star, British actor Jonathan Pryce, who plays her onscreen husband, Juan Perón. There were also some fun aspects of the shoot, notably the gorgeous haute-couture costumes. Eva Perón had been a fashion icon of her day, and top costume designer Penny Rose created no fewer than 85 different outfits for Madonna to wear. New pieces in the style of the originals were made to measure by Christian Dior, from the fashion house's headquarters in Paris, while Salvatore Ferragamo provided the shoes to match. The outfits—which also included 39 hats, 45 pairs of shoes, and 56 pairs of earrings—would eventually earn Madonna an entry in Guinness's *World Records* book for Most Costume Changes In A Film.

Any other problems the film faced were mostly incidental, such as the day shooting began in a nearby shantytown—used as the village Eva lived in before moving to Buenos Aires—only for the cast and crew to discover that they would be spending the entire day beside an abattoir and the accompanying stench of rotting animal flesh. Realistic locations were nevertheless clearly of benefit to the film. When it came to the key scene in which Madonna sings 'Don't Cry For Me Argentina' to the crowds from the balcony of the Casa Rosada—Buenos Aires's Presidential Palace—she was understandably keen to film at the Palace itself.

As with so much of the filming, this proved to be far from straightforward. President Menem was apparently reluctant to allow a foreign crew to film in the country's most regal Palace, and it was only after some nine months of diplomatic negotiations between *Evita*'s producers, Madonna herself and Palace officials that an agreement was reached. This culminated in a secret meeting between Madonna and the President at the statesman's remote private home on a small island off the coast.

In true superstar style, Madonna arrived by helicopter and was offered champagne and caviar by way of refreshments. The President meanwhile seemed enchanted by her; she played him the song 'You Must Love Me,' which she sings in the film as Evita is dying, in the hope of demonstrating the serious and respectful mood she and the producers hoped to create. When Madonna thought she saw a tear fall from the President's eye, she finally plucked up the courage to ask about filming at the palace. "Anything is possible," he replied, enigmatically.

President Menem subsequently gave his permission, and in their last week in Buenos Aires, Madonna and crew set off to shoot 'Don't Cry For Me Argentina' on the famous balcony of the Casa Rosada. The crowds waiting down below were due to be filmed later on with extras, during the next phase of filming in Hungary, but rather than singing to an empty courtyard, Madonna asked Alan Parker if the rest of the crew might temporarily stand in. Parker agreed, and the scene proved to be one of the most memorable for Madonna, seemingly giving her an eerie sensation of connection with the woman she was portraying. "In the exact place she had stood so many times before, I raised my arms and looked into the hungry eyes of humanity," she wrote in her diary, "and at that moment I felt her enter my body like a heat missile, starting with my feet, traveling up my spine, and flying out my fingertips, into the air, out to the people, and back up to heaven."

Filming the Casa Rosada scenes brought a triumphant close to Madonna's time in Argentina. A week later, she returned home to her Manhattan apartment for a short break. Shooting was due to resume a few weeks later in Budapest, Hungary, and Madonna had planned to spend some of the intervening period on holiday in Miami. Instead she decided to stay in New

An early portrait of Madonna, taken in 1979, shortly after she arrived in New York City.

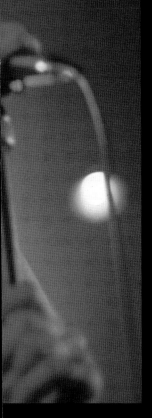

LEFT: *A still from the 1985 film* Vision Quest, *in which Madonna sings two songs, 'Crazy For You' and 'The Gambler.'* **ABOVE:** *Madonna and DJ John 'Jellybean' Benitez at the opening of the Private Eyes club in New York City, July 1984.*

ABOVE: *Madonna performs at John F. Kennedy Stadium, Philadelphia, during Live Aid, July 1985.*
ABOVE RIGHT: *Madonna on stage at the third annual MTV Video Music Awards, September 1986.*
BELOW RIGHT: *Madonna and her then husband, Sean Penn, attend the heavyweight title fight between Mike Tyson and Michael Spinks in Atlantic City, New Jersey, June 1988.*

PREVIOUS SPREAD: *Madonna performs 'Vogue' at the MTV Video Music Awards, September 1990.*
LEFT: *Madonna on stage at the Memorial Sports Arena, Los Angeles, during her Blond Ambition World Tour, May 1990.* ABOVE: *Publicity stills for the album* Bedtime Stories *(1994) and the musical film* Evita *(1996).*

ABOVE: *A still from the video for 'The Power Of Good-Bye,' the fourth single from Madonna's 1998 album* Ray Of Light.

RIGHT: *Madonna on stage at the Roseland Ballroom in New York for an intimate show in support of* Music, *November 200*

LEFT: *Madonna makes an in-store appearance to promote her ninth studio album,* American Life, *April 2003.*
ABOVE: *Madonna performs—and shares a controversial kiss—with Britney Spears at the 2003 MTV Video Music Awards as Christina Aguilera looks on.*

ABOVE: *Madonna and Stuart Price, co-writer and producer of* Confessions On A Dance Floor, *at Koko, London, November 2005.* **ABOVE RIGHT:** *Madonna with her adopted son David Banda in Mphandula, Malawi, April 2007.*
BELOW RIGHT: *The Sticky & Sweet Tour hits the Boardwalk Hall in Atlantic City, New Jersey, November 2008.*
FOLLOWING PAGE: *Madonna and her daughter Lourdes at the launch of their Material Girl fashion line at Macy's, New York, September 2010.*

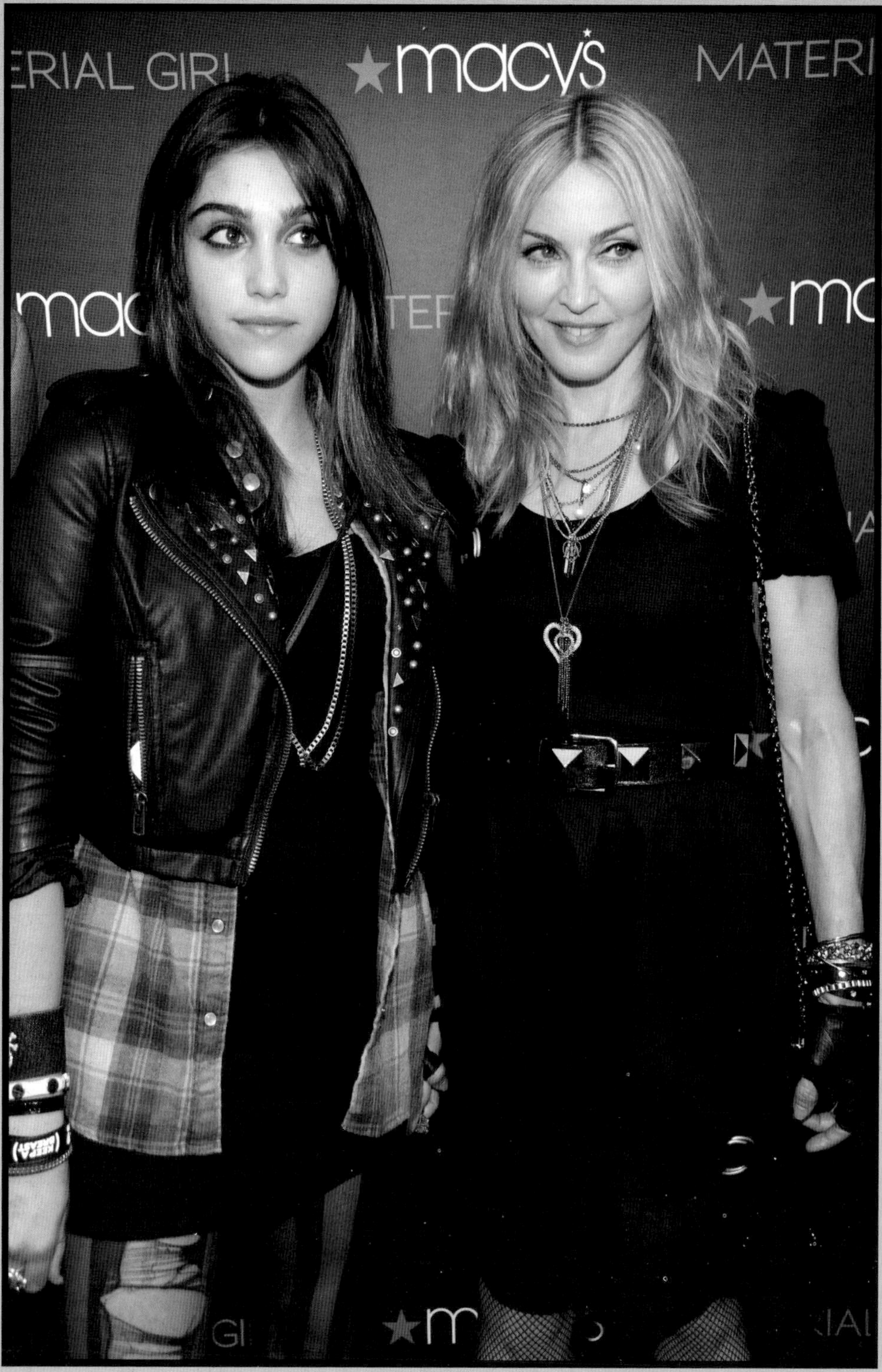
macy's

York and visit her doctor. She had been feeling nauseous for some time in Argentina but presumed that it was just the heat and rich food (which likewise seemed to have affected half the cast and crew). Nonetheless, she wanted to make sure. The doctor's diagnosis left her stunned.

Far from having some kind of stomach infection, Madonna was in fact 11 weeks pregnant. This was not something she had ever suspected—as she later explained in her diary, she often missed periods through stress, travel, overwork, or lack of sleep—and came as a complete shock. Despite the surprise, she was delighted with the news. Her primary concern now would be keeping herself and her unborn child as healthy as possible while she finished filming *Evita*'s final scenes in Hungary.

After the intense, stifling heat of Argentina, Hungary was bitterly cold, but Madonna had to spend the next few days filming in lightweight summer dresses. "Last week—heat, exhaustion, and sunburn," she wrote. "This week—pneumonia." She did get a chance to warm up from time to time in Budapest's grand 19th-century coffeehouses, however, and enjoyed indulging in the exceptional marzipan cakes and thick hot chocolate as well as visiting the historic castle and narrow, cobbled lanes high up on the hill above the River Danube.

By the time it came to filming the scene where Evita is told she is dying, Madonna felt that little acting was required. She had been on her feet for 14 hours with an irritated sciatic nerve and what she later described as "pain like lightning bolts shoot[ing] down my leg." She had wanted to play Evita more desperately than any other role in her career, but by the time filming was complete she was undoubtedly ready to move on. She felt as though she had been vicariously living Evita's life for two years; now it was time to devote herself to the new life she would soon have as a mother.

Lourdes Maria Ciccone Leon, named for the French center of Catholic pilgrimage Madonna's own mother had always wanted to visit, was born by caesarean section at the Good Samaritan Hospital, Los Angeles, on October 14 1996. Although Madonna's relationship with Lourdes's father, Carlos Leon, came to an end in 1997, the pair have remained on excellent terms.

Leon now runs a chain of upmarket gymnasiums in New York and has acted on screen and on stage but has generally been successful in avoiding the glare of publicity. Esther Haynes, who interviewed Leon for the *New York Post* in 2008, concluded that he "certainly has had the best of both worlds: American, Cuban; fame, privacy; father, bachelor." He sees Lourdes regularly, and both he and Madonna ensure that he has a strong presence in their daughter's life.

Despite accusations that Leon was simply a 'baby daddy' whose purpose was solely to provide what was needed, Madonna has however remained loyal to him. "I was madly in love with him," she said in 2004, dismissing suggestions that she used him as a 'sperm-donor' as "ludicrous ... It's not fair to me and it's not fair to him ... He's an excellent father."

Meanwhile, *Evita* was released on Christmas Day 1996 and was later nominated for five Academy Awards, winning Best Original Song for 'You Must Love Me' (which Andrew Lloyd Webber and Tim Rice had composed especially for the film). It was also nominated for five Golden Globes, winning three, including Best Actress In A Film Or Musical.

Madonna's portrayal of Evita Perón confounded those critics who had dismissed her film career to date and finally brought her a level of respect in Hollywood that had remained elusive since her debut performance in *Desperately Seeking Susan*. Although the role had proved challenging and sometimes uncomfortable, she had achieved exactly what she wanted. She had always seen the movies as the ultimate route to immortality, and *Evita* would prove to be one of the greatest film triumphs of her career.

The accompanying soundtrack album was also a resounding international success, reaching Number One in the UK and Number Two in the USA, where it eventually went five times platinum. 'Don't Cry For Me Argentina'—the song that had caused Madonna so much distress—reached Number Three in the UK and Number Eight in America, and also topped the charts in France. The idea of a song penned by Andrew Lloyd Webber and Tim Rice becoming a hit for Madonna may have surprised some, but if anyone had any doubts about her ability to score contemporary hits of her own, they were soon to be proved wrong.

CHAPTER 11
BEAUTIFUL STRANGER

With post-production of *Evita* completed and the film shortly to be released, Madonna began to think about returning to the studio to make a new album of her own. Her next release would prove to have a dramatic impact on her career, but before that news started to emerge that Madonna would soon be featured in another commercial outing—one that she had not planned. Stephen Bray, her old Michigan songwriting partner, drummer, and boyfriend, with whom she had lived and worked when she first came to New York, was planning to release *Pre-Madonna*, an album of demos the pair had recorded together at the Music Building in New York.

Rescued and restored from the original cassettes and quarter-inch tapes, the songs included the four tracks from 1980–81 that had eventually secured Madonna's record deal with Warner Bros: 'Everybody,' 'Stay,' 'Don't You Know,' and 'Ain't No Big Deal.' Madonna had never intended these tracks to be anything more than demos to show her potential. Listening to them some 30-odd years after they were recorded, they certainly sound raw, if not 'unplugged.' They do nevertheless offer a musical snapshot of Madonna in those very early days of her career, and provide one or two insights into her musical influences. They also give us the chance to play A&R man or woman for a day and ask ourselves: would *you* have signed Madonna on the basis of these tracks?

'Ain't No Big Deal,' a Bray composition, was the opening track on the original tape, and the one that Seymour Stein, the Sire Records supremo who eventually signed Madonna, originally believed should be her first single. The song later surfaced as the B-side to 'Papa Don't Preach,' but the original version from 1981—which is more or less as Stein would have heard it—has a much grittier, looser, clubbier feel, with 80s-sounding slap-bass and treble-laden guitar.

'Everybody' became similarly important for her. This was the track she had originally played to influential Danceteria nightclub DJ Mark Kamins, which in turn led to the Warners deal. The version Bray unearthed for *Pre-Madonna* is slower than the better-known single, however, with a chugging, reggae-lite feel, while the vocal is much less polished.

'Stay,' meanwhile, is another early Madonna and Bray co-composition that again sounds less polished than the version that would later appear on *Like A Virgin*. Incorporating elements of the synth-laden, almost scratch-style 'Don't You Know,' the song here has a break-dance vibe, another typically early-80s sound.

The other tracks on the album show just how quickly Madonna's music evolved during her initial time in New York. This was Madonna in her original New Wave incarnation, before she and her fellow Big Apple scenesters became immersed in the dance-friendly sounds of House. On numbers like 'Burning Up,' a straight rock song with a new-wave edge, we hear Madonna in Joan Jett mode, while 'Laugh To Keep Me From Crying,' another co-write with Bray, is clearly an homage to The Pretenders, with choppy rhythms, chiming Rickenbacker guitar, and Madonna's best Chrissie Hynde-like husky warble.

Along with Debbie Harry, Chrissie Hynde had made a powerful impression on both the young Madonna and Bray. "There was something so powerful about The Pretenders," Bray later recalled on the *Naked Ambition* television special. "The music was so evocative and the energy of the band was so intense that I think we just hoped that some of that would rub off on us. 'Laugh To Keep From Crying' was definitely out of that school."

While some of the tracks on *Pre-Madonna* reveal her musical roots, others, like the previously unheard 'Crimes Of Passion,' sound, as you might expect, more like prototypes of Madonna's early releases. With its sweet, smooth vocals and funky, clubby, syncopated groove, 'Crimes' could almost be an out-take from the *Madonna* or *Like A Virgin* sessions.

When *Pre-Madonna* was released in late 1996, Madonna made it clear that it was not an authorized release. In the decade and a half since she had recorded the demos, she had moved on considerably—not just in terms of styles and songwriting but also, having learned so much through her vocal training for *Evita*, as a singer, too. The album nevertheless sold moderately well, but it was clear that the majority of Madonna's fans were less concerned with dwelling on her past and more interested in her next contemporary release.

Few artists are able to stay at the top for more than a year or two, and fewer still for more than a decade. For those who remain, there is usually at least one album that marks a pivotal moment in the artist's career. For Madonna, *Ray Of Light* was one of those albums.

In 1997, Madonna was one of the world's most famous women, her iconic status unquestionable. Critical success had been more elusive, however. Several years had passed since Madonna's last studio album, *Bedtime Stories*, and during that time she had not only been through the challenges of filming and recording *Evita* but had also become a mother. It was unclear which musical direction she might take next. *Ray Of Light* was to change this irrevocably, bringing her not only commercial success on a scale unseen since the 80s but also a newfound artistic credibility within the music industry itself.

Ray Of Light sounded radically different from her previous albums. After the power-pop of the 80s and low-key experimentation of *Bedtime Stories*, this time there was a more contemporary, electronic dance sound, and lyrics that reflected a woman who had matured and now felt differently about herself and her life. This was no longer the work of a material girl. It also introduced a softer, mellower Madonna—one who, in place of her earlier forthright sexuality, was now concerned not only with her own welfare but also with that of her fellow human beings.

"It's just an evolution really," she told Gerri Hirshey of *Rolling Stone* magazine. "Going down to South America and getting beaten up the way that I was in the newspapers every day—and sort of living vicariously through what happened to Eva Perón—then finding myself pregnant. Going from the depths of despair and then coming out the other side ... you know, becoming a mother. I just have a whole new outlook on life. I see the world as a much more hopeful place. I just feel an infinite amount of compassion toward other people."

Part of the change had come about as a result of her recent discovery of Kabbalah—a 20th century form of spiritualism loosely based on an ancient form of Jewish mysticism. While the original religion centered around numerology, astronomy, and astrology, the new doctrine—entirely separate from conventional Judaism, focuses on reflection and meditation, suggesting that one can reach a higher state of consciousness and bring about change not only in oneself but in the wider world.

Madonna had first been introduced to modern Kabbalah in 1997, in between work on *Evita* and *Ray Of Light*, when she attended a dinner party in Los Angeles at which her old friend the actress and comedienne Sandra Bernhard happened to mention that she was taking classes with a Rabbi. They were tremendously inspiring, Bernhard said—why didn't Madonna come along? Madonna asked whether it would matter that she had been raised as a Catholic. Bernhard said it made no difference, as long as you were inspired by the teachings, so Madonna agreed to go along and find out for herself.

What Madonna heard and would subsequently learn through her own studies with the Rabbi would, as she later put it, "change my whole outlook on life." Madonna had for some time already been studying various other spiritual schools of thought, from Taoism to Gnosticism and early Christianity—in the hope of finding some kind of meaningful, philosophical truth. She felt that although she had traveled the world, performed to thousands of fans, and dined with state leaders—all the while achieving the kind of wealth and global fame few ever attain—something was somehow missing. (As she later wrote in *Yedioth Ahronot*, Israel's biggest daily newspaper: "I learned a lot and I was very inspired but I still could not connect the dots and find a way to take this knowledge and apply it to my daily life.")

Madonna was pregnant at the time, and had come to realize that she had spent almost her entire life worrying only about herself. Now, with the imminent birth of her child, she would obviously soon be responsible for another life, and she began to wonder what kind of spiritual life guidance she would be able to provide as a parent. What she heard at The Kabbalah Center's Spanish-style stucco-fronted premises on the outer reaches of

Beverly Hills provided her with many of the answers she had been seeking. She was particularly taken by Rabbi Yardeni, a good-looking Israeli in his forties with a quiet but charismatic manner. He had been instrumental in setting up Kabbalah Centers across America, and talked to Madonna about physics, astronomy, nature, and the laws of cause and effect.

"I heard what he had to say," Madonna later explained, "and I knew at this moment my life would never be the same. All the questions I had about life began to be answered and I realized I had finally found a 'belief system' or philosophy that incorporated science and spirituality.

"All the puzzle pieces started falling into place. Life no longer seemed like a series of Random events. I started to see patterns in life. I woke up. I began to be conscious of my words and my actions and to really see the results of them. I also began to see that being rich and famous wasn't going to bring me lasting fulfillment and that it was not the end of the journey; that it was the beginning of the journey."

Madonna felt that, where Catholicism had failed, Kabbalah could give her the tools for modern living she had long been seeking. In an interview with *Elle* magazine, published around the time of *Ray Of Light*'s release, she described how, to her, the teachings of Kabbalah "embody modern living. Catholicism is a religion based on shame and fear. And while there are some really beautiful rituals in Catholicism—and, you know, there is a certain kind of darkness I find erotic—it's not a very loving religion, not very flexible. It doesn't make room for human error."

Madonna was far from alone in her espousal of Kabbalah. Since the Center was first set up by Dr Philip Berg and his wife Karen, first in Tel Aviv and then in New York, more than 50 centers have opened worldwide, attracting over three million followers, including celebrities such as Lindsay Lohan, Demi Moore, Barbra Streisand, Elizabeth Taylor, Britney Spears, Roseanne Barr, and the fashion designer Donna Karan.

Kabbalah would play a significant part in Madonna's life. In recent years, she has often been seen sporting the red Kabbalah wristband—worn to ward off the 'evil eye'—and has spoken of having taken the Hebrew name of Esther, after the Jewish historical heroine who helped save her people from a plot against their lives in ancient Persia. She has also shown her commitment to Kabbalah by funding a $20 million Kabbalah Center school in New York, and reportedly diverts a portion of her touring income to the organization. But the most visible sign of her conversion to the Kabbalah way of thinking, at least to begin with, was in her songwriting. The songs she wrote for *Ray Of Light* speak of the hollowness of fame and the realization that she had "traded fame for love / without a second thought." She wasn't complaining about fame or saying that she wanted to relinquish it, she said, but wanted to make clear that "the approval, the headiness of being swept up and being popular and loved by people in universal ways, is absolutely no substitute for truly being loved."

Ray Of Light took Madonna four-and-a-half months to complete—more time than she had spent on any of her previous albums. But then ensuring its success was particularly important for her. Her last two albums, *Erotica* and *Bedtime Stories*, had sold only a few million copies each—the kind of numbers that most artists would be delighted with, but which were disappointing for someone with Madonna's track record. As a major star, and one of the world's biggest selling artists of the 80s, she was keen to regain her earlier success.

In early 1997, just a few months after Lourdes's birth, Madonna started thinking about what form a new album might take. To kickstart the songwriting process, she began looking around for writing partners. Her first thought was to call on her old co-writer Patrick Leonard, with whom she'd had such success before on hits like 'La Isla Bonita,' 'Like A Prayer,' and 'Live To Tell.' But she also wanted to try different styles, and so approached other writers including Kenneth 'Babyface' Edmonds, with whom she had worked on *Bedtime Stories* in 1994, and Rick Nowels, who had made a name for himself as the author of Belinda Carlisle's 80s hits 'Heaven Is A Place On Earth' and 'Circle In The Sand.'

Before starting to work with anyone new, Madonna always likes to have an initial meeting to see whether she'll be able to work with them. She and Nowels quickly found they had a rapport, both musically and personally. Madonna was full of talk of discovering parenthood for the first time, while Nowels himself had a three-year-old son. A few weeks later, they began working together.

Madonna believed in taking a structured approach to her songwriting. In contrast to those musicians and songwriters who like to spend days waiting for the muse to visit, Madonna liked to keep more regular hours. She drove over to Nowels's small studio high in the Hollywood Hills every day, always arriving at three o'clock in the afternoon. They'd then settle down to the task of writing until seven o'clock sharp, when Madonna would leave to go home to see young Lourdes (or Lola, as she quickly became known).

Nowels was immediately taken with Madonna's skill as a songwriter. "She's a real artist," he later told writer Lucy O'Brien. "She understands how to channel and compose a song. It's not just jamming melodies. She understands what a chorus and verse should do, where to put a bridge, how to work her melodies."

Most days the writing came easily, but there were also days when progress was less smooth. In the case of 'To Have And Not To Hold,' Nowels had an idea to create something with the gentle, hip-swaying feel of a Latin samba to suit a verse Madonna had written. She liked the idea but Nowels was struggling to work out a chorus. Scouring around for inspiration, the pair began listening to the soft, breathy sounds of Brazilian chanteuse Astrud Gilberto, famously used to great effect on her 1964 hit 'The Girl From Ipanema.' Suddenly, something in the way Gilberto made unusual harmonic leaps provided the answer they were looking for and you can indeed hear her influence in the gentle "ba ba da ba ba da" chorus.

'Little Star' also required some long hours of trial and error. Madonna had written the deeply personal lyrics for her new baby daughter, revealing how Lourdes had "breathed new life into her broken heart" and given her life new meaning. At pains to find an appropriate musical setting, Nowels remembered that he had recently come across the newly reissued soundtrack to the cult 70s film *Vampyros Lesbos* and brought it along to play Madonna. "[She] thought it was a cool title," Nowels recalled, adding that she liked the idea of creating something around a sample "from this weird, freako film."

Several hours later, however, the track had still not come together the way they had hoped it would. Nowels began to panic until suddenly, as he began playing a few chords, Madonna started to sing. "I followed her," he recalled, "and the rest was just stream of consciousness."

After ten days, Madonna and Nowels ended up with no fewer than nine songs. Three of these appear in succession on the finished album: 'The Power Of Good-Bye,' 'To Have And Not To Hold,' and 'Little Star.' The first of these would prove to be one of Madonna's most enduringly popular songs.

Madonna also completed a few songs with Pat Leonard—'Nothing Really Matters,' 'Skin,' 'Sky Fits Heaven,' and 'Frozen'—all of which would become key tracks on the album. She then recorded several more with Babyface, but in the end decided that they were too close in feel to 'Take A Bow' (from *Bedtimes Stories*) and didn't fit with the rest, so they were not included.

While the quality of the songwriting was obviously crucial to the album's success, Madonna's most important new collaborator on the album would prove to be the man who would not only co-write but also produce much of the album—the left-field English dance producer William Orbit. She had been listening to the series of ethereal, melodic albums Orbit had made under the name *Strange Cargo* and loved the poignancy and what she called the "haunting, trancelike quality" of the songs. She had also heard Orbit's remixes of some of her earlier work, such as 'Justify My Love' and 'I'll Remember,' and had been suitably impressed.

"I've always found something melancholy about his music," she later recalled. "Since I'm attracted to that sound, and since I tend to write a lot of sad songs, we seemed like a good match."

Orbit was not necessarily an obvious choice of collaborator. He had chanced upon life as a musician almost by accident after leaving school at 16 and working as a fruit picker. He had then worked in a shoe factory before spending several years living on a houseboat in the Netherlands. It was not until the 80s, when Orbit was in his early twenties and living in a squat in London, that he began to create music. "I'd make cassettes and send them to everybody in the industry," he later recalled, "which is basically how my music career began."

Shortly thereafter he began releasing records under the name Torch Song, while also co-producing Sting and remixing artists such as Belinda Carlisle. By the 90s he was working at a prolific rate. As well as releasing his ambient electronic *Strange Cargo* albums, he was also developing treatments of classical works by Henryk Górecki and Arvo Pärt, co-producing projects with Peter Gabriel, and remixing Depeche Mode. If there was any doubt about his pop sensibility, he had also scored a chart hit with the funky, reggae-tinged 'Fascinating Rhythm,' fronted by a pop combo he had put together called Bass-O-Matic.

Despite having built a reputation internationally as a sought-after remixer and producer, Orbit was still surprised when, in May 1997, he received a phone call from Madonna's Maverick Records partner, Guy Oseary. "Guy rang and suggested I send some tapes to her," Orbit later told *Q* magazine. "I didn't take it very seriously, so I didn't send anything. Then he rang again, so I sent a DAT with 13 tracks on it. Five days later, sitting in my garden, I got a call from Madonna. She said she was working on my tracks, and would I like to come out and meet up with her. They sent me a plane ticket and off I went."

Theirs was destined to be an interesting collaboration from the start. The angular, slightly gauche Orbit got caught in a downpour on his way to meet Madonna and arrived at her chic Manhattan apartment soaked through, armed only with a plastic carrier bag of DAT tapes. Clearly this was not some slick, jaded, music-business professional. "He arrived at my door looking like a drowned rat," Madonna recalled. "He looked really fragile. He was very humble and unassuming and endearing, like a little boy. As soon as I met him, I liked him."

The comedy of errors continued when Madonna tried to play Orbit some of the tracks she had been working on, only to discover that her living-room hi-fi system wasn't working. Adjourning to her gym instead, Orbit was finally able to hear her new and already quite polished-sounding material.

"She played me the stuff she'd written with Babyface and Pat Leonard," Orbit later told *Q* magazine. "I'm sitting thinking: these tracks sound very slick. What can I contribute? We spent the next week at the Hit Factory getting my backing tracks up in stereo, and she sang what she'd worked out, and it was clear that something was happening. At the end of that week, she said: would you work on my record? And I said: I'd love to."

The pair quickly fell into a regular pattern of work: Madonna would listen to Orbit's samples and song fragments over and over again until an idea came for a lyric. Then, once she had a sense of the lyrical direction of the song, she would take it back to him, and they would expand on his original idea.

One particular track on the tape Orbit sent Madonna had a lyrical, otherworldly feel that caught her attention. Using Orbit's backing tracks as a starting point, one of his regular vocalists—Christine Leach, had begun singing over it. Listening to Orbit's music, Leach had remembered the lyrics to a song called 'Sepheryn' which her uncle, Clive Muldoon, had written with his partner Dave Curtiss back in 1971. She started singing the words over the track: "Sepheryn the sky at night I wonder," it began. Orbit loved it and—not realizing that Leach hadn't written the lyrics herself—promptly included the track on the tape he sent to Madonna. It would prove to be a fateful move not just for Orbit, Muldoon, and Curtiss, but also for Madonna herself.

Having successfully worked on new songs with Orbit, Madonna liked the idea of him also bringing a new feel to the production. In the past, Pat Leonard had often played a key role in writing and producing, but this time, Madonna decided to do things differently. While Leonard would still have some involvement in the final production of one or two tracks (and in providing some of the masterful string arrangements), it would be Orbit who was to put his musical stamp on the album as a whole.

When she first started work with Orbit in the studio, however, Madonna became wary. Orbit had a loose, spontaneous, and rather organic working style, whereas she was used to a much more regimented, disciplined, and— as she saw it—professional approach. She was particularly unimpressed when he came to her house one day to play back some work he had done on 'The Power Of Good-Bye,' only to discover that he had brought the wrong DAT with him.

Nervous of whether the album would work out as she wanted, Madonna called on Pat Leonard to see whether he might come to the rescue if necessary. But once Madonna started to get used to Orbit and his way of working, she contacted Leonard again, telling him this time that she had a gut feeling she couldn't quite explain that this English eccentric might in fact be significant to her career. Later, she would also credit him with helping her develop a whole new sound. "William turned my songs into a daring mix of trance sound, warm-blooded trip-hop, catchy drum'n'bass rhythms, a lot of pop, and beautiful orchestra arrangements in abundance," she told *NY Rock* magazine. "That's what makes the songs on *Ray Of Light* sound modern and old-fashioned at the same time. You can dance to them but at the same time they invite you to dream."

You can indeed dance to many of the tracks on *Ray Of Light*, not least the title track. Orbit's hypnotic, pulsating, shimmering rhythms add a dynamic new backdrop to Madonna's vocal, which likewise has a much freer, almost trance-like form. This was another of Orbit's suggestions. Although she had at first been reluctant to sing outside of her usual range, Orbit encouraged her to sing higher, insisting that the strain would benefit the song in the end.

"'Ray Of Light' is just a semitone higher than she's comfortable with," Orbit explained, "but we thought the strain really helped. She got frustrated when we were recording but you want that bit of edge with singers, that thing of reaching. You can't fake it, and you can hear it when she cracks on the record."

The tactic of taking Madonna's distinctive pop vocals into a new dimension while never straying too far from mainstream accessibility was seemingly very much Orbit's game-plan throughout the making of the album and Madonna's faith in Orbit—and her courage to adapt to his looser working methods—had paid off.

Orbit, meanwhile, was equally impressed with Madonna's hands-on approach and talent. "Madonna's a sleeves-rolled-up kind of girl," he later recalled. "She didn't have any airs and graces. She drove to work. She was very civil and polite to everybody. And she is a genuinely clever songwriter in that larger-than-life Broadway musical kind of way. I was more impressed by her as a producer, musician, and songwriter than as an icon."

Ever keen to keep producers on their toes—and just in case Orbit became too comfortable—Madonna also brought in Marius de Vries, the British programmer, keyboard player, and producer with whom she had previously worked on *Bedtime Stories*. De Vries ended up co-producing some of the tracks on the album as well, with Madonna cannily setting him and Orbit up almost against each other. On 'Skin,' for example, she had them working in parallel studios on the same material to see who could come up with the best musical solutions.

"We hadn't met before," de Vries recalled, "and our work covered the same sort of territory, so we circled each other warily at first. 'Skin' was an icebreaker. The track started as a couple of simple beats and a lyrical idea. We constructed that in a very collaborative way, from the ground up— which is why it was so packed with detail. We were trying to fill out each corner of it with our own favorite sounds."

At Madonna's request, de Vries also added his distinctive programming details to 'Frozen,' one of the standout tracks on the album, and one of its most successful singles. Madonna and Orbit had worked long and hard on it but still felt there was something missing, so de Vries spent an afternoon programming some beats and effects, adding the texture the tracks needed.

De Vries also lent his personal touch to 'Little Star,' Madonna's ode to Lourdes, on which he was credited as co-producer after giving the track an edgy undercurrent of drum'n'bass. "The subject matter in itself is quite dangerous," he later said. "It's easy to get sentimental. It's a delicate tune so I knew it had to be handled with butterfly-like delicacy, but I also knew it needed an engine room to it, an energy, so it didn't become mawkish. That's why I did something with this skittering, unsettled, never quite resolving beat—to counteract the warmth and coziness of the central idea."

Little Lourdes had in fact made her presence felt throughout the album. Madonna would bring her into the studio most days to play in one of several leisure rooms that had been converted into a kind of crèche. She was just beginning to walk and would occasionally try to take an executive role in the sound of her mother's new album. "Like any toddler she'd make a beeline for the knobs and buttons," Orbit recalled. "We'd look away and the whole sound had changed. We had to keep an eye on her."

While Madonna's mood was often lifted by her daughter's presence in the studio, other external events were also to have a significant effect on the recording. On July 15, Madonna was in the studio working with Orbit on 'Swim,' an exploration of her concerns about the state of the earth and the "sins" we "carry on our back." Gradually, news began to filter through on the television that Italian fashion designer Gianni Versace had been shot.

Madonna had been friendly both with Versace and his sister, Donatella, who immediately phoned her, distraught. Orbit suggested that she might want to leave the vocal for another day but Madonna, ever the professional, insisted they carry on. "[That's] probably why it has such an emotional impact," Orbit told Q magazine.

If death was only indirectly present in 'Swim,' it took centre stage on the album's surreal and psychological closing track, 'Mer Girl.' One of Madonna's most deeply personal and self-explorative songs, it bears the influence of the 20th century poets she had loved since her teens, Sylvia Plath and Anne Sexton. Here she takes listeners on an eerie journey that starts with her running in the rain from her house to the trees, "up into the hills," away from the traffic and the "daughter who never sleeps." All the while she is haunted by her own mother. The song then takes us through Madonna's fear of death as the earth reaches up to bury her alive. She runs away and continues to run, only to realize that she has been running throughout her life.

"There seemed to be so much death actually around the time that I had written it," she explained a few years later. "There's the obvious thing about my mother's death, but also Princess Diana's and Versace's death." As had been the case with 'Swim,' Madonna's performance sent shivers down the spines of everyone in the studio. "She stepped out of the vocal booth," Orbit later recalled, "and everybody was rooted to the spot. It was just one of those moments. Really spooky."

With Princess Diana uppermost in so many people's minds, it was perhaps unsurprising that the man Madonna would choose to take the cover shot for the album was Mario Testino, the Peruvian fashion photographer who had become world famous when his iconic photos of the Princess were published in *Vanity Fair* magazine just months before her death.

Testino's photographs of Diana were groundbreaking in the way that they showed her looking natural, spontaneous, and happy, in contrast to the more traditionally posed, formal style favored by the Royals and aristocracy. It was this loose style that now appealed to Madonna. She had had the courage to fill *Ray Of Light* with songs that expressed a new depth and candor, now she wanted the cover image to do the same.

Instead of dramatic studio lighting and the monochrome Hollywood diva look of her earlier albums, the *Ray Of Light* shoot shows a more relaxed Madonna, at ease and in touch with herself. She is still glamorous and still unquestionably sexy but also softer than the hard-edged, steely polish of the platinum blond of old, her loose, golden curls allowed to fly freely as she tosses back her head, throwing her cares to the wind.

When *Ray Of Light* was released in March 1998, many in the music industry were surprised by what they considered to be a daring musical left-turn. It could not possibly succeed, they believed—it was not 'radio-friendly' enough, they thought—and surely Madonna, closing in on her 40th birthday, was too old to get away with venturing into the primarily youth-driven dance market.

Both critics and listeners felt differently, however. On *Ray Of Light*'s release, *Rolling Stone* declared it to be "brilliant," while *Slant* magazine described it as "one of the great pop masterpieces of the 90s." The album would go on to sell four million copies in the USA and 12 million internationally. Three of the singles released from the album made the US and UK Top Tens, with 'Frozen' topping the British chart and reaching Number Two on *Billboard*.

Some were quick to credit William Orbit with transforming Madonna's sound and career, but Orbit himself has always been at pains to stress that Madonna is due at least as much credit as he is. "Madonna was itchy to make a change," he told *Q* magazine in 2002, "and I came along at the right time. It bothers me when the press say: William Orbit revived her dwindling career. If anything, she revived *my* dwindling career."

Ray Of Light brought Madonna the artistic credibility that had previously eluded her despite her huge commercial success. "I've been in the music business 16 years," she told the audience at the 1998 Grammy Awards in Los Angeles. "This is my first Grammy—well, actually I've won four tonight," she said, showing visible signs of emotion. "It was worth the wait."

More than a decade on, *Ray Of Light* remains one of Madonna's most acclaimed albums among fans and critics alike. It was also voted the 29th greatest recording of all time by readers of *Rolling Stone*.

Despite William Orbit's claims to the contrary, he clearly had a radical impact on Madonna's sound, and Madonna herself was the first to acknowledge that. But when it had come to the album credits on *Ray Of Light*, there was someone else in particular she wished to thank. The liner notes include a "Special Thanks" to two people for "creative and spiritual guidance." One was Rabbi Eitan Yardeni of The Kabbalah Center. The other was Andrew F. Bird.

Madonna had first met the Englishman Bird through her friend, *Truth Or Dare* director Alek Keshishian, in early 1997. Bird was an aspiring actor and screenwriter with shoulder-length dark hair who dressed head-to-toe in black and was never without a Gitanes cigarette. He happened to be with Keshishian one evening when Madonna happened to call; Keshishian passed him the phone. "Say hi to Madonna," Keshishian told him. Bird was nonplussed. "Hi to Madonna," he said. She laughed and the pair began chatting. In fact, they got along so well, that after a long conversation, Madonna suggested Keshishian pass on her phone number. By now her relationship with Carlos Leon had petered out and, although the couple still had feelings for each other and agreed that Leon would continue to play an active role in daughter Lourdes's life, they had decided to be friends rather than lovers.

When Bird visited Los Angeles a few months later, he and Madonna arranged to have dinner at a discreet restaurant in the Hollywood Hills. She was enchanted with this tall and strikingly handsome man, who within days would move from staying on friends' couches to living chez Madonna. He soon had to return to London, but for the next few months they maintained a relationship across the Atlantic. Although there was a ten-year age gap—Bird was only 29—and a small gulf in their respective financial statuses, Madonna found a kind of emotional and intellectual connection with Bird that she felt had been absent in many of her previous relationships.

Once she had finished recording *Ray Of Light*, Madonna decided to spend a couple of months in London, renting a house in Chelsea, at least in part to give the relationship more of a chance. Bird encouraged Madonna's interest in mysticism and Eastern philosophy, and the pair were soon snapped by the paparazzi as they went hand in hand to yoga classes at the Inergy Centre in Northwest London. As the relationship developed further, Bird took Madonna to meet his parents, who lived in Stratford-upon-Avon, the Warwickshire town most famous for being Shakespeare's birthplace, while the pair continued to travel to and fro between Britain and America to spend time together.

The relationship gradually dissolved over the course of the next year, the discrepancy in their lifestyles, ambitions, and ages proving to be too great, but Bird clearly had a lasting effect on Madonna. Early the following year, she recorded a new song, 'Beautiful Stranger,' for the film *Austin Powers: The Spy Who Shagged Me*. The song was co-written with William Orbit, but Madonna told Bird she had written the lyrics for him.

"I looked into your eyes / And my world came tumbling down," she sings. "I looked into your face / My heart was dancing all over the place." Madonna's final single of the decade, 'Beautiful Stranger' peaked at Number Two in the UK and Number 19 in the USA during the summer of 1999, selling more than 2.5 million copies worldwide.

The combined effect of her relationship with Bird, motherhood, her discovery of Kabbalah, and the new working partnership with Orbit had transformed Madonna from an 80s star to a 90s superstar. She would build on her new persona for her next album, but first she was due to return to the cinema for a new acting role.

CHAPTER 12
HEY, MR DJ

One day, while basking in the success of *Ray Of Light*, Madonna received a call from her old friend, the British actor Rupert Everett, who wanted to tell her about an exciting new script he had read, *The Next Best Thing*, which told the story of Abbie, a single woman in her late thirties who accidentally becomes pregnant by her gay best friend. Everett had just had a huge hit of his own playing opposite Julia Roberts in *My Best Friend's Wedding* and felt he could repeat the success with this new screenplay. What was more, he thought Madonna would make the perfect female lead.

Madonna was initially unsure, however, and felt the scenario was a little too sitcom-like, but Everett managed to persuade her, partly by explaining that he would amend the script himself, and also by mentioning that legendary British director John Schlesinger would be assigned to the film. Schlesinger was most famous for directing *Midnight Cowboy* and *Marathon Man* but had come to fame in the 60s with films like *Billy Liar*, *A Kind Of Loving*, and *Darling*, which Madonna later described as one of her all-time favorites. The tale of a young woman who uses her femininity and sexuality to gain fame and fortune, *Darling* had made a star of the then relatively unknown Julie Christie, who won an Academy Award for her performance in it.

Three years had passed since Madonna made *Evita*, and despite its success she was still keen to prove her worth as a serious actress in a non-musical film. Working with a director as eminent and revered as Schlesinger might, she hoped, be a good move.

She also felt some empathy with the character of Abbie, just as she had with Eva Perón. "It's a real statement for the 21st century," she told *Jane* magazine. "I think few people have conventional family situations. Look at me. I have a baby with somebody I'm not with. I'm really good friends with him and I value my relationship with him a great deal. When I had the baby with him I had every intention of being with him, but things didn't work out."

Madonna felt that the premise of the script was important in terms of changing preconceptions about gay men raising children. "I think gay men truly are interested in raising families and being parents," she told *Next*, "but I don't think many people take that very seriously. I hope [the film] changes that misconception. And I think Rupert is a fantastic gay role-model because he doesn't really fit into middle America's preconceived notion about what gay men are: that sort of effeminate, Nellie, queeny, gay personality. I think he kind of defies all of that. He's actually quite butch."

The Next Best Thing's script underwent numerous rewrites—mainly by Everett, and not all of them with Schlesinger's blessing. The result fell somewhere between lighthearted rom-com and serious drama and although the film was not exactly welcomed by the critics, Schlesinger felt that Madonna had acquitted herself well.

Happily for Madonna, she had also been able to introduce a musical element to the film—one which was destined to fare much better than the film itself. During the course of filming, Everett suggested that Madonna record a version of the old Don McLean hit 'American Pie,' which he thought would work well within the film. As with the script, however, Madonna was at first unsure. Although she had loved the song while growing up, it had never occurred to her to record her own version, and she thought the idea was "too corny for words." She also felt that the length of the song, which ran to eight minutes in its original version, meant that it would be unlikely to get radio play. But Everett persisted, and eventually Madonna agreed to record it on the basis that she would only sing two of the song's five verses.

Fresh from their success on *Ray Of Light* and 'Beautiful Stranger,' Madonna once again called on William Orbit to produce the song, returning to the sound they had created together on her album, similarly blending her sweet, sinuous vocals with his rhythmic electronic wizardry. The result was a completely transformed version of the folky original. In a statement issued by Maverick Records, Don McLean described Madonna's version as "mystical and sensual" and "a gift from a goddess."

Although it was never released as a physical single in America, Madonna's 'American Pie' nonetheless managed to reach Number 29 on the *Billboard* Hot 100 on airplay alone. The single was a massive worldwide hit, reaching Number One in the UK, Canada, Australia, Italy, Germany, Switzerland, Austria, and Finland, proving that although her acting career had once again faltered, Madonna could still top the charts with ease.

The success of 'American Pie' left Madonna hungry to get back into the studio and record another album. Apart from her role in *The Next Best Thing* and her brief sojourns into the studio for one-off singles with William Orbit, she had spent most of the previous two years looking after young Lola. Now that Lola was old enough to start school however, Madonna had more time to devote to recording and felt a renewed sense of energy.

"Everything in life moves in cycles," she told *Billboard*. "There's a period when you're quiet, and there's a period when you explode. In the time leading up to *Ray Of Light* I was in a quiet space—making lots of discoveries and going through lots of changes. It was an introspective, questioning time. Then, almost without warning, I felt like I needed to explode. I didn't feel the need to be so introspective. I felt like dancing. And that's reflected in these [new] songs."

Previously, Madonna's albums had tended to be either pop records or dance records. "There's the frivolous side of my life and then there's the—hopefully—non-frivolous side of my life," she told *The Face*. "I usually make a record that's one or the other." With *Music*, she did both. Also unlike her earlier albums, this one was to be made in England, at the state-of-the-art SARM Studios in West London's Notting Hill. She had spent time in London before although she had never recorded an album in the city, but this time she had a new reason to want to be there. Her friend Trudie Styler (Sting's wife) had hosted a garden-party lunch the previous summer, at which Madonna unexpectedly found herself sitting next to the up-and-coming British film director Guy Ritchie.

The attractive, urbane, and well-connected Ritchie had just made his first full-length feature, *Lock, Stock And Two Smoking Barrels*, a postmodern take on the gangster movie genre whose rapid-fire pop-promo editing and quirky effects came off like a British Quentin Tarantino on amphetamines. The pair felt an immediate rapport and Madonna was charmed by his sense of humor. "He has a great wit," she later revealed. "That's the first thing I noticed when I met him, his incredible sense of humor and his use of language—I found that very attractive. He made me laugh, but he was funny in a clever way, not in an obvious way. He made me think. He's very well read, very curious, inquisitive."

Ritchie was equally captivated. Over the next year the relationship gradually developed on a long-distance basis, despite the transatlantic divide, and eventually reached the point where Madonna realized that if she wanted this to become something more serious they would, at the very least, need to be based in the same country. Since Ritchie was unprepared to relocate to America, she would therefore need to move to the UK. And so she did.

By the time the *Music* sessions began in September 1999, Madonna had set up home with Ritchie in a four-story mansion in South Kensington, a short drive from SARM Studios. Recording in London may have been a new experience for Madonna but she was certain in illustrious company. SARM's client list reads like a *Who's Who* of rock and pop, with Sir Paul McCartney, George Michael, The Rolling Stones, Christina Aguilera, and Radiohead all having worked there. Madonna found these new surroundings stimulating. The studio offered both state-of-the-art technology and, rather more surprisingly, natural daylight—something she really appreciated, having previously worked in unfailingly subterranean American studios. Being able to see street life outside the studio's windows she felt, helped the creative process and she found herself "stimulated by the cool, creative vibe" and "really connected to the world."

When it came to deciding on producers for the album, Madonna's first thought was to call on William Orbit, but since the success of *Ray Of Light*, Orbit had worked with so many other artists that his distinctive sound was beginning to lose its cachet. Madonna therefore decided that although she would still work with him on a few tracks, she would draft in someone new for the rest. The question was: who to use? The solution came one day when she happened to listen to one of the many demos sent in to Maverick by songwriters and producers (aspiring and established alike). This one was by a Swiss-born, half-Afghan producer from France who, like Madonna, was known only by his first name.

Mirwais Amadzaï's musical roots were a combination of driving electronic rock and lush acoustica. He had been the lead guitarist with cult 80s French synth-pop outfit Taxi Girl—a kind of early Depeche Mode-meets-Kraftwerk combo later cited as an influence by both Air and Daft Punk. He had then formed the softer, more guitar-based Juliette Et Les Indépendants. Both had achieved cult followings, but the lack of mainstream success left Mirwais feeling that the French music business had more or less ignored him and his groups. As a result, he felt no pressure to conform to any predetermined rules or expectations in the studio. On the contrary, his mantra was more along the lines of 'anything goes' and his last studio outing had been a solo funk-electronica album called *Disco Science*.

His musical influences meanwhile were diverse and included 70s disco and Kraftwerk, who he idolized for inventing what he called "electronic disco." He was also enchanted with punk, in particular the early pre-punk stance of The Stooges on the album *Fun House*, which he admired for both its experimentation and its sexuality. "For a lot of people it's not music," he explained, "but for me it's incredible. It's like John Coltrane. I'm not into jazz but I love Coltrane. There is a correspondence—totally free, you can't find something more wild. Iggy Pop's lyrics are so strong; there is some kind of sexuality."

Madonna soon saw that they shared more than a little common ground and was impressed with Mirwais's original approach. Despite his low profile, she once again decided to follow her nose when it came to sourcing new and innovative collaborators. "I'm always searching for something new and edgy and undiscovered," she told *Billboard*. "I love to work with the weirdoes that no one knows about—the people who have raw talent and who are making music unlike anyone else out there."

At first the collaboration proved hard work, mainly because of the language obstacle. Mirwais's English was severely limited, and Madonna spoke very little French, so his manager had to translate. But Madonna realized they were both equally keen to create something that mixed experimentation and commerciality, and gradually, with particular effort on Madonna's part, they began to make themselves understood. "I was intent on making it work," she said, "because I truly believe that this man's a genius."

Mirwais was obviously similarly determined to make the partnership work and also felt a genuine kinship in their musical approach. "Madonna is quite an extremist," he told *Crash* magazine, "and I am too. That's why we understand each other well."

It seemed to Mirwais that Madonna, by virtue of her phenomenal success, was no longer hampered by the same commercial constraints as most other musicians. The certainty that every time she made an album it would sell several million copies gave her freedom when it came to the studio. "You notice that what she wants is exactly the same as everyone else, except she takes more risks," he said. "She doesn't pose the same questions."

Like other young producers and collaborators before him, Mirwais found the more experienced artist easy to work with. Madonna had mentioned that she had liked a couple of pieces on the original tape he had sent Maverick, and wanted to use them, but Mirwais explained that he wanted to save those for his own solo album. Madonna accepted his argument. Instead she suggested that they begin work writing some new material together.

This time, however, perhaps intimidated by the pressure to follow up the huge success of *Ray Of Light*, Madonna felt less sure of the sound she wanted. What she did know was that it had to sound different, so she consequently ended up discarding dozens of songs before settling on the final ten. "I just kind of threw myself into it," she explained. "I wanted everything simple, direct, and meaningful. I've never written as many good songs and not used them before. But if it wasn't new, if it wasn't important, I wasn't interested."

Despite the initial language barriers, Mirwais was immediately impressed by Madonna's directness and decisiveness. "If she said she liked something," he later recalled, "she never changed her mind." *Music* would prove to be just the first of many collaborations between the pair.

The first song Madonna and Mirwais worked on together was 'Paradise (Not For Me),' the penultimate track on *Music*. With its spoken lyrics (in English and French) and ethereal mix of lush strings, gamelan-like xylophone, and 70s-style electronic undulations, the song recalls the edgy, beat-laden, filmic sound of British trip-hop groups Portishead and Massive Attack. If Madonna had wanted to do something new and different, this was certainly it. But the other tracks on the album were to sound quite different again.

Their next collaboration, the album's title track, was the one that really set the tone for the whole record. Here was a return to Madonna's dance-floor disco roots, with its 'let's get down and groove' vibe and call-out to "Mr DJ." It was a far cry from the soul-searching introspection of *Ray Of Light* and clearly marked the start of a new musical phase for Madonna. While Orbit had created ethereal, melodic soundscapes around her voice, Mirwais chopped it up, played around with it, and fed it back into an audio collage of bleeps, beats, and spiraling electronica.

The buoyant 'Impressive Instant'—one of several songs on the album clearly inspired by Madonna's new relationship with Guy Ritchie—is another case in point. She sings of the joyful abandon and heady intoxication of instant attraction and falling heart-over-head in love. "I don't want nobody else / All the others look the same," she whispers, breathily, before letting herself free to sing: "My world is spinning / I let the music take me / Take me where my heart wants to go."

She had clearly let the music take her where her heart wanted to go—not only emotionally but musically. For a woman known for her precision and almost regimented working methods, the line about wanting to "singy sing like a bird on a wingy wingy wingy" is wonderfully silly and testimony to Madonna's new mood. "We were working on that song," she explained, "and I thought: oh, fuck it, let's just have fun. Life would be such a drag if it was deep and probing all the time."

If 'Impressive Instant' and 'Music' demonstrate the upbeat dance sound of Madonna and Mirwais, 'I Deserve It' evokes the quieter, more acoustic side (albeit still with an experimental edge). It has a soft, almost demo-like rawness, with little to accompany Madonna's voice beyond a few gentle, tinny-sounding beats and a swirling, hypnotic, siren-like 70s synth effect that elevates the track from a simple acoustic love song to something much more unsettling.

This juxtaposition was exactly what Madonna wanted, but she also appreciated the fact that in this instance Mirwais had left her voice alone. 'I Deserve It' is one of several *Music* tracks about which Madonna would later claim that Mirwais had almost hoodwinked her into leaving her voice completely untreated. It was an effect she would eventually warm to, however—so much so that she would later insist that the other producers working on the album did the same.

Her voice is again very much to the fore on another of the album's standout tracks, 'Don't Tell Me,' which subsequently became one of its biggest hit singles. Written by Madonna's brother-in-law, Joe Henry, an acclaimed jazz and alt.country songwriter, musician, and producer, the song had originally been called 'Stop.' Madonna's sister Melanie had sent her husband's song over to Madonna, thinking that she might like it, and she was right. Henry's original version was more of a bluesy torch song but Madonna worked with Mirwais to significantly change the musical style while making sure to leave in the sense of defiance that had so appealed to her when she first heard the song.

"To me it is a romantic song," she told *Interview* magazine. "Do not tell me who I should love, or how I should love. Don't tell me to give up. To me, in a way it's like that Frank Sinatra song ['New York, New York']: If I can make it there, I'll make it anywhere." New York was clearly on Madonna's mind at some level, and despite Mirwais's chopped-up, cut-and-paste treatment, 'Don't Tell Me' sounds more unflinchingly American than anything else on the album, conveying the very notion of Americana that Madonna would go on to address in the album's artwork.

The Mirwais tracks on the album very much carry his personal stamp, but then so do William Orbit's contributions. 'Amazing'—described by Madonna in *The Face* as an "I-love-you-but-fuck-you song"—features his hallmark shimmering, melodic backdrop and effects. A tale of doomed love, it seems to recall Madonna's earlier liaison with Andy Bird. Around the time of the album's release, she described 'Amazing' as "a song about loving someone that you wished you didn't love, because you know that you're doomed, but you can't stop yourself, because it's amazing." When questioned as to exactly what the "it" might be, she replied, coyly: "You figure out what 'it' means."

In her drive to make the album sound as fresh as possible, Madonna also engaged Guy Sigsworth to work on one of the other key tracks, 'What It Feels Like For A Girl.' Like Nellee Hooper and Marius de Vries, with whom Madonna had worked on *Bedtime Stories* and *Ray Of Light*, Sigsworth was someone Madonna had admired for his work with Björk. He had experience of producing mainstream artists like Britney Spears and Seal as well as more alternative artists such as Kate Havnevik and Imogen Heap and his musical taste and experience had the mix of commerciality and experimentation that Madonna shared with Mirwais.

Sigsworth had originally sent Madonna a tape containing musical ideas, one of which was a short piece of speech by Charlotte Gainsbourg, the singer/actress daughter of cult French songwriting genius Serge Gainsbourg and his English wife Jane Birkin. The clip was taken from *The Cement Garden,* the 1993 movie based on the eponymous novel by Ian McEwan about an incestuous affair between a brother and sister.

"It's OK to be a boy, but not OK for a boy to look like a girl," Gainsbourg says in the clip, "because being a girl is degrading." It was a sentiment that Madonna had felt intensely in both her professional and personal life. She immediately knew she wanted to use the phrase and build a song around it.

Madonna took the idea and expanded it to express her feelings of frustration at having to hide her strength and intelligence, particularly in her personal relationships with men. The result was one of her most heartfelt vocals. This, she told *Interview* magazine, was a song about "swallowing that bitter pill. Our generation has been encouraged to grab life by the balls, be super-independent, get a great education, follow our dreams, kick ass, all that stuff, and I feel like I woke up one day holding the golden ring and realized that smart, sassy girls who accomplish a lot and have their own cash and are independent are really frightening to men. I felt like: why didn't somebody tell me? Why didn't somebody warn me?"

The other major factor that informed the writing of the song for Madonna was yet another change in her personal circumstances. Shortly before making the move to London and starting work on recording the album, she discovered she was pregnant again. She had decided to make the move from America to the UK to begin a settled relationship and family life with Guy Ritchie but, just as had been the case during the filming of *Evita*, she once again had to conceal her pregnancy. Press photos showed Madonna coming to work in the studio every day wearing an all-encompassing, slightly oversized coat; for Madonna to have to pretend that things were still 'business as usual' while she was pregnant served only to highlight how much women are often obliged to conceal.

"My life was just a roller coaster at that point," she recalled. "I would think: God, if people only knew. So that's what that song came out of: you're pregnant, your hormones are raging, and you can't tell anyone."

Shortly after the album was finished, Madonna flew back to Los Angeles, having decided that she wanted to give birth in America, where she could be nearer to family and friends. On August 11 2000, she gave birth to a baby boy, named Rocco after one of her uncles. Madonna and Guy, who was with her in LA, were both overjoyed. *Music* was released a month later.

In many ways, *Music* was Madonna's first European album, inasmuch as it had been recorded largely in London with British and French producers. But the artwork—based around photographs by another Frenchman, Madonna's old video-artist friend Jean-Baptiste Mondino—was decidedly American. In a kind of bubblegum version of Americana, Madonna is presented as a glamorous cotton-candy cowgirl in baby blue and sugar-pink Stetsons, rhinestone encrusted shirt, and resolutely feminine stilettos.

Being away from one's homeland often crystallizes one's sense of identity, and Madonna's time in London had unquestionably intensified her sense of being American. "Everyone thinks and writes that I've become a complete Anglophile," she lamented. "They say I've got no interest in America. But that's so not true. In fact, sometimes you have to go away from something to really appreciate and see it."

Mondino's album artwork—and indeed his video for 'Don't Tell Me'—was a kind of homage to Americana, albeit in a way that took a traditionally macho genre and feminized it. The video shows Madonna, once again in plaid shirt and Stetson, walking along an empty highway in the midst of the vast empty plains of the American Midwest before kneeling down to pick up handfuls of earth, savoring them in an image starkly evocative of Scarlett O'Hara at the end of *Gone With The Wind*.

"I just love the whole iconography of the West," Madonna noted. "The kind of sturdy earthiness of it, the earthy, rural poet. But it's got to have an edge to it, too. I think there's something really folky about a lot of the stuff that I wrote. It's really simple and lyrical, but then you combine it with modern technology."

Both the video and the album artwork have a soft, airbrushed sensuality about them, with an undercurrent of sexuality running subtly throughout. If *Ray Of Light* represented Madonna's spiritual quest, this was clearly a return to a more visceral reality.

"I like to boogie-woogie," Madonna wrote on the penultimate page of the CD booklet, and the video for 'Music' left no doubt about it. It shows Madonna on a night out with her 'homegirls' in a limousine driven by Sacha Baron Cohen (in his Ali G incarnation) intercut with animated sequences of Madonna as cartoon superhero disco-girl. The image was not so far from the reality: while writing the album, Madonna had tested out the songs by playing them on her car stereo out on the town with what she called her 'pussy posse.' If a track got the thumbs-up from her girlfriends, she knew to include it on the album. If it didn't, it would be rejected.

Madonna knew that the opinion of 'real' people was a much better litmus test than that of any record company executive, and once again she was proved right. *Music* went to Number One in the UK and numerous countries across Europe as well as and America, where it sold more than three million copies. It won an MTV Award for Best Dance Record, while Madonna herself won Best Female Artist. The 'Music' single, meanwhile, was equally successfully, reaching the top spot in Britain, America, and across Europe.

With another global hit on her hands, Madonna began to feel, as did her management and record company, that the obvious next move would be to go out on tour. But first she had some personal matters to attend to.

Soon after her brother Rocco, was born, four-year-old Lola asked: "Mom, are you going to get married before I get married?" At the time, Madonna was non-committal. But Lola got her answer on December 22 2000, when Madonna married Guy Ritchie at Skibo Castle—a pink-turreted Edwardian folly set amid 7,500 acres of private parkland near the highland village of Dornoch in rural Scotland. Guests at the castle included Sting, Trudie Styler, Rupert Everett, and Madonna's new friend Gwyneth Paltrow. The maid of honor was another new close friend, fashion designer Stella McCartney, who had also designed the bride's £30,000 strapless, ivory silk gown.

After the fiasco with the helicopters at her first wedding to Sean Penn, Madonna's second wedding certainly seemed to live up to the fairytale she had always dreamed of. The following day, four-month-old Rocco was christened at nearby Dornoch Cathedral. Nearly 400 fans—and even more press, radio, and television crews—gathered outside the cathedral in thick fog, eagerly awaiting a sighting of the famous family and their friends. Local fans waved banners with messages of support like 'Rocco Is Our Ray Of Light To Dornoch.'

After a honeymoon at Sting's lavish country estate in Wiltshire, Madonna wasted no time in getting back to work. A month before her wedding she had played a one-off show at London's 3,500-capacity Brixton Academy, performing songs from *Music*. This was her first stage show since giving birth to Rocco, but what had originally been planned as a relatively low-key performance for invited guests nevertheless soon became an international sensation when no fewer than nine million fans logged on to the live webcast.

Delighted with the show's success, Madonna was eager to plan a full-scale international tour. It would be her first tour since 1993, and her circumstances had changed radically in the intervening years. She now had a husband and two children to consider, and she planned the tour with them in mind. First of all, she would tour in the summer, since this would suit the children best. She also wanted to make sure that instead of jetting off on a madcap schedule from one European city to another—as she had often done previously—she would spare the children the ordeal of constantly getting on and off planes by staying in each city for at least a week.

Madonna had decided that almost everything about this tour had to be new and different, and that extended to the dancers. In March 2001, hundreds of hopefuls queued for hours on the streets of New York to audition for the potentially life-changing opportunity to dance on her new tour.

For her live band, Madonna brought in drummer Steve Sidelnyk, who played on *Music*; guitarist Monte Pittman, who was also Madonna's own personal guitar tutor; percussionist Ron Powell; and Stuart Price, a young British keyboard player whom Madonna had been introduced to by Mirwais. Price also doubled as a remixer, DJ, and composer, and had recorded with his own act, Les Rhythmes Digitales. Madonna quickly sensed in him the hip, finger-on-the-pulse vibe that she had always gravitated toward, and within a few weeks of rehearsals had promoted him from keyboardist to Musical Director. "There was a certain direction she was looking for," Price later explained, "and she put me in control of making music the right side of cool."

The plan was for Madonna to perform 22 songs, mostly from *Ray Of Light* and *Music*, with 'La Isla Bonita' and 'Holiday' as the finale to keep her old fans happy. Rehearsals began in the spring at Culver City Sound Studios in LA and, in true Madonna-style, this was by no means a half-hearted operation. She and her band spent nearly a month rehearsing 13 hours a day, five days a week, and when the songs were finally ready they moved over to the Staples Center, home of the LA Lakers, to begin full rehearsals for choreography, staging, and lighting.

Madonna was determined to make this new show more spectacular than anything her fans had seen before by taking the conventional pop tour to new levels of artistry. "I never want to repeat myself," she told *Interview* magazine. "I don't see the point of doing a show unless you offer something that is going to mind-boggle the senses. It's not enough to get on stage and sing a song. It's all about theater and drama and surprise and suspense."

As it turned out, there would be plenty of all four. The concept of the show was loosely inspired by JG Ballard's 1962 novel *The Drowned World*, which had at one time been the working title for *Ray Of Light*. The book is the second of four novels set in the future in which the protagonists make their way through dangerous and fantastical landscapes before finally finding "the truth." The Drowned World show similarly comprised its own series of fantastical scenarios and was divided into four separate sections, each one almost a stand-alone mini-opera. The various sets and costumes drew on ideas and genres as far-flung as 70s punk and flamenco, country & western and rock'n'roll; Japanese *butoh* dancing and martial arts, geishas and circus imagery. This was indeed going to mind-boggle the senses.

To mastermind the staging of this extravaganza, Madonna brought in a longstanding friend, director and choreographer Jamie King. King had been a protégé of Prince and a dancer with Michael Jackson; more recently, he had staged Ricky Martin's Livin' La Vida Loca World Tour. Madonna was so impressed with Martin's tour that she also hired the core members of his production crew, including production manager Mark Spring and technical consultant Joyce Flemming, as well as lighting designer Peter Morse, video director Carol Dodds, and—perhaps most significantly of all—production designer Bruce Rodgers, who had also created the video wall for Madonna's opening of the 2000 Grammy Awards.

The Drowned World Tour would be much more elaborate than that, however. Madonna told Rodgers that she wanted a set like Ricky Martin's— something "silver and shiny and modern." She also gave him a few other pointers: "I want to arrive on a spaceship. I want to ride a mechanical bull. I want to have a disco party, dance a redneck hoedown, put on a gypsy performance, and have a kabuki style dance scene."

This was to be the last conversation they had before production rehearsals began, but Rodgers managed to deliver exactly what Madonna wanted, producing a series of vast, apocalyptic, *sturm und drang* sets. Similarly, Jamie King created a back-to-back sequence of show-stopping dance numbers, while Madonna's costumes were designed by Dolce & Gabbana, Versace, Gaultier, and DSquared at a total cost of around £130,000.

Unsurprisingly, Madonna was meticulous about every aspect of the show, right down to the smallest detail. For the 'western cowgirl' section, she calculated exactly how high she could lift her leg in relation to the weight of the costume, while for the martial arts section—for which King had devised a *Crouching Tiger, Hidden Dragon*-style flying battle—she learned to leap and fly in an uncomfortable harness suspended on cables high above the stage. Choreography and rehearsals for that segment alone took two weeks.

Before the tour began, Warner Bros issued a statement telling fans that it would be "the most extravagant stage spectacle of [Madonna's] illustrious career." They were not wrong. The show made use of over 100 tons of equipment, including giant TV screens and a mechanical bull, as well as a traveling entourage of nearly 200 people. The stage itself, meanwhile, was nearly 5,000 feet wide. Tickets sold out within an hour of going on sale.

Perhaps unsurprisingly, even Madonna was now beginning to feel anxious. "I'm looking forward to it," she said, "but I'm also nervous about it. I'm always saying: can I do it? It's a massive undertaking." But she was also buoyed by the certainty that it felt like the right time for her to be touring again and getting back out on stage in front of her fans. "It does feel right," she explained. "It's like when I got married. Certain things happen, and there isn't a doubt in your mind. You know there's going to be challenges, you know that it's going to be a rocky road and all those things, but you also know in every cell of your body that it's the right thing to do, so you just do it."

The Herculean task of preparing such a vast production perhaps inevitably meant that there were some technical hitches at the last minute. The opening show, scheduled for Cologne, Germany, in early June, had to be canceled. But a week later, on June 9 2001, Madonna launched her Drowned World Tour at the 27,000-seater Palau St Jordi stadium in the Spanish city of Barcelona.

The opening sequence included 'Drowned World/Substitute For Love,' 'Ray Of Light,' and 'Impressive Instant,' which Madonna performed in a Gaultier-designed punk kilt flanked by dancers in boots, Mohicans, and cyberpunk gas masks. As well as singing, Madonna also played guitar on stage, wearing the instrument low-slung in the insouciant grunge style (and occasionally swearing at the audience to complete the effect).

From grunge-punk it was on to the darkest section of the show: a series of numbers drawing on *butoh*, the Japanese style of movement and dance which traditionally involved absurdist moves, grotesque imagery, and the breaking of taboos. Against a menacing blood-red and black backdrop, Madonna rose up from the centre of the stage in a black wig and breathtaking red kimono with sleeves spanning a staggering 52 feet. It took seven people to help her into it.

A samurai swordsman appeared during 'Nobody's Perfect,' Madonna kneeling submissively before him while he symbolically cut off her ponytail, holding it high like a prize as she fell to the ground. Meanwhile, the vast screens showed images of Madonna looking ghostly pale and bruised, blood pouring out of her nose.

'Mer Girl' came next, only to be interrupted by 'Sky Fits Heaven,' during which Madonna and her dancers crisscrossed through the air, flying over the stage in a martial arts battle before a reprise of the first song. The section closed with the screen showing violent Japanese-style cartoons and dark pornographic imagery; Madonna, of course, was eventually the victor in this mini-war. After dramatically pulling off her wig, she shot the samurai dead.

Madonna was of course no stranger to provocative imagery and controversy. Although some of the disturbing images came as a shock to some fans after the New Age spirituality of *Ray Of Light*, the new show was very much about the artist she was now rather than the pop star she had been in the past. "Her music for that moment was really kind of introspective and dark," Jamie King later explained, "so the tour had to reflect that phase. I thought it was really important that Madonna didn't sell out and that she didn't just do the hits, but she did really cover her new material because that was who she had evolved into and ... who she was."

Prior to the tour, Madonna had felt emboldened once again to tackle difficult subjects and was not afraid to confront them headlong. The video for 'What It Feels Like For A Girl,' directed by her new husband Guy Ritchie, features a kind of dystopian vision of a dirt-car race. Madonna plays a macho female, driving around in a high-speed performance car with a fragile elderly woman in the passenger seat. She then proceeds to rob a man at gunpoint at an ATM machine and aim her gun at two police officers before showing that it is in fact a water pistol. Next she rams her vehicle into a passing car, steals another racer's car, and sets fire to a gas station. Finally, she runs the car into a lamppost, presumably killing both herself and her passenger.

This, said Madonna, was a way of acting out a fantasy and "doing things girls aren't allowed to do." Both the video and the tour addressed many of the issues that had always interested her, notably the repression and suppression of women in a male-dominated society and the conflicts, both internal and external, that women face.

The samurai scene in the Drowned Word Tour was a return to these ideas, but for the final quarter of the show the setting moved from Japan to America's Wild West, striking a slightly more upbeat tone for 'I Deserve It,' 'Don't Tell Me,' 'Gone,' and two older songs, 'Secret' and 'Human Nature.' Dressed once again as a cowgirl, Madonna jumped rodeo-style aboard an oversized bucking mechanical bull. For 'Don't Tell Me,' it was line-dancing hoedown time; the mood then changed to one of spiritual awakening for 'Secret,' with the video wall showing a film by Melodie McDaniel about baptism alongside images of orthodox Jews praying at the Western Wall in Jerusalem.

The show's finale brought things very much back down to earth—and a more uplifting one at that—with Madonna singing 'What It Feels Like For A Girl' and 'La Isla Bonita,' this time in a kind of R&B take on Spanish flamenco, with images of the singer throughout her career projected on the screen. The grand closing number was 'Music,' for which Madonna spun around on a giant, revolving seven-inch single after an extended intro based on the main rhythmic phrase from Kraftwerk's 'Trans Europe Express.' "It's basically one note played a million times," Stuart Price recalled. "It can sound minimal on your kitchen hi-fi, and it can be massive in a stadium. I found it really exciting as the climax of the show."

After a triumphant opening night in Barcelona, the tour then continued around Europe before hitting the USA in late July for two nights in Philadelphia followed by five nights at New York's Madison Square Garden.

By August, Madonna was exhausted and suffering from laryngitis, but she carried on regardless until September, when the tour came to a short but unexpected halt.

Madonna was scheduled to play the first of a series of shows at Staples Center in Los Angeles on September 11 2001 but canceled the show in the light of that day's unimaginably catastrophic events. The tour resumed two days later, but Madonna was determined not to ignore what had happened. Instead, she turned the performance into her own form of memorial and rallying call.

For the opening section, Madonna appeared in a skirt made out of an American flag, and over the next few nights she held several moments of silence at each show in memory of those who had been killed in the terrorist attacks. She also announced that she would be pledging the proceeds of the remaining shows to the families of the victims.

"Violence begets violence," she told the crowd as she led them in prayer, encouraging President George Bush to practice restraint. "What happened was horrible, but I'd like to think of it as a wake-up call. There's terrorism every day all over the world."

When a bunch of fans began an urgent chant of "U-S-A," Madonna took the opportunity to expand on her view of the situation. "OK, USA," she told them, "but start looking at the whole world. If you want to change the world, change yourself. We're not doing this show because we want to forget, but because we want people to remember how precious life is." With that, she closed the show with 'Holiday.'

Madonna's Drowned World Tour would later be confirmed as the third-highest grossing concert tour of the USA in 2001. For Madonna, it was an unquestionable triumph in every respect. The production had been her most artistically daring to date in the way it renewed her earlier attacks on society's preconceptions and sensibilities. It seemed as if the newfound stability in her personal life had given her the courage to return to the fight.

Shortly after the end of the tour, a live video of the show was released. To accompany it, Warner Bros issued *GHV2* (Greatest Hits Volume 2), bringing together all of Madonna's 90s hits, just as *The Immaculate Collection* had done for the 80s. The album sold more than seven million copies worldwide.

GHV2 had various working titles, including *The Second Coming: Hit Lady* and *The Immaculate Collection Part Deux*, but in the end Madonna decided on *GHV2*—partly because she thought it was a title people would remember but also out of sheer laziness as she was exhausted from the tour. When deciding which tracks to include, Madonna certainly had no shortage of hits to choose from. Among those included were 'Erotica,' 'Take A Bow,' 'Don't Cry For Me Argentina,' 'Ray Of Light,' 'Drowned World/Substitute For Love,' and of course 'Music.' But rather than using the original single versions, ten of the tracks are in fact new edits, with an explicit line from 'Human Nature' omitted in order to avoid a Parental Advisory sticker.

In an interview with the BBC's Jo Whiley, Madonna explained that her selection criteria had been based on finding songs that she could listen to five times in a row. 'American Pie' was left off, she said, because she regretted including it on *Music.* "It was something a certain record company executive twisted my arm into doing," she told Whiley, "but it didn't belong on the album, so now it's being punished."

No singles were drawn from the album, but a 'GHV2 Megamix' was given a limited release around the same time. A month later, Madonna also issued a promotional double-album, *GHV2 Remixed: The Best Of 1991–2001*, featuring lengthy club-oriented re-workings of tracks such as 'What It Feels Like A Girl,' 'Don't Tell Me,' 'Frozen,' and 'Erotica' by producers and DJs like Victor Calderone, BT, Sasha, and Timo Maas.

Although well short of matching the phenomenal success of *The Immaculate Collection*, *GHV2* was nonetheless one of the bestselling albums of 2001 and served as a suitably successful summation of Madonna's second decade in pop. The success of the album and the Drowned World Tour proved that whatever persona she portrayed—be it was the New Age neophyte of *Ray Of Light,* the iconoclastic cowgirl of *Music*, or the politically outspoken performer of her tour—it would have little effect on her capacity to sell records. This was just as well, since there was to be yet more controversy when it came to her next album release. In the meantime however, she had another film to make.

CHAPTER 13
DIE ANOTHER DAY

After a tour on the epic scale of Drowned World, many artists would have taken some well-earned time out. Not Madonna. Within weeks of the final dates, she and husband Guy were sailing in the Mediterranean just off the coast of Malta, where they were scheduled to start making their first film together.

Swept Away was to be a remake of the 1974 film *Travolti Da Un Insolito Destino Nell'Azzurro Mare D'Agosto* (released internationally as *Swept Away*), a torrid romance with a feminist subtext set amid the deserted sands of a Mediterranean island. This would be Madonna's first acting role since *The Next Best Thing* and her first with her new husband as director. In Ritchie's film, which had the working title *Love, Sex, Drugs & Money*, Madonna was to play Amber, a wealthy and arrogant American socialite who goes on a yachting holiday but, through her own pigheadedness, ends up stranded on a deserted island. With her is Guiseppe, a communist sailor she has earlier chastised and humiliated on her yacht. Those roles are soon reversed as the sailor takes control; he knows how to survive on the island but she does not. Perhaps inevitably, it is not long before the pair become romantically involved.

Lina Wermüller, who made the Italian original, was known as a feminist director with an interest in politics of gender, suppression of women, and role reversal. For Madonna, the appeal was obvious. "It was a great part to sink my teeth into," she told *Genre* magazine. She also liked the fact that Amber goes through a spiritual awakening and epiphany during the course of the film after starting off as an unlikeable character.

"I liked the challenge of playing somebody who's so unsympathetic," she told the *New York Times*. "Hopefully she is sympathetic by the time you get to the end of the film. I like the idea that there's some kind of transformation; that she starts out clueless about what matters in life, completely self-obsessed and spoiled and unhappy. And by the end, she has figured it out. Or at least she starts to get a feeling for what is important. So I liked the journey that she went on."

Ritchie, meanwhile, liked the idea of remaking a film that was barely known outside Italy. "I just thought it was an interesting film, and very fresh, comparatively," he said. "I knew no one was going to watch it who wasn't Italian. It was made in 1974, and I'd never heard of it. I thought it had some pertinent points in it: rather politically incorrect, but nevertheless pertinent."

When the film was released in 2002, the media was unsurprisingly keen to know whether the film's plot in any way reflected the dynamic between Guy and the new Mrs Ritchie, as Madonna now liked to be known. "Mrs Ritchie," Alan Riding of the *New York Times* asked, "I was wondering whether, when you saw the original film again, you saw an echo of your own relationship with Mr Ritchie? You once called your husband a great macho ..."

"I expected this question and I rehearsed," Madonna replied sassily. "There are elements in the movie that I would say are reflective of the politics in our relationship. Guy's a real macho and I'm a real hard-nose, too. And sometimes we come to blows: not physically, but mentally and emotionally. And there is an element, a tiny little element of that in there. I'm attracted to men who are going to stand up to me. Now I'm only attracted to this man. But before I met Guy, my idea of the perfect man would be someone intelligent and clever enough, but also kind and compassionate enough to stand up to me: to stand up to me with compassion. And I think that's ultimately why Amber falls in love with Giuseppe: because he stands up to her and her husband doesn't."

Friends had frantically advised Madonna and Guy not to work together, insisting that it would destroy their marriage. For Madonna, however, the idea of idling around while Ritchie worked was anathema. "I think it would have been much harder for me to hang around on the set with two kids, doing nothing, while he directed a film," she said.

Reporters were also keen to know what it had been like for the married couple to work together, with Guy literally calling the shots as director. But Madonna had of course acted before, and was well used to letting the director take charge. This time was—in theory, at least—no different.

In fact, because of the situation, Madonna tried harder than usual to hide her emotions on set. She knew that observers would seize on any instance of Ritchie paying her extra attention—and on any on-set arguments between the pair—so hid any nerves or vulnerability she may have felt during filming. "Because people were expecting Guy and I to fight," she explained, "I had to even be more of a warrior and have a stiff upper lip and be the first one there and the last one to leave and always on my best behavior to, in a way, prove everyone wrong. And there are probably times, if Guy hadn't been my husband, where I might have started sobbing or fallen apart. But I couldn't in this situation."

Swept Away was received poorly when it was released in 2002, and despite the Ritchies' higher-than-usual profile in Britain, it went straight to DVD. But this was not going to deter Madonna from seizing upon the next film role she was offered. This time the part combined both film and music, and although it was only to be a cameo appearance, it just so happened to be in the most successful film franchise of all time. Madonna had been given the role of Verity, fencing instructor to none other than James Bond in *Die Another Day*—007's 20th film outing. She was also due to write the high profile title song.

In the 60s and 70s, film composer John Barry had created the Bond song genre with classics like 'Goldfinger', 'You Only Live Twice,' and 'Diamonds Are Forever,' and Madonna's 'Die Another Day'—once again co-written and produced by Mirwais—certainly has the minor key poignancy associated with those earlier Bond themes. But Madonna also introduced a new edginess and experimental darkness to the theme which was very much her own. When it came to the lyrics, meanwhile, she sought to bring a new, more psychological approach to the standard Bond premise of good versus evil.

"The song I wrote for the Bond film is about destroying your ego," she explained in an interview with her brother, Christopher, for *Genre* magazine. "It's juxtaposing the metaphor of the fight against good and bad. It's set inside the whole universe of Bond. James Bond is in prison and he gets out of prison. Like all Bond films, somebody's chasing him or he's chasing somebody, and it's always a fight against good and evil. I wanted to take it to another level. It's kind of a metaphor of … I'm fighting myself."

Madonna's approach was certainly different and the accompanying promo video seemed similarly distanced from the James Bond traditions of old.

Directed by the Swedish team Traktor, who had previously worked with The Flaming Lips, Basement Jaxx, and Fatboy Slim, the clip shows Madonna trying to escape being tortured and is intercut with scenes from her appearance in the film. The single was released in late 2002, and although some Bond fans may have found its new approach to the genre a little too radical for comfort, the record was nevertheless another success. It reached Number Four in the UK charts while spending 11 weeks at Number One on the *Billboard* Singles Sales chart. Its dark mood would also set the tone when it came to recording her next album.

For some artists, going from sugar-coated blond cowgirl to gun-toting militant guerrilla in the space of a few short years might be considered a bit of a leap. But reinvention and the manipulation of her visual identity have always formed an integral part of Madonna's career.

When her ninth studio album, *American Life*, was released in April 2003, the CD artwork showed stark monochromatic images of a dark-haired Madonna sporting a beret and combat pants in the style of 60s Argentine revolutionary Che Guevara. Instead of dallying playfully in the hay, as she did on *Music,* she was shown here against a bare white background brandishing a machine-gun with splashes of blood red dotted around—a radical change from the love-and-disco incarnation of her last album. This time, Madonna's entire motivation for making a record had changed.

She had started work on the album shortly after finishing the Drowned World Tour, and the September 11 terror attacks, which occurred near the tour's close, had colored her mood. Rather than just wanting to write songs that reflected her own experiences, Madonna wanted to create something that she might offer some kind of spiritual awakening and enlightenment.

"The point of this record is to bring up subjects that aren't terribly popular," she told Dutch journalist Eddy Zoey. "How obsessed we are as a culture with superficial things, with the way things look, the surface of life, and how we don't pay attention to what really matters in life—the way we treat one another; the kind of love and compassion that we show to one another. Those kinds of things aren't really focused on in our society, so what I'm trying to do is bring that up in my record. I'm trying to inspire people: I'm trying to bring about unity in the world. I'm not just putting out a record for the sake of putting out a record to get more rich and more famous."

These ideas were very much a return to the kabbalistic philosophy she had first espoused around *Ray Of Light*. They form the basis of the entire record. Lyrically, *American Life* can be seen almost as a concept album, and the music likewise reflects Madonna's newly impassioned stance. Again co-produced—and for the most part co-written—by Mirwais, it built on the combination of analogue and digital, commercial and experimental the pair had first explored on *Music*. "We set out to put the two worlds of acoustic and electronic music together," Madonna told *Q* magazine. "It is another step on, but I've never wanted to repeat myself. I don't ever want to make the same record twice."

The title track seemed to sum up both the musical character of the album and Madonna's worldview. On the edgy opening verse, over Mirwais's trademark beats and electronic tricks, Madonna parodies the questions asked by a million teenage wannabes as they look at themselves in the mirror: "Do I have to change my name? / Should I lose some weight?" In the softer, more melodic chorus, she sings about how, after trying to live the American dream and play the part, she "forgot just what I did it for."

At the end, in a rap that harks back to 1990's 'Vogue,' she lists the extensive trappings of her fame and fortune—the lawyer, the agent, the gardener, the chef, the three nannies—before explaining that "nothing is what it seems." She wasn't complaining about her fame, she told Zoey, but she did feel that, despite receiving opportunities not offered to people in other countries, "we as Americans are completely obsessed and wrapped up in life with the wrong values."

The other key aspect of Madonna's message was the importance of love. The centerpiece of the album is a triptych of songs written for her husband—'Nothing Fails,' 'Intervention,' and 'X-Static Process'—that leave no doubt as to how she was feeling at the time. The couple had by now set up home with their two children at Ashcombe House, a stylish country estate in Wiltshire that was once home to the fashion and society photographer Cecil Beaton. Ritchie regularly visited Madonna in the studio, and she was keen to have him around, seeking his advice on whatever track she was working on.

On 'Intervention,' co-written by Mirwais, Madonna sings of the redemptive power of love, while on 'X-Static Process,' co-written by the Drowned World Tour's Musical Director, Stuart Price, she laments its unsettling impact. "When you're around," she sings, "I don't know how I am." Both songs are low key, gentle, and largely acoustic, with Madonna's voice supported by only the sparsest of accompaniment.

Perhaps the most touching of the three songs however is 'Nothing Fails,' originally co-written by producer and programmer Guy Sigsworth, with whom Madonna worked on *Music*, and the Welsh singer-songwriter Jem Griffiths. The song had had more of a folk feel on Sigsworth's original demo, but Madonna and Mirwais gave the melody line a slightly poppier (and more typically Madonna-like) feel before further transforming the song into a big production epic.

The track opens with a soft, country-meets-trip-hop feel before entering the multi-tracked chorus, which gradually builds in a sweep of strings arranged by the legendary French composer Michel Colombier. It continues to build until the grand finale, for which The London Community Gospel Choir joins Madonna in a rousing, celebratory coda of "I'm not religious but I feel so moved."

'Love Profusion,' another of Madonna's softer pop ballads, continues the central love theme. Accompanied only by acoustic guitar, she sings again of love's redemptive qualities before returning to her own spiritual quest. "I have lost my illusions," she sings. "What I want is an explanation."

There are plenty of other intimate moments on the album. If listeners thought *Ray Of Light* sounded personal, songs like 'X-Static Process' and 'American Life' take Madonna's introspection and self-exploration further still. She delves deep into her childhood on 'Mother And Father,' singing about the innocence of early childhood, the loss of her mother, and her sense of loneliness and rejection—all of which is presented in a rather unlikely pop-disco-rap setting.

Madonna was not just letting it all out for the sake of it. By talking about the unhappy aspects of her own past, she said, she felt she might be able to help others. "I want to write about something so that other people who have had similar experiences can go away with some kind of feeling of being able to heal themselves as well," she said. "I take certain situations that could be perceived as painful and turn them into something that's hopeful, that can be educational and enlightening rather than something that paralyses you.

"I'm talking about something that can be perceived as a tragedy," she continued, "but ultimately something that you can become stronger from ... If you have an emptiness inside yourself and you want a certain kind of love, the only way you're going to get it is to give it. That's the message that I want to get across, not that I want everybody to dwell on the aspect of my mother dying."

Madonna's most regularly used source for lyrics was her journal, in which she keeps ideas from newspapers and books as well as her own personal thoughts and sometimes fragments of free verse. But the initial starting point almost always came from the music itself. "The songs just come to me when I hear music," she explained. "Something jars and I have an emotional reaction and I have to start writing."

This was certainly the case with 'Easy Ride,' the album's beautifully poignant closing track. She co-wrote the song with Monte Pittman, the guitarist on the Drowned World tour, from whom she also been taking guitar lessons for some three years by the time of the *American Life* sessions. During one of their lessons, a musical phrase suddenly suggested a lyric to her.

"I want the good life / But I don't want an easy ride," she sings, gently, during the pared-down opening, backed only by softly strummed acoustic guitar. She wants to work for it, she explains—to feel the sweat on her brow and to feel that she's earned it. The song gradually builds, with lush strings once again arranged by the late Colombier.

When it came to devising the artwork for the album, the link between guerrilla imagery and the lyrical themes of love and goodness may not have seemed obvious, but to Madonna it made perfect sense. As she explained in an interview with the BBC's *Top Of The Pops*, she had been "feeling revolutionary" when she wrote the songs, and that was where the idea for the visuals came from. "I see Che [Guevara] as a revolutionary," she said. "I don't necessarily agree with the Communist Party *Manifesto*, but there are aspects of socialism which are good, and I like what he represents."

Mirwais had also clearly played a part in Madonna's choice of imagery. In a later interview, she described him as "very cerebral, very philosophical, and very intellectual" and they had, she said, "got sucked into the French existentialist vortex. We both decided we were against the war, and we both smoked Gauloises and wore berets, and we were against everything ... I was in a very thoughtful mood, a very angry mood."

The cover shot was taken by British fashion photographer Craig McDean, who had also photographed Madonna for *Vanity Fair* magazine in 2002; the rest of the artwork was created by the French design team M/M Paris, best known for their work with Björk. (All in all, the artwork was rumored to have cost most than £250,000.)

Released in April 2003, *American Life* made its debut at Number One in the UK charts as well as on the *Billboard* 200, selling nearly 250,000 copies in its first week. Reviews were mixed, however, and the album's total worldwide sales of four million copies were among the lowest of her career. Many also considered the drop in sales to be not entirely unconnected with the controversy surrounding the promo video for the album's title track and lead single.

Shot by Swedish director Jonas Akerlund, who had directed the 'Ray Of Light' clip, the 'American Life' video picked up where the militant artwork left off. Set at a fantasy fashion show, it has models stalking the runway in surreal, provocative versions of military fatigues. Madonna plays a gun-wielding resistance fighter: she and her crack team shoot into the crowd from the runway amid flashing images of bombs exploding and wounded Muslim children roaming around in rubble. The video ends with a grenade exploding in front of a President Bush lookalike in the audience.

The Iraq War had not started when Madonna conceived of the idea, but it was already evidently a possibility, and clearly the motivation behind the video. "I wanted to wake people up to the idea that war isn't far away, that people suffer," she said. The message was: People, wake up, this is right around the corner. But the post-production work took almost a month, and by the time the video was ready for release, war had broken out.

Both Madonna and her record company consequently felt that the video was too sensitive to be released and so set about making a second video, in which Madonna sings in front of various flags of the world. In the interim, she issued a statement explaining the original video. "I have decided not to release my new video," she said. "It was filmed before the war started and I do not believe it is appropriate to air it at this time. Due to the volatile state of the world, and out of sensitivity and respect to the armed forces, who I support and pray for, I do not want to risk offending anyone who might misinterpret the meaning of this video."

When later pressed about the intentions behind the video, she acknowledged that it was indeed an anti-war statement, but made clear that it was not necessarily against *this* war. "At any given moment, there's at least 30 wars going on in this world," she told *Q* magazine. "I'm against all of them."

Further controversy ensued when she attempted to preempt illegal internet downloads of the album. Her team planted a number of fake song files on the internet. Anybody who attempted to download them received an audio file containing nothing but a short message from Madonna herself, asking: "What the fuck do you think you're doing?" Others contained a rap-style "thought you'd sneak past me, didn't you?" and a loop of the "soy latte" part of 'American Life.'

If Madonna thought she had been smart enough to outwit those attempting to illegally distribute the album online, there was at least one person out there who was smarter still—someone who managed to successfully hack into Madonna's official website and post a message stating "This is what the fuck I'm doing," followed by links that enabled visitors to the site to download the correct versions of each of the tracks from the album. It was a far cry from the message of love and healing that Madonna had hoped to spread.

The subsequent single releases from the album proved rather more straightforward. 'Hollywood,' 'Nothing Fails,' and 'Love Profusion' were all solid international hits even if they failed to make a significant impact on the US charts. *American Life* may not have sold in anywhere near the quantities Madonna had become accustomed to with her previous albums—and certainly not when compared with *Ray Of Light*—but it has in the years since come to be considered by some as one of Madonna's strongest artistic statements.

That same year, Madonna celebrated her 20th year in the music business. She had released her debut, *Madonna*, back in 1983, and it seemed fitting to issue some kind of commemorative release. A 20th anniversary boxed set was discussed, but eventually Madonna decided to put out an EP of remixes, mainly of songs from *American Life*, but with a few added extras.

The result was *Remixed & Revisited.* Released on November 24 2003, the EP features four *American Life* tracks—'Nothing Fails,' 'Love Profusion,' 'American Life,' and 'Nobody Knows Me'—reinterpreted by a varied cast of DJs and producers, as well a previously unreleased track from the *Bedtime Stories* era, 'Your Honesty.' As an added bonus, the EP includes a live recording of the 'Like A Virgin' / 'Hollywood' medley Madonna performed with Britney Spears and Christina Aguilera at the MTV Video Awards, as well as a brief duet with Missy Elliott from the same show, 'Into The Hollywood Groove.'

On the whole, the *American Life* remixes take the basic melody and vocal parts from the originals and give them a hardcore club makeover. 'Nobody Knows Me,' remixed by the American-born, Berlin-based DJ and performance artist Mount Sims, is a case in point. Sims is known for taking ideas from somewhere way left of what might normally be described as left-field and the story goes that, for this remix, he made the drum sounds from time-compressed segments of a speech by Charles Manson.

Elsewhere, 'Nothing Fails' is re-imagined as a dance-rock ballad by DJ/producer Jason Nevins, best known for his hit remix of Run DMC's 'It's Like That,' while 'Love Profusion' and 'American Life' are each given a heavy-rock overhaul by Headcleanr. The track most fans cited as their favorite, however, was 'Your Honesty,' which was co-written and produced by Dallas Austin, the Atlanta-based producer best known for his work TLC, and gave fans a small but thrilling glimpse of the 'pop' Madonna of old.

It seemed that with the anniversary of her second decade in pop, Madonna herself began to re-acknowledge the potency of her own past. In August 2003, when she was asked to appear at the 20th MTV Video Awards, it seemed appropriate for her to reference what was still one of her most memorable incarnations. The plan was for her to sing 'Like A Virgin,' but rather than performing the song alone, she was to sing alongside two new young female pretenders to her pop crown who had both recently become huge stars: Britney Spears and Christina Aguilera.

Spears had become Madonna's biggest rival on the pop charts, having sold more than 27 million copies of her 1999 debut album, ... *Baby One More Time*, while Aguilera looked set to follow suit on the strength of her recent hit, 'Beautiful.' But despite the presence of these two and other younger stars such as Beyoncé and 50 Cent, it was nevertheless Madonna who made the headlines.

The MTV spot began with Spears and Aguilera singing 'Like A Virgin.' Both were dressed in virginal white—albeit in the form of micro-dresses with stockings and suspenders—in a raunchy homage to Madonna's original video. Madonna then rose up from a wedding cake on the stage to appear dressed as the supposed groom in head-to-toe Gothic black with a satin top hat and tails and tight trousers tucked into spike-heeled leather boots. As the song segued into her recent 'Hollywood,' Madonna took the lead, seductively caressing her two young 'brides' before giving each of them a kiss. But while the kiss with Aguilera looked relatively innocent, the one with Spears was a lustier open-mouthed affair. And it was this that caused the real sensation, in the USA and beyond.

In the media frenzy that followed, even feminist author Camille Paglia was moved to add her two cents' worth. The kiss, she wrote, was Madonna's way of telling Spears: "I'm passing the torch to you." Madonna later said she had got straight on a plane to Scotland in the immediate aftermath of the event, oblivious to the mounting furore. It wasn't until two weeks later, when she appeared on *The Oprah Winfrey Show*, that she came to face any questions about the performance.

"Was that planned or was it spontaneous or what was it?" Oprah asked. Madonna replied that it was intended as a playfully ironic comment, "'cause I had two brides and I was going to kiss both of my brides." In rehearsals, she said, it had been no more than a light air-kiss. "If Britney looks like she's kissing me in an aggressive manner, it was a surprise to me. I swear to God!"

At this, the studio audience erupted into laughter. Knowing how to keep the crowd with her, Madonna expanded further. "I'm a showgirl," she said. "After 20 years in show business, you learn how to roll with the punches." While to some the incident was little more than a highly successful publicity stunt, she insisted that she had not been trying to make a statement. "I made those statements ten years ago," she quipped.

Whether out of genuine admiration or a desire to identify herself with the new kid on the block, Madonna has spoken in the past of her empathy with Spears. (She also wore a 'Britney" T-shirt during promotional interviews around the turn of the millennium.) "I feel really protective of her," she told *Interview* magazine. "Even though she's terribly successful, for some reason I think of her as an underdog. ... It's like when you go to a party and there's a girl, and everyone's avoiding her because she's really pretty, or whatever. I always want to go over and talk to that person.

"Maybe to a certain extent I can relate to it, because I feel that I was certainly a victim of snobbery when I first started," she continued. "I can't even count the number of things that I read about myself that kept dismissing the fact that I had talent or that I could sing or any of those things. And now I just see everybody doing it to her, so I feel defensive of her and protective of her."

Some seven years after the MTV Awards was broadcast, a poll conducted by Selfridges declared Madonna and Britney's moment the 'Kiss Of The Decade.' "Madonna performing with both Britney and Christina was a big enough event in itself," a spokesperson for the department store noted, in a mood of sober understatement, "but nobody—even the MTV people—expected what happened. It was one of the most memorable moments ever."

It may indeed have been memorable, but what was perhaps in fact much more impressive was Madonna's seemingly unending capacity to magically transform her image from one moment to the next—as would be seen with her next project.

If her appearance at the MTV awards had seemed shocking to some, her next venture would come as even more of a surprise. Not content with a highly successful music career and an ongoing (if uneven) film career, in September 2003 she published her first children's book, *The English Roses*.

The idea for the book—the first in a series—had first come up in the early 90s, when American publisher Nicholas Calloway watched Madonna read one of his children's titles, *Miss Spider's Tea Party*, during a show to promote her *Bedtime Stories* album on MTV. The young studio audience was clearly captivated, and Calloway was immediately impressed with Madonna's ability to convey a story and suggested that she might like to think about writing some children's tales of her own.

The timing was perfect. Madonna's daughter Lola was now seven years old and when it came to reading to her at bedtime, Madonna became increasingly impatient with the lack of realism in traditional children's stories. "While there were lots of cute books and fantastic illustration, there weren't that many stories that were actually about anything," she told the Home Shopping Network's Callie Northagen. "If you read the classic fairy tales, there's always the princess who gets the guy. I would find myself getting to the end and saying to my daughter: wait a second ... they didn't even ask the princess whether she *liked* the prince! So I felt that I wanted to write stories for girls who want to think."

Once Madonna had decided to take up Calloway's suggestion that she write a story of her own, she knew that she wanted to address the unrealistic nature of existing children's literature. She was also keen to bring in a moral element, and to introduce the values she had learned from her study of Kabbalah—particularly the central message of being kind to those around you.

Having developed a story idea, Madonna needed to work out exactly how to put it together to convey what she wanted. "I didn't really know what I was doing at first," she told NBC's Matt Lauer. "Trying to get a good narrative, trying to tell a unique story, trying to tell something that's timeless and classic—that was a challenge for me."

The next challenge was to find the right illustrator. This took some time, since both Madonna and her publisher wanted to give the books a classic, timeless feel rather than something strictly contemporary. They eventually settled on Jeffrey Fulvimari, an Ohio-born Andy Warhol protégé whose graphic, linear, and often whimsical, colorful style harks back to earlier children's classics like *The Cat In The Hat* or *Madeline*.

The central character in *The English Roses* is Binah, a young girl with more than a touch of Cinderella about her—and likewise more than a few echoes of Madonna herself as a young girl. Binah is beautiful and good but she is also sad because, since her mother's death, she has spent her days cooking and cleaning for her father. She is also sad because she has no friends. The other girls her age have ostracized her—they assume she must be spoiled and rich, not realizing that she is neither.

The other girls in the book are named after four of young Lola's friends—Nicole, Amy, Charlotte, and Grace—nicknamed The English Roses by the teachers at Lola's London French Lycée. In the book, the girls' attitudes are transformed when they all have a dream in which a fairy godmother shows them how lucky they are compared with Binah. "When morning came," Madonna writes, "the girls told one another about their dreams, and they promised each other that, from that day on, they would be kinder to Binah and stop complaining about their own lives." They start off by inviting Binah to a tea party; before long they are walking to school and doing their homework together. The English Roses soon find out that Binah is, in fact, "very likable indeed."

Madonna launched *The English Roses* by hosting a children's tea party in Kensington, where she read to the assembled crowd from her new book. The images that subsequently appeared in the world's press couldn't have been any further from her previous raunchy personae. Instead of the brazen, circus mistress predator of the MTV Awards, what we now saw was Madonna surrounded by children and dressed in a knee-length, white silk dress with a romantic red rose print. She looked like the ultimate respectable children's author.

The book was published simultaneously in more than 100 countries worldwide and translated into 30 languages. Madonna's own children were fans of the book, but so too it seems were millions of others around the world. *The English Roses* became the fastest-selling book ever published by a first-time children's author. It debuted at Number One on the *New York Times* Best Seller list for Illustrated Children's Books and remained there for no fewer than 18 weeks.

Madonna was understandably delighted not just to have achieved success in another new field but also to be doing something she considered morally and financially worthwhile. All proceeds from the series would eventually be donated to Raising Malawi, the children's foundation she would set up a few years later, and so for Madonna, this was indeed a tangible way in which she could help children less fortunate than her own. "I feel like it's a privilege," she told Callie Northagen, "to write books which I enjoy doing and I can take that money and help children who don't have parents and don't have their basic needs met—for me it's just full circle."

Madonna was also thrilled to receive letters from children who had read the book and taken onboard its central message. "It felt really good to publish a book and to know it got into the hands of lots of kids," she explained, "and to start reading letters from children who read *The English Roses* and said: you know, when I read your book it made me think of how horrible me and my girlfriends were to this girl in school. I thought it was so cool—I'm helping kids, and I never thought I'd be doing that."

Madonna published the second *English Roses* book, *Too Good To Be True*, in 2006, and by 2010 the English rose foursome had made a dozen further appearances in print. By launching herself as a children's writer, Madonna had once again taken fans and observers alike by surprise with her ability to pursue ever new projects, but she had also recently begun to look to her own past for reference, and she would do so still further in her next venture.

CHAPTER 14
RE-MAKE, RE-MODEL

Since celebrating 20 years in music, Madonna had gradually begun to reference her own past, both musically and visually. When it came to her next album, she would also acknowledge her own musical influences, but wherever she looked for inspiration there was still a virtual pendulum swinging between two extremes. On one of the tracks on her new album, 'Like It Or Not,' she would sing "You can call me a sinner / You can call me a saint." Over the next two years, on tour, on record, and during one-off performances, she would do her best to be both.

While The Drowned World Tour had been very much a reflection on her most recent material, when it came to her next foray into the live arena, Madonna would take a different approach. She had recently become more and more conscious of the value of her own back catalogue, and this time she planned to give her fans what she knew they wanted, offering more of an overview of her entire career. She would showcase all of the old hits, but rather than merely packaging nostalgia she intended to bring the songs up to date. She was, after all, best known for her capacity to tirelessly reinvent and evolve and her approach to her own songs was to be no exception.

Madonna herself had long been frustrated by the media's emphasis on her talent for reinvention, but with this, her sixth major concert tour, she decided that rather than trying to flout the pundits, she would tackle them head-on. The working title for the tour had originally been Whore Of Babylon, a reference to the character from *The Book Of Revelation*, with the idea being that Madonna herself was to play the whore. In the end, this idea was ditched, and the Re-Invention World Tour was born.

With Re-Invention, Madonna wanted once again to create a grand spectacle. The new show would have its dark moments but it would in general be much more of an upbeat crowd-pleaser. That did not mean there would be any less of the 'wow' factor, however. The official tour poster showed Madonna in a shimmering gold bolero evening gown and a towering Marie Antoinette-style white-blond wig. With costumes designed by Arianne Phillips, Stella McCartney, Karl Lagerfeld, and Christian Lacroix, The Re-Invention World Tour took the theatrics and choreography of Drowned World and incorporated them into a show that may have been hard to define, but however you chose to label it, was unquestionably crowd-pleasing. "Madonna has created a new performance hybrid," the *Washington Post* proclaimed, "one that lifts and blends elements of Broadway, Cirque Du Soleil, Rock The Vote rallies, art installations, extreme sporting events, church sermons, disco dances, and gun-spinning military drills."

As with Drowned World, Jamie King and Stuart Price were re-hired as Artistic and Musical Directors respectively, and also as per the previous tour, the Re-Invention shows were divided into five acts: French baroque, military, cabaret/circus, acoustic, and finally Scottish/tribal. The linking theme was unity versus violence, using Steven Klein's photographs from his X-STaTIC Pro=CeSS installation of images of Madonna as a starting point.

The shows opened with a short film, *The Beast Within*, shot by avant-garde director Chris Cunningham, best known for his provocative music videos for The Prodigy and Aphex Twin. Echoing X-STaTIC Pro=CeSS, the macabre film was edited in a static-heavy, montage style and showed Madonna writhing on a prison-style bed while reading from *The Book Of Revelation* as wolves looked on, barking savagely. This was conceptual art for the sports arena. Madonna may indeed have been 'reinventing' herself once again, but even at her edgiest, an air of high-camp glamour was never far away.

Madonna next appeared on stage on a rising platform, dressed in a gold-embroidered Christian Lacroix bustier and boots. She coaxed herself against an elaborate Rococo-style backdrop into sinew-straining yoga positions to the opening strains of 'Vogue,' striking a pose as she performed a yogic headstand, swinging her stockinged and booted feet high into the air. Next came 'Nobody Knows Me,' an energetic and ingenious performance on a conveyor belt, before 'Frozen,' which was accompanied by a video—projected onto vast custom-made screens—of a naked, androgynous couple wrestling underwater.

The dazzling second act began with the sound of a helicopter droning in the background as Madonna returned to sing a hard-rock rendition of 'American Life' dressed in khaki fatigues and Che Guevara beret. The backing dancers crawled on their stomachs in battle-mode as footage of bombed-out villages, war-ravaged children, and general death and destruction raged on the video screens around them.

If that wasn't enough to stun the audience, a show-stopping V-shaped catwalk then descended from the ceiling and extended right out into the audience, where it hung some 20 feet above the crowd. Both Madonna and designer Jamie King had wanted to find a practical but striking way of getting Madonna closer to her fans and this had been the solution. A circular section of the stage then turned to reveal stacks of sky-high television screens.

A rifle-twirling 'Express Yourself' followed, with Madonna still in Sergeant Major mode, before she strapped on her guitar for rocked-up versions of 'Burning Up' and 'Material Girl.' The dancers paraded the stage and runway in various types of religious dress—there was a cardinal, a nun, a rabbi, and a woman dressed in a super-short mini burka—before whipping off their costumes to show that, in the end, they're all the same. "I am a material girl," Madonna sang, before adding "but not really!"—just in case anybody had forgotten her much trumpeted new life ethos.

The show then left the world of war for a big-top circus, with 'Hollywood' accompanied by a more lighthearted blend of vaudeville tricks and cabaret including break-dancing, skateboarding, and belly dancing. This led into a similarly showy rendition of 'Hanky Panky,' and a jazzy 'Deeper And Deeper,' before the mood darkened once again for 'Die Another Day.' Images of an old man on his deathbed flashed on the screens before Madonna, dressed in a Wild West outfit of stars and stripes, sang the closing part of the song—followed by *Evita*'s 'Lament'—while strapped into an electric chair that rose high above the stage. She would later say that this had been her favorite part of the show. "I like the idea of being restrained," she explained. "I'm singing about all the things I could have had, but my ego got in the way and I destroyed all my happiness."

The high-octane razzle-dazzle factor was then turned down several notches for the show's acoustic section, for which Madonna wore a sleek Savile Row-style three-piece suit designed by Stella McCartney. Strapping on her guitar, she treated the crowd to poignant, low-key renditions of 'Nothing Fails' and 'Like A Prayer,' with outsized Hebrew letters appearing on the screens around her.

These were replaced by Catholic images for 'Mother And Father' before Madonna surprised the audience with a cover of John Lennon's 'Imagine,' accompanied by more images of war-ravaged children—something Madonna later explained she felt was vital to bring home her point. "I wanted to make a statement," she said. "I feel like that song is the ultimate peace song, and it was important to have the stuff going on behind me, the pictures, and really hit home that children are involved in all this chaos and destruction. I don't think people remember that all the time."

Madonna sang the closing words—"We can live as one"—to the plaintive strains of a Scottish bagpiper before being lowered beneath the stage for one final costume change. Gradually, the pipes began to build to a rousing wail for 'Into The Groove,' with the lone piper—flown in especially from Scotland—joined by a drum corps.

Madonna and her dancers then emerged in matching black-and-white tartan kilts, with Missy Elliott appearing on the video screens. Building toward the show's close, Madonna then moved from John Lennon's past to her own with a crowd-pleasing run through of 'Papa Don't Preach,' 'Crazy For You,' and 'Music.' Aware as ever of the power of the slogan, Madonna wore a black T-shirt bearing various "... Do It Better" lines that varied from show to show: one night it was "Kabbalists," while others included "Irish," "Italian," "Midwesterners," and so on.

'Music' closed with Madonna and her dancers lifting up their kilts to reveal red underwear emblazoned with the word "Freedom." For the grand finale, she sang the song that was always guaranteed to delight her fans—'Holiday'—before a flurry of canons fired wedding-style confetti through the air and the words "REINVENT YOURSELF" appeared in giant letters on the screens. Madonna had made sure that nobody was allowed access to her Scottish wedding to Guy Ritchie, but here it seemed as if she wanted to bring some aspect of the day to her fans after all.

The tour was well received by the critics. The *Washington Post*'s David Segal commented that he had been "entertained into submission" while the *Independent* concluded: "She's a woman of many flaws, but in terms of theatricality and spectacle, there's no one who can touch her."

Madonna played 56 shows in 20 cities across Europe and North America on the Re-Invention World Tour, reaching a total audience of around 900,000. It was the highest-grossing tour of 2004, with estimated takings of nearly £80 million. Even so, Madonna still made sure that those who hadn't been able to catch the tour in person would not be left completely bereft.

Back in 1991, she had redefined the 'tour film' genre with *Truth Or Dare*, and while planning the Re-Invention World Tour she had decided to do something similar. This time the film was to be part tour journal, part spiritual quest. It would show Madonna not just on her physical journey around Europe and America but also on an emotional trail as she continued her search for personal growth. "If I'm going to take people through a journey of my life," she told *Vogue*, "they are going to see all my journeys, and I hope they will also be moved by it."

Madonna had originally discussed the idea of a tour film with campaigning filmmaker Michael Moore, who had made a name for himself with films like *Bowling For Columbine*, his look at guns, violence, and the 1999 Columbine High School massacre. Moore had helped Madonna with the initial concept and might have directed the film had he not been busy making his own *Fahrenheit 9/11*. Instead, in the hope of recreating some of the edgy spirit of *Truth Or Dare*, Madonna hired Jonas Akerlund, her collaborator on the videos for 'Ray Of Light,' 'Music,' and the controversial 'American Life.'

As with most Madonna projects, it was clear from the start that this was not going to be your average 'pop star on the road' affair. It begins with a voiceover reciting a doom-laden passage from *The Book Of Revelation*, warning viewers that the material world will be our undoing. "I refer to an entity called The Beast," Madonna says in the film. "To me the beast is the modern world that we live in: the modern world, material world, the physical world, the world of illusion, which we think is real. We live for it, we're enslaved by it, and it will ultimately be our undoing."

The rest of the film mixes black-and-white concert footage and rehearsal scenes with reportage-style shots of Madonna's life with her husband and children, her musical director and record producer Stuart Price, and also her father. We see 72-year-old vineyard-owner Tony Ciccone, a longstanding Republican and practicing Catholic, wandering calmly through the mayhem of his daughter's working life. "My dad sent me an e-mail after he watched the movie," Madonna told *Rolling Stone*. "At the end of it, he wrote: In spite of our differences—I don't agree with everything that you say—I'm very proud of you. That's the only time my father's ever said that. I mean, he's only liked certain things I've done: my last tour, *Evita*, *Dick Tracy*, and a couple of my ballads. That's about it ... It's terrible. All my life I've been going out of my way to get my father's approval. And he's never been impressed."

The film follows Madonna as she visits key cities including Los Angeles, New York, Las Vegas, Dublin, and Paris, and along the way we hear some revealing comments about her marriage to Guy Ritchie. "I got married for all the wrong reasons," she says at one point. "My husband did not turn out to be the person I imagined him to be. ... There is no such thing as the perfect soulmate. Your soulmate is the person who pushes all your buttons, pisses you off on a regular basis, and makes you face your shit. It is not easy having a good marriage, but I don't want easy."

The final section of the film shows Madonna on a Kabbalah-inspired visit to Israel. She visits Rachel's Tomb in Jerusalem and explains that she had "a sense of really going back in time ... that I was being pulled into something." The sequence closes with a final image of peace in which two children—one Israeli, one Palestinian—walk down a road, hand in hand.

When *I'm Going To Tell You A Secret* aired in a commercial-free premiere on MTV on October 21 2005, some critics were skeptical of Madonna's desire to preach to her fans while criticizing the material wealth from which she had greatly benefited. She in turn seemed at pains to explain herself. "All I'm saying is that it took me a very long time to grow up and realize how myopic my world was," she told *Attitude* magazine, "and I'm just sharing my story. If you're going to make a documentary about yourself, you've got to tell the truth. I'm sharing my journey and if people get something out of it, great; if they don't, then that's fine, too."

The following year, *I'm Going To Tell You A Secret* was released on DVD, packaged alongside a CD of highlights from the Re-Invention World Tour. It debuted at Number 33 on the *Billboard* 200 and also appeared on the European Top 100 Albums chart.

Madonna had made it clear throughout her recent albums and tours (and indeed in *I'm Going To Tell You A Secret*) that her new worldview was very much concerned with the welfare of her fellow human beings and so it was perhaps only natural that she would be eager to take in part in two new concert broadcasts, both dedicated to human aid.

The first, in January 2005, was a star-filled two-hour concert organized by American broadcaster NBC in response to the Asian Tsunami disaster which had happened a month earlier. The show was broadcast simultaneously from Universal Studios in Los Angeles and the Rockefeller Center in New York as part of a Telethon in aid of the American Red Cross International Response Fund. Madonna was just one of the many international stars who agreed to take part.

The two-hour show, entitled *Tsunami Aid—A Concert For Hope*, began with the actor Morgan Freeman recounting tales of survival and hope from the tsunami, including that of a 60-year-old man who had survived for two weeks before being found by rescuers. Madonna then gave a performance of John Lennon's 'Imagine,' broadcast live from London, for which she wore an elegant black, knee-length dress.

The show's other performers included Elton John, Stevie Wonder, Eric Clapton, and Diana Ross. Manning the phone lines to take donations, meanwhile, was an equally dazzling array of Hollywood A-listers, including George Clooney, Brad Pitt, Leonardo DiCaprio, Uma Thurman, Nicholas Cage, and Halle Berry.

Madonna's second benefit show that year came six months later, on July 2. Twenty years after Live Aid, Bob Geldof organized another historic intercontinental event: ten concerts held simultaneously in the G8 nations and South Africa, timed to precede the G8 Conference & Summit, with proceeds to be donated to the Make Poverty History campaign in Britain and the Global Call For Action Against Poverty worldwide.

Madonna was at home in Wiltshire when she received a request from Geldof to appear in the show. She was keen to do anything she could to help, but the timing was far from ideal. "It was during the only holiday I had with my children," she told *Attitude* magazine. "When Bob Geldof started writing me letters, I thought: oh no, I just finished recording, and I just finished my film—and I'd promised my children I'd go to the countryside. They'd just finished school, and they were really mad at me."

Geldof was insistent. "Africa's more important than your children!" he told her. Before she even had had a chance to reply, she read in the newspaper that she was due to be appearing at the show in London's vast Hyde Park. Joining her on the bill were U2, Pink Floyd, Elton John, and Paul McCartney, who opened the show with 'Sgt Pepper's Lonely Hearts Club Band.' Microsoft founder Bill Gates and UN Secretary General Kofi Annan also made appearances.

Before Madonna's set, Geldof came out onto the stage to introduce 24-year-old Birhan Woldu, the young woman who had featured as a child in the 1985 CBS News report on the Ethiopian famine that had first prompted him to organize the original Live Aid. Madonna then appeared in a sharp white tuxedo. "Are you ready to change history?" she asked the 200,000-strong crowd as she took Woldu's hand. She opened her set with 'Like A Prayer,' for which she was accompanied by The London Community Gospel Choir, before moving on to a super-uptempo rendition of 'Ray Of Light' complete with body-popping and head-spinning from two freestyle dancers.

For her final number, Madonna launched into 'Music,' with almost the entire crowd swinging their arms and singing in unison to the song's chorus. She even got the paparazzi to down their cameras and join in. "That was my favorite moment," she later explained. "They were all at the front, and everyone in the park was clapping their hands except them. They were taking pictures and I looked down and said: you too! I know one of the paparazzi, Richard Young, and I said: come on, Richard, do it! He dropped his camera and the rest of them did too."

The Live 8 shows were broadcast on 182 television stations and 2,000 radio networks around the world. Madonna said it was the biggest crowd she had ever played to. Although she had performed at the Live Aid concert at the JFK Stadium, Philadelphia, 20 years earlier, she was nevertheless delighted to be on the bill once again.

"I think it's an amazing event and I was really flattered to he asked to be part of it," she told *Now* magazine. "Bob Geldof is the most dedicated, inspiring man and this really is his achievement. People have to remember what this is all about. It's so important that it's not just seen as a series of pop concerts. If it can effect change, make sure that laws are changed, infrastructure put into countries and money into the right hands, then that's something major that had been done. To me, this is all about thinking of other people. If Live 8 makes you think even for just a few minutes, then that can't be a bad thing."

After the physical strain of the Re-Invention World Tour, two global benefit shows, and a series of epic editing sessions for the subsequent *I'm Going To Tell You A Secret* DVD, Madonna may have felt understandably exhausted but she was also ready to have some fun. After all, sometimes a girl just has to let her hair down. Rather than just putting her feet up, however, Madonna went back into the recording studio. Recording her new album, she told the *Observer*, "was the antidote for the stress of that film. It was: I want to dance, I want to feel free, buoyant, happy, placated."

Since the late 90s, Madonna's album had alternated between the more cerebral, at least as far as the lyrics are concerned, with *Ray Of Light* and the more straightforward 'get down and boogie' approach. Her new album *Confessions On A Dance Floor*, was definitely more of the latter, musically at least. Although when it came to lyrics, she would continue to tackle some of the major life issues he had touched on in *American Life*, Madonna wanted her next album to be much more upbeat and direct, revisiting some of her own musical roots in 70s and 80s disco.

The result was an album which—musically at least—is pure groove from start to finish, with barely a pause for breath. From the Abba sample on the opening 'Hung Up' onward, Madonna seems intent on taking her fans on a nonstop roller-disco bonanza. Along the way there are references to her own back catalogue, with snatches of 'Papa Don't Preach,' 'Like A Prayer,' and 'Die Another Day,' alongside a kind of Greatest Dance Hits of previous decades, with samples lifted from tracks by Giorgio Moroder, The Pet Shop Boys, The Jacksons, and Tom Tom Club. It's almost as if this is Madonna's own version of the extended mixes of disco and club classics that hip DJs pioneered on the original Kiss FM radio station in New York in the 80s. Lyrically, the songs are at points as 'confessional' as the title suggests, but this rarely gets in the way of the party.

Some of the *Confessions* songs had in fact originally been intended for another project altogether. Shortly after completing the Re-Invention World Tour, Madonna agreed to collaborate with French director Luc Besson, known primarily to many for *The Fifth Element*, on a musical film about a woman looking back on her life from her deathbed, sifting through memories tainted by amnesia and senility.

Madonna had started to write material for the film, in which she was also in line to star, with Mirwais, Pat Leonard, and Stuart Price, the Musical Director on her past two world tours. The songs ran the gamut of 20th century styles, from big band swing and 60s folk to punk and contemporary electronica, but the project was never to reach completion.

"I made my own research book, and I had tons of reference material," Madonna told Simon Garfield of the *Observer*. "But when I finally got the script, it was 300 pages long and I was really not happy with it. It just wasn't what I wanted it to be."

Around the same time, Madonna's record label, Warner Bros, reminded her that she was contractually due to make another album. Loath to abandon the material she'd already written for the Besson project, she decided to incorporate it into her new album. The original plan was for her to work once again with Mirwais but, after Madonna and Stuart Price wrote 'Hung Up' together, she felt that it "resonated so monstrously" that Price should produce the whole album.

The musical connection she felt with Price, she explained, was not dissimilar to the effect of meeting a new lover. "You meet somebody, and you're already going out with somebody else, so you have this fantastic date with them, and when you go back to this other person you're with all you can do is think about that other new person," she said. "I couldn't stop thinking about how fun it was to work with Stuart. It took me a minute to decide which boyfriend I wanted to have."

When it comes to choosing producers, Madonna has always gravitated toward young, hip DJs and musicians. Price was no exception. He was 28 years old—almost 20 years younger than Madonna—and inevitably had a fresher approach than some of his older, more established colleagues. And, as a practicing club DJ, he was also very much in touch with exactly the audiences Madonna wanted to reach. "I try to keep working with interesting, creative people who are hungry, who are curious and innovative, people who aren't jaded," she told Dutch journalist Eddy Zoey. "I like to explore new territory. I like to find collaborators who think the same way."

Madonna and Price had also toured together twice by now and had got to know each other well, so their working relationship was inevitably less formal than some of the other musical collaborations she had had in the past. "It was more relaxed," she explained, "because we've toured together and been in many rehearsal situations together. We've been on planes, trains and automobiles together. And stuck in hotels. He's like my brother. I feel very comfortable with him. Usually, [when] I work with people in the studio … we have a slightly more formal relationship. That's not how it is with Stuart and me."

Madonna enjoyed Price's dry English humor as well as his capacity to work relentless hours, often staying up all night to develop tracks. She was also so delighted with the upbeat, infectiously danceable feel of 'Hung Up' that, once she and Price had finished it, she decided that it should be the model for the rest of the album. Picking up where 'Hung Up' left off, she wanted to make the ultimate house-disco album. While well aware that her own clubbing nights were behind her, she nevertheless hoped to create something that would resonate with clubbers of the current generation.

"Once we decided we were going to make a dance record, there were two promises that I made [Stuart] swear by," she recalled shortly after the album's release. "One was that that we wouldn't make any record that he wouldn't play in a club or that he couldn't make a dub version or remix of. The other was that we had to immerse ourselves in all kinds of dance music. That was our homework."

Price had a sizable collection of old vinyl, including numerous 12-inch dance mixes. The pair spent several weeks soaking up the disco glitter-ball sounds of Chic, The Bee Gees, and Hi-NRG supremos Donna Summer and Giorgio Moroder. Listening to these records over and over again, the pair would notice different elements—a bassline here, a bell sound there—that would serve to inspire their own collaborations.

The records Madonna and Price were listening to often felt like a trip down memory lane—at least for her—and the studio surroundings offered a similar source of nostalgia. Madonna had worked in super-slick, state-of-the-art studios on her previous records, but *Confessions On A Dance Floor* was for the most part recorded in Price's modest, two-room attic apartment in Kilburn, West London. The main 'studio room' contained Price's collection of old keyboards and a mixing desk, but the ceilings were so low that he couldn't stand up straight. For Madonna, however, this was all part of the charm.

"*Confessions* brought back the time I was recording my first record with Steve Bray," she recalled. "We worked in a very casual way in his apartment on the Lower East Side of Manhattan with these street sounds coming in through the windows being recorded, and not giving a shit. In a recording studio, you always sing in isolation, and I hate that. I hate being cut off from everybody … and that I can't hear what they're saying in the control room. To me, recording this album was like going back. It was so liberating. I want to be in the shit-holes. I want to be in a small place with no furniture. I want to keep it the way it was when I started, sitting on the floor and scribbling in my notebook. I work best under those circumstances."

The decision to avoid an expensive, commercial studio had evolved gradually once Madonna and Price began working together. As Price explained: "We just wanted to experiment with ideas, and seeing as I do all my other music here it made sense for Madonna to come over. Once we started working here we didn't feel the need to go anywhere else, so we just stuck with it. She likes the vocal sound here and I like being able to get up in the night and have everything there.

"When you work out of your flat you're less concerned about the money you have to spend on a studio, and more relaxed because you don't feel silly messing around with ideas in front of people you don't know," he continued. "Most dance records that I like aren't made in commercial studios. They're made in rooms like this, by someone with a little bit of equipment but the desire to get something they like out of it, and that mentality was an important part of the process."

In fact, the environment proved to be more than just stimulating for the pair—Madonna loved it. She said she found it "very magical"—so much so that after the album was completed she was keen for Price to hang on to the flat as it contained so many special memories. "I've told him that he has to keep this place because so many great things have happened here," she explained. "It feels historical to me. We've been to a thousand recording studios in New York, London, LA, everywhere, and you cannot get the same vocal sound anywhere as you get here."

Madonna's vocal sound is something she and Price play around with on the album, but on many of the tracks, it is their clever use of samples that gives these songs their extra drive. When 'Hung Up''s "tick tock, tick tock" opening leads into the powerful surge of Abba's 'Gimme Gimme Gimme (A Man After Midnight)' it gives the album an irresistibly euphoric start. The Abba original was, in fact, one of the group's darker, late-period singles, but once combined with Madonna and Price's new melody lines, it's all about the groove.

As it turned out, Madonna had been lucky to be able to use the song at all. Abba's Benny Andersson and Bjorn Ulvaeus rarely grant sample requests but the pair eventually agreed to this one after a particularly impassioned entreaty from Madonna. She had always felt a personal attachment to the group, with many of their hits coinciding with key episodes in her own younger life. "Every one of their songs is like the soundtrack to something that happened in my life," she said. "I'm sure 'Dancing Queen' was written about me! It's not just dance music, to me there's something really poetic about it. They really inspired me so to me it made sense to have an Abba sample on my record."

'Hung Up' segues neatly into 'Get Together,' which itself eases seamlessly into the majestic orchestral overture of 'Sorry.' Here Madonna solemnly recites the words "I'm sorry" in different languages as the bassline from The Jacksons' 1980 hit 'Can You Feel It' gradually rises to the fore. Once the driving disco beat kicks in, Madonna describes a scene that reflects one of the more strained moments in a marriage: "Don't explain yourself 'cause talk is cheap / There's more important things than hearing you speak."

As the final chorus of 'Sorry' fades, in comes the instantly recognizable, turbo-charged synth-bass from Donna Summer's classic 'I Feel Love,' the sample once again serving as the backdrop to a spoken intro and an almost 'Ray Of Light'-style verse. 'Future Lovers' is a clear nod to Madonna's sizable gay following, and also her own homage to the disco divas like Summer and Gloria Gaynor who both she and her fans adore. Madonna had danced the nights away to their songs back in Detroit at a time when her dreams of stardom were no more real than Tony Manero's in *Saturday Night Fever*.

The mood darkens on the ironic 'I Love New York,' the celebratory air of the previous tracks replaced with the toughness of the city itself. Over the doomy, minor-chord riff from Iggy Pop's 'I Wanna Be Your Dog,' Madonna sings a snippet of 'Love Song'—her duet with Prince from *Like A Prayer*—before deadpanning: "If you don't like my attitude, you can F off."

Madonna is in typically strident, defiant mood, but then that very defiance and "brutality" had formed a big part of her love for New York. "It's like putting your finger in a socket," she told *Attitude*. "Even though I grew up in Michigan, I really grew up in New York. Aside from when my mother died, the toughest time in my life was living in New York; being broke, having no friends, and struggling, trying to find my place in the world."

The album then returns to gentler pastures on 'Forbidden Love,' an ethereal blend of Euro-disco beats and the kind of ambient electronica popularized by French synthesizer maestro Jean Michel Jarre. The Euro-disco feel continues on 'Jump,' which has a sample from Pet Shop Boys' 'West End Girls' at its heart and a central message about facing your fears and running with them that harks back to her earliest hits.

A rare moment of pause leads into the minimalist opening of 'How High,' on which Madonna returns temporarily to the world of 21st century pop for a song that sounds not unlike 'Can't Get You Out Of My Head' by Kylie Minogue, her main rival in the hearts of her gay following. The lyrics, meanwhile, are once again more confessional than dance floor. "It's funny / I spent my whole life wanting to be talked about," she sings, before referencing a track from *Music*: "Nobody's perfect—I guess I deserve it."

After 'How High' fades out, we get a bolt seemingly from left field on 'Isaac': the voice of Yitzhak (Isaac) Sinwani, an Israeli friend of Madonna's, singing a slow, mournful version of the Hebrew poem 'Im Nin'alu,' originally made famous by Ofra Haza and successfully sampled in the 80s by the hip-hop duo Eric B. & Rakim. The beats slowly build around pizzicato strings before Madonna come in to sing a few extra stanzas.

Like Madonna, Sinwani was a student of Kabbalah, but despite coming from a family of singers he had never made a record. Madonna and Price suggested he come to the studio although they had no particular idea as to how they might use him. Once he began to sing however, they were left in no doubt. "He's flawless," Madonna recalled. "One take, no bad notes. He doesn't even need a microphone. We took one of the songs he did and I said to Stuart: let's sample these bits. We'll create a chorus and then I'll write lyrics around it. That's how we constructed it."

Madonna's lyrics once again return to the theme of addressing one's fears. "I toyed with the idea of calling the song 'Fear Of Flying,'" she recalled, "because it's about letting go ... people who are afraid to fly obviously have control issues. We all have fears in many areas of our lives. Some people can't commit to relationships. The song is about tackling all of that: will you sacrifice your comfort? Make your way in a foreign land? In other words, will you go outside of your comfort zone?"

By the time of the closing track, 'Like It Or Not,' the listener has experienced something akin to the musical arc of a DJ set, with the carefree 'Hung Up' giving way more intense and personal themes as the album progresses. "It's like: now that I have your attention, I have a few things to tell you," Madonna explained. For this final electro-chant anthem, written and co-produced by the Swedish songwriting duo Bloodshy & Avant, Madonna revisits the public's perception of her. "You can call me a sinner / You can call me a saint," she sings, before announcing—or perhaps confirming—that this is who she is, whether you like it or not. It's Madonna at her most personal, and indeed her most confessional.

The final mixing stage took place in Los Angeles, with Madonna insistent that Price also audition the tracks live in clubs. After the intimacy and cocooned comfort of Price's home studio, she needed to make sure that these new songs sounded good not just out in the real world but also—most importantly—on the dance floor itself. She was well aware that her current 'Lady Of The English Manor' lifestyle meant that she was no longer in touch with the clubbing scene, and as *American Life* had sold relatively poorly she was keen to ensure that this new batch of songs would appeal to a younger generation.

"Because Stuart DJs all over the world, we tried it all out—dub versions so they wouldn't know it was me or [versions with] only a strain of my vocal in the background," she explained. "I even made him film things for me on his telephone so I could see the crowd reaction." This was Madonna's own form of market research, and it was a failsafe. "You know within the first ten seconds if the mix is right," Price recalled, "and the first 20 if the track is good at all."

After getting to the point where she and Price were happy with the music, Madonna still needed to take care of the artwork for the CD and videos. She once again called on Steven Klein to photograph the album images, and they were, perhaps predictably, quite a radical change from the beret-and-fatigues look of *American Life*. The new-look Madonna was softer and more feminine, a *Saturday Night Fever* disco diva complete with leotard and long, strawberry blond, Farah Fawcett-style flicked hair.

Madonna planned to continue the disco theme in the video for the first single, 'Hung Up,' but was forced to change her plans shortly before filming was due to start. On August 16 2005, her 47th birthday, she was out riding on her country estate in Wiltshire, England, when suddenly and without warning her horse faltered, throwing her to the ground. It was a serious fall. Madonna suffered three cracked ribs, a broken collarbone, and a broken hand. Her doctors told her it would be 16 weeks before she could do yoga, dancing, or indeed much else.

Ever the showgirl, Madonna was however determined to prove them wrong. Within ten weeks she was on her way to Los Angeles to film the 'Hung Up' video with Swedish director Johan Renck, who had previously created the Japanese-inspired images for 1999's 'Nothing Matters.'

This time there were no guns, no explosions, and no violence. Instead, 'Hung Up' picked up where Madonna's 70s disco-flicks left off. In a clear homage to *Saturday Night Fever*, we see her swaggering along the streets of Compton near Los Angeles, (standing in for the original movie's Brooklyn) in a black leather bomber-jacket—just as John Travolta's character, Tony Manero, famously does in the film. We also see her practicing in her leotard in a mirrored dance studio accompanied only by her cassette-playing boom box (a nod to Karen Lynn Gorney, Travolta's dancing partner in the film).

Madonna's dance sequence was choreographed by Jamie King and took three hours to film. She was in significant pain for much of that time as her bones had not yet fully healed, but having already had weeks of enforced rest she was more than ready to get back on the dance floor. "Pharmaceuticals and my will got me through the shoot," she told *Harper's Bazaar*. "I felt so much inspiration and so much joy to have my body back and to feel strong again."

As had been the case so often in the past, the long hours of toil and pain paid off when *Confessions On A Dance Floor* became one of Madonna's most successful albums. Released in November 2005, it was an immediate bestseller, debuting at the top of the charts around the world. It was her sixth Number One on the *Billboard* 200, while 'Hung Up' entered *Guinness World Records* after topping the singles charts in 41 countries.

The album was not merely a commercial success. The critics loved it too. The *Village Voice* described it as "an almost seamless tribute to the strobe-lit sensuality of the 80s New York club scene that gave Madge her roots," while for *Billboard* it was "swirling, throbbing, and altogether great." Madonna was named Best International Female Solo Artist at the 2006 BRIT Awards while *Confessions* won a Grammy for Best Dance/ Electronic Album.

Madonna had proved once again that whether she appeared as virgin or whore, sinner or saint, she could make a record on her own terms and make it a success. Disco nostalgia, despite being dressed up in Price's up-to-the-minute styles, may not necessarily have been in line with the sounds which were at that point filling either the pop or dance charts, but Madonna had never been one to be cowed by musical convention. She loved every minute of her new disco queen incarnation and her fans would soon be seeing much more of it.

CHAPTER 15
TRUE CONFESSIONS

When Madonna said she had always thought of herself as Abba's 'Dancing Queen,' she clearly wasn't joking. She had made it clear on *Confessions On A Dance Floor* that she was in the mood for dancing so the obvious step was to go out on the road and take the disco with her. But although there was clearly an emphasis on fun, this was by no means to suggest that her show would be any less provocative than her audiences had come to expect. Indeed, over the coming year, controversy would feature not only on her tour but also in her personal life.

With the Confessions tour, rather than the 'greatest hits' approach of the Re-Invention World Tour, the idea this time was to support the album and simply get down and boogie, while also illustrating some of the more confessional aspects of the album. "I want to make people feel like they're inside a disco ball," she explained. "I want to explore the idea of making the dancers more personalities in the show and having their stories come out."

In March 2006, Madonna and her family headed to Los Angeles to begin rehearsals for the tour. Jamie King was once again appointed as the tour's choreographer, with Stuart Price back as Musical Director. Madonna and King had talked about wanting to the make the tour feel as intimate as possible but that did not mean that it was going to be any less dazzling than her previous shows. No fewer than 24 trailers were hired to transport the stage sets and props for the two-hour extravaganza, which included a rising and lowering 40-foot turntable that formed the centre of the main stage.

As with her previous tours, the show was divided up into different sections: equestrian, bedouin, glam-punk, and (of course) disco. Once again, the opening was nothing less than spectacular. Giant screens flashed images of Madonna, riding crop in hand, with horses cantering across windswept plains in the background. And then came the grand entrance: to the tune of 'Future Lovers' a two-ton disco ball—shimmering with $2 million worth of Swarovski crystals—lowered to the stage and opened up, lotus-like, to reveal Madonna, kitted out in Jean Paul Gaultier jodhpurs, cravat, and horse-tail hat.

The equestrian theme took its lead from a photo shoot Madonna had done some months before with Steven Klein for *W* Magazine. Provocative as ever, the shoot showed Madonna dressed in S&M-style black rubber panties, fishnet pantyhose, long PVC gloves, and a riding crop alongside six black and white stallions. But this was not about sleaze: the photographs were all shot in the monochrome style of Old Hollywood (and indeed her own *Vogue* video), lending them a high-art elegance and glamour.

The equestrian theme continued as 'Future Lovers' segued into Donna Summer's 'I Feel Love' (from which it had borrowed a bassline). For 'Get Together,' Madonna's dancers were kitted out in horses' reins; during 'Like A Virgin' she rode a diamond-encrusted carousel horse on a pole. But just in case the audience began to think the show was all fun and nothing else, the backdrops displayed the X-rays of Madonna's recently broken bones from her riding accident as well as footage of jockeys being flung from horses and other savage riding accidents.

'Jump' was accompanied by a quite literal interpretation of the song's title. Madonna had recently discovered *parkour*—the French non-competitive mix of martial arts and acrobatics in which participants run along an urban route and jump, leap, or climb over anything in their way, be it a wall, a building, or something else—and recruited some genuine *traceurs* (as *parkour* practitioners are known) from the Paris suburbs to perform on the tour. Against images of skyscrapers and vertical urban skylines, the *traceurs* ran, leaped, and indeed jumped to the music.

Madonna then left the stage, leaving the opening act to close with voiceovers of three of her dancers revealing 'confessions' about themselves. ("I live with my past tucked away deep inside of me," one said, while another spoke of cutting her arms.) Some members of the audience found this sequence surprising, if not alarming, but it was the next section of the show that was to cause major international furor.

The bedouin part of the show began with Madonna wearing crimson blouse, velvet pants, and a crown of thorns as she hung from a giant, mirrored crucifix that gradually rose from the floor. As she sang 'Live To

Tell'—her own act of confession—images of African children appeared on the screens alongside a counter that started at zero and gradually rose to a horrific 12,000,000, an estimate of the total number of African children to have been orphaned by the AIDS pandemic. The final image on the screens was a quote from *The Book Of Matthew*: "For I was hungry and you gave me food. I was naked and you gave me clothing. I was sick and you took care of me and God replied: Whatever you did for the least of my brothers … you did it to me."

Madonna stepped off the cross for 'Forbidden Love,' backed by a pair of entwined male dancers and video images of blood corpuscles connecting to form symbols of hope and unity. Moving from one world religion to another, she next welcomed Yitzhak Sinwani to the stage to blow a *shofar*—the ram's horn traditionally played during the most important Jewish festivals—and duet with her on 'Isaac.' While they sang, a female dancer clad in an oversized burka danced in a giant cage in front of footage of famine in Africa and the war in Iraq.

In the space of three songs, Madonna had managed to upset leaders from all three monotheistic world religions. "I think her idea is in the worst taste and she'd do better to go home," Mario Scialoja, the head of Italy's Muslim League, remarked, while the Russian Orthodox Church and the Federation Of Jewish Communities Of Russia described Madonna's performance as amoral and urged all members to boycott her upcoming concert in Moscow (her first ever show in Russia). Catholic leaders condemned her performance at Rome's Olympic Stadium, not far from the Vatican, as an open act of hostility toward the Roman Catholic Church, with Italian Cardinal Ersilio Tonini describing the concert as "a blasphemous challenge to the faith" and a "profanation of the cross" and calling for Madonna to be excommunicated.

As the controversy escalated, Madonna fell under increasing pressure. "My performance is neither anti-Christian, sacrilegious, or blasphemous," she said in a statement. "Rather, it is my plea to the audience to encourage mankind to help one another and to see the world as a unified whole. I believe in my heart that if Jesus were alive today he would be doing the same thing. My specific intent is to bring attention to the millions of children in

Africa who are dying every day, and are living without care, without medicine and without hope. I am asking people to open their hearts and minds to get involved in whatever way they can. Please do not pass judgment without seeing my show."

If the bedouin section of the show was unerringly provocative, the glam-punk act was considerably more straightforward. Dressed in black swans' feathers and a bomber jacket, Madonna strapped on a guitar for rocking versions of 'I Love New York' and 'Ray Of Light' while her dancers, kitted out in gangster-style black suits and white ties, performed against a backdrop of the New York skyline.

An upbeat rendition of 'Let It Will Be' followed before the mood changed once again as Madonna sat on the stage for an acoustic version of 'Drowned World/Substitute For Love.' She then brought back Yitzhak Sinwani for a similarly stripped-down take on 'Paradise (Not For Me).'

By this point, there was no doubt that the audience had witnessed the 'confessions' element of the show. Madonna now had every intention of making sure she brought them back to the dance floor on their feet. She came out for the final section—a mega-mix of 'Music' and The Trammps' 70s classic 'Disco Inferno'—in a butterfly-collared pant suit reminiscent of the iconic white suit worn by John Travolta in *Saturday Night Fever*, her dancers skating around the stage in true roller-disco style.

On the screens behind her, Madonna then took her audience on a trip to the tropics with Technicolor images of exotic islands and their fauna for 'La Isla Bonita' and 'Holiday.' Then came the grand finale—what else but 'Hung Up'? The song had by now become one of the biggest hits of her career and was here turned into an audience singalong complete with golden balloons and confetti falling from above. As Madonna left the stage for the last time, the words "Have You Confessed?" appeared on the giant screens.

Whether or not Madonna herself had confessed was moot. She has never strayed too far from controversy, and the Confessions Tour was no exception. But the by end, after 60 shows in the USA, Europe, Russia, and Japan, the tour had brought in some $200 million, making it the highest-grossing tour ever staged by a female artist. Further controversy was still to come however, this time, in connection with her personal life.

In 2006, Madonna became the center of a media furore that even she could not have predicted. Whereas in the past it had usually been her provocative stage performances or videos which had upset people, this time it was her plan to adopt a small boy from Africa.

As a result of her performance at Live 8, Madonna had begun to hear from Bob Geldof about the severe plight of children across Africa orphaned by AIDS. Some time after that, she received an unexpected call from Victoria Keelan, Managing Director of an agricultural supply company in Malawi, a small, impoverished country in Southeastern Africa, who wanted to tell her about the plight of a million children in her country. These children, Keelan explained, had been orphaned by AIDS, and many were living on the streets and sleeping under bridges. Many were also being kidnapped and raped. Madonna asked how she could help. "You're a person with resources," Keelan replied. "People pay attention to what you do."

Madonna was not entirely sure where Malawi was at that point but she began to look deeper into what Keelan had told her and was soon so struck by what she found that she decided to take action. She discovered that Malawi is in fact one of the world's poorest nations, and one of the most densely populated countries in Africa. She also learned that this small country—landlocked between Zambia, Tanzania, and Mozambique—had been hit hard by drought, had a spiraling AIDS crisis, and that the average life expectancy for its 14 million inhabitants was just 40 years old. More than half the population lived below the poverty line.

With Rabbi Michael Berg, co-director of the Kabbalah Center, Madonna founded Raising Malawi, a charitable foundation that aims "to bring an end to the extreme poverty and hardship endured by Malawi's two million orphans and vulnerable children once and for all." As the foundation's website explains: "Raising Malawi supports community-based organizations that provide vulnerable children and caregivers with nutritious food, proper clothing, secure shelter, formal education, targeted medical care, emotional care, and psychosocial support."

Madonna was also keen for the foundation to try to bring support to the people of Malawi at a grassroots level by supporting non-government organizations that offer impoverished families new opportunities for self-sufficient sustainability. In addition, the foundation pledged to raise over three million dollars. But she knew that there was no use having a foundation if nobody knew about it. What she needed to do next was to raise awareness of what she was doing. The best way to do that, she decided, was to make a documentary that showed the situation of the children in Malawi and the work of her own foundation while also following her and Guy Ritchie's progress during the course of several visits to the country.

Over the years, Madonna had often mentioned that she would one day like to try producing a movie herself. This new film seemed the perfect opportunity. But the question remained as to who she should hire as director. Her husband was an obvious possibility, of course, but in keeping with her fondness for encouraging new talent, Madonna decided to work with someone else albeit someone equally close to home.

Nathan Rissman had first worked for Madonna as a gardener, research assistant, and video archivist. "He's a brilliant, lovely guy," she told *Interview* magazine. "One of those guys who came into my life and did every job. He was a runner, an intern, a gardener. He took care of my kids. He did everything, and he did it with humility. Everyone just grew to love him and then he started doing these little movies of my children and sending them to me, and making films out of photographs and just being really creative. So one day I said I needed somebody to document this, and then I looked at him and I said: I think that person is you! And he really stepped up to the plate."

As had so often been the case in the past, Madonna's gamble appeared to have paid off. She was sure she had made the right decision as soon as they started shooting. "He cares deeply about everybody in the film," she continued. "He's spent a lot of time in Malawi, literally sleeping on the floors of people's huts and waking up with chickens on his head. He really lived it and approached it with an open heart and so much gratitude. And I think that really comes through in the movie as well—the way he films people ... people opened their hearts to him. I couldn't have done that. I don't have his simple approach."

The film opens with Madonna walking amid a crowd of Malawians. In a voiceover, she tells us: "People always ask me why I chose Malawi, and I tell them I didn't. It chose me." The movie then goes on to trace Madonna's own voyage of discovery to Malawi as she finds out more herself.

"When I went there for the first time, I saw that I needed to document my journey," she explained. "More specifically, I wanted to go on a journey with these children to find out for myself what was going to make a difference in their lives and document that. ... The more I went to Malawi and observed things, the more I realized that people are layered, so solving their problems is layered. The worst thing you can do to help a person is to just throw a bunch of stuff at them and run away. That doesn't work with anybody."

I Am Because We Are details Madonna's various visits to the country's orphanages as well as the work of Raising Malawi in helping to improve the children's lives. "To say that this film is a labour of love is trivial," she explained at Cannes. "It's also the journey of a lifetime. I hope you all are as inspired watching it as I was making it."

As the film continues, we see harrowing black-and-white photography of AIDS sufferers alongside moving footage of Malawian life. Intercut with these scenes are candid interviews with world leaders including Bill Clinton and Desmond Tutu—the result of many petitioning letters from Madonna—as well as some extraordinary stories from ordinary citizens. Some of these convey indescribable suffering: a woman who was subjected to a sexual ordeal in order to be 'cleansed' after the death of her child; a boy who was mutilated in a brutal superstitious ritual; a dying mother who wonders what will become of her soon-to-be-orphaned son. Other scenes show women and children dying of AIDS right in front of the camera.

When asked whether she had intended the film to be so disturbing, Madonna explained: "I wanted to tell the truth. Believe me, I took out some of the incredibly harrowing stuff. My goal was to make a film that would serve the interests of the people of Malawi."

When it came to naming the film, Madonna took inspiration from *ubuntu*, an African philosophy that acknowledges "the common links and bonds between peoples of all kinds," and which contains the saying "I am because we are." As Madonna notes on raisingmalawi.com: "Translated simply, it means: without you there is no me. Your fate is mine. We are all inextricably connected. This is why we strive to raise Malawi."

I Am Because We Are premiered at the Tribeca Film Festival in New York and the Cannes Film Festival in France during the spring of 2008. It then began airing on the Sundance Channel in the USA on December 1 2008—World AIDS Day—and received almost universally positive reviews. The UK's *Times* newspaper called it a "shocking and incredibly moving film," adding: "If Madonna wants us to see her as more than the gyrating, gym-obsessed Queen of Pop, she has succeeded powerfully." A companion book containing color photographs taken during the visit and stills from the film was released in January 2009, with all author proceeds donated to Raising Malawi.

But it was not the film itself which was to cause an outcry. During one of their first trips to Malawi, Madonna and Guy visited the Home For Hope orphanage, where they met 13-month-old David Banda. They were immediately enchanted by the small boy. Madonna had been thinking of adopting for some time, and following her discovery of the situation in Malawi she began to think that, as she had set up the foundation and was campaigning on the country's behalf, it made sense to adopt from there.

"There are no accidents," she told the BBC's *Newsnight*. "Right around that time, I started my foundation, Raising Malawi, and the more information I got about the children and the number of orphans that were there, it seemed quite obvious: if you want to go to Africa and adopt a child, you might as well go to Malawi."

Madonna had seen film footage of David before she met him and felt drawn to him from the start. "I kept saying: who's that baby? Who's that boy?" she explained. "I was drawn to something about his face, his eyes." When the Ritchies arrived in Malawi, however, they were alarmed by how ill he was. David had a high temperature, was bleeding from diaper rash, and was having difficulty breathing. Madonna arranged for him to be taken to a clinic where, after tests, he was diagnosed with pneumonia.

Conditions at the orphanage were far from ideal, with 500 children living in one hall and receiving only one frugal meal a day. Concerned for David's survival, Madonna enquired about his personal circumstances. The Reverend who ran the orphanage told her that David's father was in fact alive but lived far away and had no car, so subsequently he never visited.

Madonna enquired about the possibility of adopting David and taking him home to live with her family. She discovered that the adoption process was relatively informal in Malawi, but that one of the few laws that did exist stated that provisional parents wanting to adopt children from the country needed to have lived there for at least 18 months before an adoption could be granted. Madonna's unusual circumstances were taken into consideration, however, and an exception was granted. (She later explained that she had also offered financial support to David's father, should he wish to care for the child himself, but that he had declined the offer in favor of the proposed adoption.)

Once news of this was publicly announced, the international reaction was far from unanimous. While many considered Madonna's adoption of a child from an impoverished situation to be admirable, others were highly critical. Some felt that she had bent the rules; ordinary people, without either money or celebrity, often find it much harder to adopt. The international aid community felt particularly strongly about it—so much so that a coalition of more than 60 aid agencies and children's charities mounted a legal challenge to get the adoption blocked.

Madonna was shocked by the extent of the antagonism toward her, not to mention the level of international coverage the story generated. "What happened with the adoption and the world's reaction to it was quite shocking," she told *Newsnight*. "There was no way I could have prepared myself for it." She had anticipated some cynicism, but not on this scale. "I didn't expect to be accused of kidnapping or doing something illegal," she told Meredith Vieira on NBC's *Today*. "I didn't expect to be demonized."

Under pressure from the weight of the scandal, Madonna issued a public statement. "After learning that there were over one million orphans in Malawi, it was my wish to open up our home and help one child escape an extreme life of hardship, poverty, and in many cases, death, as well as expand our family," she explained. "Nevertheless, we have gone about the adoption procedure according to the law like anyone else who adopts a child. Reports to the contrary are totally inaccurate." She also confirmed that she had agreed to take David home to see his remaining relatives once every few years.

The media outrage gradually died down. Despite the distress the publicity had caused her, Madonna eventually felt that the experience had in some way been positive. "All the criticism is ultimately a blessing in disguise," she said, "because now people know about Malawi and David's home." She also wanted to get the Malawian legislation changed, she added, in order to make it easier for other people—whatever their circumstances—to adopt.

Despite years of courting controversy herself, Madonna found this latest episode more traumatic than she could have imagined. But it had by no means daunted her taste for exploring new fields and having taken her first step into film production, she now felt ready to make a further move into film, this time with a fictional plot.

While she was producing *I Am Because We Are,* she had also become involved in another movie project, this time a dramatic feature that she not only co-wrote and produced but also directed. The film—eventually titled *Filth And Wisdom*—started out as a short but gradually grew into a full-length musical comedy-drama.

The plot centers around a group of young hopefuls in London as they search for meaning in their lives (a meaning here reflected through Madonna's own Kabbalah-inspired beliefs). The main character is A.K., a lanky, mustachioed Ukrainian émigré played by Eugene Hutz. A.K. believes that the path to enlightenment—and economic survival—lies in confronting the seamy side of life, and with this in mind he funds his dreams of rock'n'roll stardom by moonlighting as a cross-dressing dominatrix who tortures masochists for money.

A.K shares his apartment in a decaying block with two attractive female room-mates: Holly, a gifted dancer who works as a stripper and pole dancer at a nightclub but dreams of becoming a prima ballerina; and Juliette, who fantasizes about traveling to Africa to help impoverished children but meanwhile works at a pharmacy, where she surreptitiously procures medicine for charity as well as for her own recreational use.

British actor Richard E. Grant—star of the cult classic *Withnail And I,* among many other films—plays Professor Flynn, a blind poet surrounded by books he can no longer read. *Filth And Wisdom* also features several performances by Gogol Bordello, Eugene Hutz's real-life New York-based gypsy-punk group, who deliver impassioned songs in a style once described as midway between Joe Strummer and Borat.

When asked why she had wanted to break into directing films, as well as writing and producing them, Madonna explained: "I've been inspired by films since I started dancing, and I'm married to a filmmaker. I think it was one of my secret desires, but I was afraid to just say: I want to be a director. But then one day I said: OK, stop dreaming and do it. But I didn't want to do it the Hollywood way, and talk through agents. I decided it all had to be generated by me, so I wrote it … it was my film school."

Madonna had long been impressed with mid-20th-century European directors like Jean-Luc Godard, and it was to Godard and his European contemporaries that she turned for inspiration. "I feel this film was seriously influenced by Godard," she said. "He's the one filmmaker I was always inspired by, but I have a lot of others I was inspired by—all dead Europeans. I went to the University Of Michigan for one year, and fortunately they had a foreign-film cinema, and I discovered it, and I thought I died and went to heaven. I discovered Fellini and Visconti and Pasolini and De Sica and Buñuel."

The film eventually received its world premiere at the 2008 Berlin Film Festival before being released, in an unusual move, through iTunes. The reviews were exceedingly mixed, with many critics highly dismissive. James Christopher of the *Times*, however, was impressed. "Madonna has done herself proud," he wrote. "Her film has an artistic ambition that has simply bypassed her husband, the film director Guy Ritchie. She captures that wonderfully accidental nature of luck when people's lives intersect for a whole swathe of unlikely but cherishable reasons. Altman-esque would be stretching the compliment too far, but *Filth And Wisdom* shows Madonna has real potential as a director."

Madonna had for many years expressed an interest in directing films herself and with *Filth And Wisdom* she had finally taken that step. The result had not received widespread acclaim but nor had it ruffled any feathers. Her next move was to return to what she had always done best and begin work on a new album. That did not mean she would stay out of the headlines for long, but next time the news would be of a different nature altogether.

CHAPTER 16
THE NEW DEAL

The history of rock'n'roll is littered with stories of artists who were financially exploited by their record companies, but from the very start of her career Madonna seemed determined not to join that particular list. On the contrary, she has built a reputation not only for shrewd artistic decisions but also for sharp business acumen.

It was to be this side of her career that would make headlines toward the end of 2007. Before that, however, Madonna was due to appear in another international benefit show, this time in aid of a cause which was starting to capture headlines worldwide.

"We're starting an avalanche of awareness but we are running out of time," Madonna told an 80,000 strong crowd at Wembley Stadium in July. "Tonight's concert and the concerts going on around the world are not just about entertainment—they're about starting a revolution! Amen!"

In February 2007, former US Vice President Al Gore and concert producer Kevin Wall had announced plans for a series of international benefit concerts to combat climate change. Inspired by the 2005 Live 8 event and the original 1985 Live Aid show, the concerts were planned to take place in July and would bring together more than 150 acts, including Madonna, in eleven cities across five continents.

Madonna had first expressed her own concerns about the environment as early as 1998's *Ray Of Light*, so was delighted to be asked to take part. Hers was to be the closing performance of the July 7 concert at London's Wembley Stadium, where she was to perform alongside Genesis, Red Hot Chilli Peppers, Black Eyed Peas, and The Beastie Boys, among others. With tens of thousands packed into the stadium and millions watching on television and online worldwide, British actor Terence Stamp introduced Madonna to the stage. "Let's not be endarkened by this, let's be enlightened by this," Stamp told the audience as all of the 'non-essential' lights in the stadium were symbolically turned off. "Let it be the beginning of an adventure."

Madonna then came out in a demure black silk dress and began her set with 'Hey You,' a new song she'd written especially for the show (and which was also used as the bridging music between the other acts playing at Wembley). The song encourage people to take action "to keep it together" and "make it all right." As Madonna began to sing, a long line of children in school uniform appeared behind her to sing backing vocals while huge screens displayed images of world leaders like George W. Bush and Gordon Brown intercut with footage of natural disasters and the earth seen from space.

After a gypsy-flavored 'La Isla Bonita,' Madonna closed the show with a triumphant, show-stopping rendition of 'Hung Up.' The stage backdrop was transformed into a *Saturday Night Fever*-style wall of disco lights as Madonna led the vast crowd into a chant of "Time goes by / So slowly."

The Live Earth shows were broadcast in over 130 countries and watched by some 19 million viewers in the USA as well as nearly half of all households in Canada, 37 per cent of all those in Brazil, and 20 per cent in Germany. Madonna's 'Hey You' was released as the main charity single for the campaign, and for an initial weeklong period it was available as a free download from websites like MSN, with Microsoft pledging to donate 25 cents per copy to the Alliance For Global Climate Change for the first million downloads.

Madonna had made her stand for a much-needed change in the way the world views its resources. Now she was about to make significant changes closer to home. In October 2007, after more than 20 years with Warner Bros, Madonna decided to leave her record label in favor of a new deal with Live Nation, the concert promoter behind the Live 8 events. Record companies and concert promoters were having to find ways to diversify in response to the threat of online piracy and dwindling album sales, and this new deal—worth a reported $120 million and covering the next ten years of her career—was a landmark for the music industry. While the traditional record deal was primarily focused on recording rights, this new agreement also covered touring, merchandising, and more.

The deal gave Live Nation exclusive rights to promote Madonna's highly lucrative tours, but was slanted hugely in her favor: she would receive 90 per cent of the profits from her live performances. She also received a signing bonus of around $18 million, and was due an advance of around $17 million for each of the three albums she had agreed to deliver. The agreement also incorporated future music and music-related businesses, including the various subsidiaries of the very profitable Madonna brand: merchandising, fan club, website, DVDs, music-related television and film projects, and associated sponsorship deals.

Madonna had not simply turned her back on her old label. Her management had offered Warner Bros the chance to match the deal, but the company refused. In a press statement, Madonna said that she was drawn to the deal with Live Nation because of the changes the music business has undergone in recent years. "The paradigm in the music business has shifted, and as an artist and a businesswoman, I have to move with that shift," she said. "For the first time in my career, the way that my music can reach my fans is unlimited. I've never wanted to think in a limited way ... with this new partnership, the possibilities are endless."

The Live Nation deal marked the end of an era for Madonna. She had been associated with Warners since that first fateful visit to Sire Records mogul Seymour Stein's hospital bed in New York in 1983. The label in turn had supported her as her career grew over the decades.

Madonna had not by any means forgotten her early years, however. A few months later, in March 2008, she received one of the music industry's ultimate accolades when she was inducted into the Rock & Roll Hall Of Fame. She accepted the award with a speech in which she sounded unusually overawed by the occasion. She thanked those who had encouraged her from the start: her first guitar teacher; Seymour Stein, who was present in the audience; managers past and present; her PR and assistants. She spoke of how she had been "miraculously and continuously possessed by some kind of magic" in her ability to write songs, and how music remained central to her career. "I have gone on to do so many things in my life," she said, "from writing children's books, to designing clothes, to directing a film. But for me it always does, and it always will, come back to the music, so thank you."

Most acts—if they are ever inducted at all—tend to receive the honor at the tail end of their career, since the rules stipulate that an artist only becomes eligible for the Hall Of Fame 25 years after the release of their first single or album. This year was the first in which Madonna could be nominated, so she was doubly honored to be inducted. Her fellow inductees in 2008 included Leonard Cohen, John Mellencamp, and two 60s groups: pop band The Dave Clark Five and guitar-twang instrumental combo The Ventures.

After a video montage showing the various stages of her career, Madonna was introduced to the stage by Justin Timberlake. The boy-band supremo turned megastar gave a long speech in which he talked about how Madonna had "changed the way our world sounded [and] the way our world looked" before noting that "the world is full of Madonna wannabes. I might've even dated a couple," he quipped, "but there's truly only one."

After Madonna herself spoke, fellow Detroit native Iggy Pop gave 'Ray Of Light' his own inimitable punk treatment. His performance culminated in one of his characteristic dives into the audience. Madonna looked nothing short of delighted.

Madonna's meeting with Timberlake was to prove fortuitous for them both. Having gone against the grain of contemporary musical trends with *Confessions On A Dance Floor,* for her next album Madonna began to feel that maybe now was the time to finally embrace the sound that was proving so successful for chart-topping acts like Timberlake and others.

In the three decades since she had started out, Madonna had tried on just about every dance style for size, from house to electronica to disco, with the exception of the one that just so happened to be the biggest-selling sound of the early 21st century. It was surely only a matter of time, then, before she decided to make an R&B album.

For *Hard Candy*, her final album for Warner Bros, Madonna chose to follow in the footsteps of the new generation of female stars—the Britneys, the Nelly Furtados, and the Gwen Stefanis—by trying to work her magic on the sound of urban R&B. She had historically always been the trailblazer herself, taking the left-field and the avant-garde and bringing it into the mainstream with her unflinchingly commercial ear (and in doing so inspiring the rest to follow in her wake) but at this point in her career it seemed to make sound commercial sense to follow the hottest trend.

Madonna was not turning her back on her own style: *Hard Candy* may have a mainstream urban-dance sound, but it still gives the nod to the 80s disco of her early work, the 70s Philly Soul sound of her youth, and the strong melodies that have always been so integral to her music. As Timbaland, one of the album's key producers, put it: "It's kinda like 'Holiday' with an R&B groove."

If *Confessions On A Dance Floor* had marked Madonna's return to the dance floor, *Hard Candy* continues in that mode, but with a frothier, more playful, and more bawdily humorous feel. And whereas *Confessions* offered light relief after the pressures of a global tour, *Hard Candy* similarly gave Madonna the chance to relax and laugh a little after the long hours spent editing *I Am Because We Are*.

"I would go from sitting watching hours and hours of footage of people dying, to going to the studio," she explained. "I cut out a lot of stuff that people just couldn't handle—a lot of really painful things. And to see this imagery over and over again, of mothers weeping, burying their children, and vice-versa … I needed a release from that."

Returning to the recording studio gave her that release. The album's opening track, 'Candy Shop,' seems to sum up the notion that the record works almost as an assortment of candy, offering up some tracks that are pure sugary indulgence and others that are a little more bitter to the taste. In a track-by-track rundown to promote the album, Madonna described the song as one of her favorites, adding that it "personifies the mood I was in when I was making the record: kind of cheeky, wanting to have fun, play on words, wanting to dance, lots of innuendo.

"I put it first because it also is a kind of illustration of the variety of songs that are on the record," she continued. "So hopefully there are more serious songs, more up-tempo songs, and more thoughtful songs." And indeed there are, from the turbo-charged '4 Minutes' and the irrepressibly anthemic 'Give It 2 Me' to the more somber and grandiose 'Devil Wouldn't

Recognize You' and 'Voices.' Lyrically, meanwhile, the album is in some ways even more autobiographical and personal than *Confessions*.

When it came to choosing collaborators for *Hard Candy*, the solution seemed obvious. After finishing work on *Confessions On A Dance Floor*, producer Stuart Price asked Madonna what she wanted to do next. "I want to make dance music, as always," she replied. "Well, what kind of music do you like right now?" he asked. "Well, the only records I love are Justin [Timberlake]'s and Timbaland's," she said. "Why don't you work with them?" Price said. And so she did.

The tall, Virginia-born Tim 'Timbaland' Moseley first rose to fame when he produced Aaliyah's *One In A Million* and Missy Elliott's *Supa Dupa Fly* in the 90s, and had since put his musical stamp on the work of everyone from Jay-Z and Nelly Furtado to Mariah Carey and Wyclef Jean. He was also closely associated with the sound of white R&B megastar Justin Timberlake, the former boy-band star currently being hailed, amid much hyperbole, as the new Michael Jackson (and a gossip-column regular for having previously dated Britney Spears). If Madonna wanted to connect with a new, younger audience, choosing to collaborate with Timbaland and Timberlake was an unquestionably smart idea.

Ever loath to assign full responsibility to just one producer, however, Madonna also approached another pair of Virginians: Pharrell Williams and Chad Hugo, aka The Neptunes. The Neptunes' list of past production credits was at least as impressive as Timbaland's, with Kelis, Britney Spears, Jay-Z, and The Rolling Stones among their clients. Between them, these were the most successful producers of the day: if Timbaland had been responsible for a sizable proportion of chart hits in recent years, then most of the others came courtesy of The Neptunes, who in 2003 were averaging around five hits a week on the *Billboard* Hot 100.

As well as producing chart hits on a grand scale, The Neptunes also managed to maintain a slightly cultish reputation as crazy sound alchemists who conjured up pop gems in their studio lab, and this was yet another aspect that appealed to Madonna. She had chosen in the past to work with less overtly commercial producers from Europe, like Mirwais, Price, and William Orbit, but on this album it was almost as if she wanted to recapture the energetic sound of her early 80s hits and come home to the sound of mainstream America.

While always keen to experiment and push artistic boundaries, Madonna has forever had one ear on the charts. She pays close attention to what the public is most likely to want, and at this point in 2007, the answer, unquestionably, was R&B-pop. Even after 25 years of chart success and some 200 million record sales, Madonna was "still trying to make those hits. Everybody wants to make music that people want to listen to—that people want to hear on the radio," she told Canada's *Jam! Showbiz*. "I've never, ever made a record where I didn't care whether people heard it or not."

Whenever she wanted to create a new sound, Madonna had always looked to her working partners not only to produce her albums but also to collaborate in the writing process. *Hard Candy* was no different. She and Timberlake eventually came up with five tracks for the album, including the first single, '4 Minutes.' The other seven songs were co-written by The Neptunes' Williams.

Perhaps inevitably, there were some battles in the studio when these four outsize characters—Madonna, Timberlake, Timbaland, and Williams— began to work together. Madonna was used to keeping to a fairly strict routine, working the hours she wanted, and, in the case of the *Confessions* album, leaving Stuart Price to burn the midnight oil while she went home to her family. Timberlake, Timbaland, and Williams were different. They were used to working nights, too, but they expected Madonna to do the same and were reluctant to change their routines for Madonna's sake.

There was also the small matter of ego to contend with. As Madonna herself put it, there were "four divas" working on this album. "It was different for me," she explained in an interview with German television's *TAFF*. "I usually work with producers who are sort of behind the scenes people—they don't go out on tour, they don't make their own records, they're not usually stars in their own right so we definitely had to get used to each other's energy. They have very strong opinions—so do I—and that was a bit of an adjustment but it turned out great in the end."

The writing process had a similarly rocky start. Madonna had got to know Stuart Price well by the time they sat down to write together. Working with Timberlake and Williams was a different story altogether. "It's not like we hit it off right away," she explained. "Writing is very intimate. You have to be vulnerable and it's hard to do that with strangers. I had ups and downs before everybody got comfortable, but I grew very fond of Pharrell and Justin."

Despite being a phenomenally successful songwriter in her own right, Madonna later told the BBC's Jo Whiley that, because she didn't really know either of her new partners, she had felt a little "nervous and intimidated" when she first sat down with them. She was used to writing melodies on her guitar but was aware that the initial acoustic sound could often be some way from the end result she had in mind.

"That's not how you mean it to sound once you put a bassline and drums and stuff, so there's that moment of embarrassment where you think: I'm gonna play this for you but it's not gonna sound exactly like this," she recalled. "You have to get over yourself and stop worrying about people not liking your lyrics and whether they're gonna think it's corny. And Justin admitted to me to me the other day that he felt the same way, so everyone goes through that."

The embarrassment soon subsided when Madonna and Timberlake began playing around with ideas and phrases. Some days one of them would come into the studio with an idea for a title and the other would pick it up and fill in the rest. On others Madonna would bring in an entire idea with a complete set of lyrics.

On other occasions Madonna would hear a brief snippet of music and be inspired to write a lyric. 'Miles Away'—one of the softer, more acoustic tracks on the album, with its Hispano-reggae ballad feel—was a case in point. "When I heard the music," Madonna recalled, "I immediately started singing and the words came and I don't know where they came from."

The words might have come to her in a seemingly random way but they clearly refer to the difficulties of maintaining a long-distance relationship— something Madonna subsequently referred to in interviews, admitting that she was "tapping into the global consciousness of people who have intimacy problems." Her and Guy Ritchie's respective work commitments often meant that they were on opposite sides of the Atlantic for days or weeks at a time. Some of the words to 'Miles Away' are intensely personal, to the extent that they added further fuel to rumors of problems in Madonna's marriage.

There is a similarly introspective feel to two of the other songs Madonna and Timberlake wrote together, 'Devil Wouldn't Recognize You' and 'Voices,' which ended up as the album's closing tracks. As with *Confessions*, Madonna wanted to take listeners on a dancehall voyage, and as such the album starts in a place of buoyancy, builds to a crescendo, and then eases down to a gentle 'chill-out' section at the end.

After a brooding, cinematic opening, 'Devil Wouldn't Recognize You' presents a typically melodic vocal about somebody who has "everyone in their life" and who "gets away with everything." 'Voices' continues the sober theme, referring, as Madonna later put it, to people who "could trick you into thinking one thing about them [when] actually they were something else. People that play mind games, and go on ego trips and they don't realize. Are you walking the dog, or is the dog walking you? Who's in control?"

Both songs started life when Madonna and Timberlake were "riffing off each other." They quickly found a strong rapport, both in terms of ideas and in their approach to songwriting. They spent long hours discussing ideas for lyrics during what Madonna later described as psychoanalytic sessions. "We'd sit down and we'd start talking about situations," she told *Interview* magazine. "Writing together with somebody is very intimate, so we had to find a place to start talking about something we cared about ... that was fun, because he's open and he's got talent." There hadn't been many other occasions, she added, when she'd felt so instantly connected to another songwriter. "He's as interested in the rhythm of the words as [their] meaning ... and so am I."

Madonna and Timberlake might have been interested in lyrics but they were also keen to make some upbeat dance music, from the nostalgic, 80s-sounding 'Dance 2Night' to the monumental, quasi-gangsta '4 Minutes,' on which Timbaland makes a cameo appearance with a guest rap. The song opens with his trademark horns and a driving, military beat before Madonna and Timberlake sing about a kind of comic-strip teen-romance scenario in which they've "only got four minutes to save the world."

The song evolved piecemeal, as did many of the other tracks on the album. It started with the beat, as provided by Timbaland; Madonna and Timberlake then wrote the lyrics and melody line around it, before Timbaland added further layers of music. Lyrically, the song seemed to sum up Madonna's approach to life at the time, tapping into ideas about taking responsibility for the world around you but also finding time to enjoy yourself at the same time. "It's about waking up to the world around you," she said. "We all have our part in it, we all need to be part of the solution, not the problem. We also want to have a good time while we're saving the world. It's not *all* serious and suffering. I do consider myself to be an activist, but I also am a person that wants to have fun."

As it turned out, some of that fun came from working with Timberlake and Pharrell Williams. Despite describing him as a "smooth operator," Madonna liked Williams's childlike sense of humor. It was clear from the start that this was not a man who took himself too seriously. Every day, on arriving at the studio, he would reach for his outsized luxury Hermes bag, take out a pair of comedy Mickey Mouse slippers, and proceeded to put them on, explaining that they were "lucky."

Williams's approach to making music was similarly unpretentious. Madonna immediately appreciated his spontaneity. "I think Pharrell is a natural musician," she told *Dazed & Confused*. "I like his inventiveness. He would grab my acoustic guitar—he couldn't play, but he start playing percussion on it. He would find bottles and start playing them with spoons. He is very inventive in the studio, he's not precious, and I like his lo-fi approach to making music."

Madonna also welcomed his ideas and suggestions. 'Spanish Lesson,' a frenetic hybrid of R&B beats and the Hispanic-influenced pop Madonna had trademarked on hits like 'La Isla Bonita,' was inspired by what Williams described as the B-More beat or "the percolator," a new style of chopped-up, staccato beats coming out of Baltimore, Maryland. Ever open to experimentation, Madonna agreed to try it out, and she and Williams wrote the song around it on the spot.

With Madonna and co working on the basis that if you couldn't dance to it, it wouldn't make it onto the record, even the more soul-searching songs were set to dance beats. 'She's Not Me' evokes Debbie Harry and Gloria Gaynor as Madonna tells a lover that "it won't feel the same" with someone new over an old-school bassline and guitar by Wendy Melvoin, formerly of Prince's Revolution. The more straightforward, low-key R&B of 'Incredible' refers in part to at least one aspect of her marriage, but there's a hint that the best is in the past. "Everything in life just goes wrong," she sings. "Feels like nobody's listening / And something is missing."

"I think every woman experiences all the emotions that are in all of those songs," she explained in a German television appearance to promote *Hard Candy*. "I think we've all been deceived before, I think we've all been left or abandoned before, I think we've all suffered loss or heartbreak, and we've also taken people for granted and wanted to make things right again. The song 'Incredible' is about … being taken for granted and taking somebody else for granted, which we're all guilty of."

If these are the album's slightly crunchier moments, there's no shortage of softer-centered toffee elsewhere. 'Beat Goes On' is a poppy nod to Detroit techno with a guest appearance by hip-hop superstar Kanye West; 'Give It 2 Me' is a similarly infectious and euphoric hybrid of trance and R&B.

Both songs are unstoppably upbeat. In the case of 'Give It 2 Me,' the sense of euphoria reflects the fact that, by the time it was recorded, Madonna had already completed most of the album, and both she and Pharrell Williams were in need of some light relief. "By the time we got to that stage of the record," she explained, "we just felt that we needed to make some crazy, uptempo dance record."

Meanwhile, when asked by *Interview* magazine about the sense of urgency in 'Beat Goes On,' Madonna laughed as she recalled that there was indeed a rush as West only had four hours to record the track before he caught a plane. The result nevertheless represents exactly what one might have expected of a collaboration between the pair: Madonna putting her own vocal and melodic stamp on Kanye West's urban club sound, and an almost 'Into The Groove'-style chorus adorned by breakout beats.

As she had done in the past, Madonna conducted her own private 'market research' while making the album, playing individual tracks to her children, her husband, and her friends to gauge reactions before releasing it to the public. Once again, her efforts paid off as *Hard Candy* debuted at Number One in 37 countries, while '4 Minutes' provided her with her 37th US Top Ten hit. She had previously been tied with Elvis Presley when it came to the highest number of Top Ten hits on the *Billboard* Hot 100, but now The Queen Of Pop had surpassed even The King.

CHAPTER 17
STICKY & SWEET

One of the problems with success on a grand scale is that it is often a hard act to follow. Consequently, when it came to thinking about building a live show around her *Hard Candy* album, Madonna had a dilemma. The spectacular Confessions Tour had been the highest-grossing tour ever by a female artist, so when you've dazzled your fans with show-stopping extravaganzas, artistic experimentation, and spellbinding visuals, where do you go next?

The answer came from *Hard Candy* itself. If the new album was the sound of her letting her hair down and taking the vibe of *Confessions On A Dance Floor* one step further, the Sticky & Sweet Tour, as it would be known, simply took the party vibe out on the road, bringing the dance floor to the stadium. The Confessions Tour had been a party show too, but it had also contained its fair share of messages. This time, the polemic would be kept to a minimum. Madonna and her dancers would be concentrating on getting into the groove for a nonstop party.

This did not mean that the show was going to be any less spectacular than her previous tours, however. A crew of 250 joined Madonna on her travels around the globe, and she was to wear no fewer than eight different outfits during the show, most of them designed by the long-serving Arianne Phillips, her costume designer of choice since *Ray Of Light*, but with some additional pieces by new Givenchy designer Ricardo Tisci, as well as Miu Miu shoes and Moschino sunglasses. Gucci designer Tom Ford provided bespoke suits for the band.

As before, the show was divided into four acts: a pimp-themed opening, supposedly a concoction of 20s Art Deco and the "modern-day gangster-pimp"; an old school journey through the hits of yesteryear; a gypsy section, which was more or less as its name suggested, a mix of Romanian folk music and dance; and, to close, a rave built on Eastern influences.

The tour opened on August 23 2008 in Cardiff, Wales, with a 3D computer animation on giant screens showing candy being manufactured and used as a pinball (described by one journalist as "equal parts *Charlie & The Chocolate Factory* and Mousetrap"). As the video ended, Madonna appeared on an M-shaped throne in a black Givenchy minidress, fishnets, and thigh-high Stella McCartney boots, legs spread apart, dominatrix-style, wielding a cane, while her dancers performed in similarly bondage-themed costumes to the sounds of 'Candy Shop.' "She's not afraid of being hard," Arianne Phillips noted. "It's a theme that runs throughout her career. She always wants to push the envelope. There are no vanity considerations based on her age."

The next two songs featured onscreen appearances by three recent celebrity collaborators: Pharrell Williams and Kanye West on 'Beat Goes On,' and Britney Spears on 'Human Nature.' For the first, Madonna and her dancers, dressed in pastel-colored hot pants, performed around an Auburn Speedster—the 1935 equivalent of a Ferrari or a Porsche; the second song was given a 2008 update with vocodered backing vocals, while the video screens showed Madonna and Britney trapped in an elevator under the gaze of a security camera.

The 'pimp' section of the show closed with a mash-up of 'Vogue' and '4 Minutes' followed by a synchronized boxing match set to 'Die Another Day.' Then it was on to the old school section, an irreverent homage to Madonna's 80s Manhattan roots and the early days of hip-hop. Madonna kicked off proceedings in track shorts and bobby pins for 'Into The Groove,' skipping over a rope as cartoon images by her late friend Keith Haring, the seminal New York graffiti artist and cartoonist, flashed on the screens behind her. The urban theme continued as Madonna strapped on a purple electric guitar for a rocked-out 'Borderline' before embarking on a typically self-referential sequence for 'She's Not Me.' A quartet of dancers came out dressed as different incarnations of Madonna's earlier self: the 'Like A Virgin' bride; the Material Girl in a silk dress; the Blond Ambition-era bombshell in Gaultier-style conical bra; and the Girlie Show gamine. Madonna tore at their respective outfits one by one, proudly ripping up the past and dragging her audience firmly into the present.

A disco version of 'Music' followed, mixed in with bursts of Fedde Le

Grand's electro anthem 'Put Your Hands Up 4 Detroit' and Indeep's 1982 club classic 'Last Night A DJ Saved My Life.' 'Rain' then brought the old school act to a close in a mash-up with Eurythmics' electro-pop hit 'Here Comes The Rain Again' while the video wall showed a graffiti-covered subway train and an animated pixie taking shelter under a petal during a rainstorm.

The gypsy-themed part of the show began with Madonna perched atop a grand piano, cloaked in a black shroud, for 'Devil Wouldn't Recognize You.' The next track, 'Spanish Lesson,' featured a flamenco-influenced solo by Russian gypsy dancer Alexander Kolpakov. After a guitar-led 'Miles Away,' it was time for the highlight of the show: 'La Isla Bonita,' complete with fiddles, flamenco, and what else but a Romanian folk tune. As the song drew to an end, Madonna marched to the front of the stage with her troupe of gypsy violinists, the Kolpakov Trio, before leaving the players to take center stage for a solo star turn.

Madonna returned after the instrumental interlude for an acoustic rendition of 'You Must Love Me' before moving on to the only message-laden part of the show. She had for the most part resisted the temptation to proselytize on this tour, but 'Get Stupid' was to be the moment in which she implored the audience to "save the world" with a video interlude showing world disasters, from global warming to famine, intercut with images of Republican Presidential candidate John McCain, Adolf Hitler, Barack Obama, Mahatma Gandhi, and other world leaders.

After the bitter pill of politics, Madonna wasted no time in offering her crowd a full array of candy-like sweeteners with a series of non-stop hits even if the next number, '4 Minutes,' was not without its own message. Except on the odd occasion when her celebrity co-stars were available to join her in person, Madonna duetted with life-size virtual versions of Justin Timberlake and Timbaland before moving on to a raved-up remix of 'Like A Prayer' (incorporating snippets of 'Feels Like Home'), 'Ray Of Light,' and a guitar-rock version of 'Hung Up.'

The show ended with the crowd-pleasing 'Give It 2 Me,' a song Madonna said she had written, in part, "so I could have a great time doing it in a stadium." As she predicted, the song had the vast crowds jumping up and down and singing along to every word of the chorus while Madonna egged them on with the autobiographical lyrics that clearly refer to her love of provocation: "Got no boundaries, got no limits ... If it's against the law, arrest me." As the song reached its climax and Madonna left the stage, the giant screens flashed the words "Game Over."

The Sticky & Sweet Tour comprised 85 dates and ran well into 2009. Perhaps inevitably, some of the shows were affected by world events. During her performance at Petco Park, San Diego, on November 4 2008, Madonna congratulated the newly elected Barack Obama on his landmark win for the Presidency of the United States. "This is a historical evening," she told the crowd during the intro to 'Express Yourself.' "This is the beginning of a whole new world. Are you ready?" The following year, during the European leg of the tour, Madonna incorporated a dance tribute to Michael Jackson into the show after hearing the news of his death in June 2009.

Further tragic news followed a month later in Marseille, Frances, where Madonna was due to play the Stade Vélodrome on July 19. While the roof of the set was being assembled, the stage collapsed, injuring eight technicians and killing two, one French and the other British. The show was subsequently canceled. "I am devastated to have just received this tragic news," Madonna said in a statement. "My prayers go out to those who were injured and their families along with my deepest sympathy to all those affected by this heartbreaking news."

Madonna subsequently visited the other technicians injured in the accident and paid her respects to the families of those who had died. She likewise interrupted her show in Udine, Italy, on the day of the accident, to speak of her devastation at the news and invite the audience to say a prayer for the two men.

It was an unforeseeably tragic episode, but the tour continued. By the time Madonna had played her final date, in Tel Aviv, Israel, she had performed to 3.5 million fans in more than 30 countries. Sticky & Sweet was the highest-grossing tour ever staged by a solo artist—and second only on the all-time list to The Rolling Stones' Bigger Bang tour of 2005–07. It brought in $408 million, easily breaking the record Madonna herself had set with her Confessions Tour and doubling what Coldplay—at the time one of the biggest rock bands in the world—had earned on their own 2008–09 tour.

Madonna celebrated her 50th birthday on August 16 2008, and it seemed somehow fitting that she should mark this point in her life and indeed her career with a new compilation of hits. The aptly titled *Celebration* was as self-referential as ever. The artwork featured a pastiche of Andy Warhol's famous screen-printed images of Marilyn Monroe, with a *True Blue*-era photograph of Madonna, designed by New York street-pop artist Mr Brainwash, in place of Monroe.

Unlike the previous *GHV2*, this collection spans and indeed celebrates Madonna's entire career, incorporating not only her major hits of recent years, such as '4 Minutes,' 'Miles Away,' and 'Hung Up,' but also older gems from the early years, from 'Holiday' and 'Like A Virgin' through to 'Into The Groove' and 'Justify My Love.' *Celebration* was released in 2009 in several different formats, including an 18-track standard edition and a double-disc deluxe version featuring two brand new recordings, 'Celebration' and 'Revolver.' A third new song, 'It's So Cool,' was made available through iTunes.

An upbeat Euro-pop house track clearly aimed at the dance floors of Ibiza and beyond, 'Celebration' was one of several new songs Madonna began working on in 2009 with British superstar DJ Paul Oakenfold, who had opened several dates on the Sticky & Sweet Tour. Just as had been the case with other collaborators in the past, Oakenfold had initially sent Madonna a selection of tracks he was working on for an album of his own. Of these, Madonna picked out 'Celebration,' which Oakenfold had co-written with two of his colleagues, Ciaran Gribbin and Ian Green. She then added her own lyrics.

'It's So Cool'—co-written by Madonna with guitarist Monte Pittman and Mirwais, and co-produced by Oakenfold—is a similar exercise in Hi-NRG Euro-disco, seemingly the default sound of Madonna's 21st century hits. She had recently confessed to having written 'Give It 2 Me' with the stadium in mind; 'It's So Cool,' with its anthemic "We need love" chorus, was surely conceived in the same way.

'Revolver' sees Madonna adopting a slightly darker cloak. It features a cameo by the US rapper Lil Wayne and is pitched somewhere between the sound of Britney Spears and British electro-pop act Goldfrapp. Lyrically, meanwhile, Madonna has her tongue very firmly in her cheek as she takes on the persona of some kind of female sex-goddess incarnation of Clint Eastwood in *Dirty Harry*. "My love's a revolver / My sex is a killer," she sings. "Do you wanna die happy?"

A DVD compilation, *Celebration: The Video Collection*, was released to coincide with the album. It features promo videos for many of the tracks as well as unedited and previously unseen footage of 'Justify My Love.' It also contained the newly completed video for 'Celebration,' which was released as the first single from its parent album in August 2009. Directed by longtime Madonna favorite Jonas Akerlund, the clip shows her partying and getting up close and personal with the DJ in a club—played by 22-year-old Brazilian model Jesus Luz—while a selection of dancers (including daughter Lourdes) break-dance.

Celebration reached the Top Ten across Europe, as well as in the USA, Canada, Australia, and New Zealand, while the title track became Madonna's 40th Number One hit on the *Billboard* Dance Club chart. *The Video Collection* debuted at the top of the *Billboard* Top Music Videos chart and was subsequently certified platinum by the RIAA.

The success of *Celebration* was further evidence, if any was needed, of Madonna's enduring popularity. But while professional glory was hers in abundance, musically at least, on a personal level, 2008 would prove to be particularly difficult year. But she would not allow that to prevent her from moving on to ever more varied and ambitious ventures.

In the summer of 2008, just as the tour was about to begin, Madonna's younger brother, Christopher, published a warts-and-all autobiography entitled *Life With My Sister Madonna*. The pair had always been fairly close. Christopher had worked for his sister as a dresser and interior designer, and had also served as a designer and director on her Blond Ambition and Girlie Show tours. Over the previous year, however, they had gradually become estranged.

Co-written by Wendy Leigh, Christopher's book not only revealed many intimate aspects of his sister's life and their relationship but also portrayed her in a less than flattering light. Sibling spats, break-ups, and make-ups are described in detail, as is Christopher's increasingly strained relationship with his brother-in-law, Guy Ritchie. The book generated huge amounts of publicity worldwide. Perhaps unsurprisingly, it debuted at Number Two on the *New York Times* Best Sellers list, and was a million-seller worldwide. Madonna was said to be furious about its very existence.

While giving media interviews about the book, Christopher also began to confirm the rumors that had begun to circulate about his sister's marriage, claiming that the relationship was held together only by regular visits from a Kabbalah Rabbi who acted as a marriage counselor. The couple had reportedly pledged to reduce their respective work schedules and ensure that they did not spend more than a week at a time apart, while also agreeing to support one another's interests and career choices where necessary.

Around the same time, Madonna was named in the divorce proceedings of 32-year-old New York Yankees baseball star Alex Rodriguez. He and Madonna had reportedly been seen dining together on several occasions in New York and were said to have developed a "close friendship." (Madonna was quick to deny any allegations of an affair.)

Eventually, on October 15 2008, after months of press speculation, publicist Liz Rosenberg announced that Madonna and Guy Ritchie were indeed to divorce. A variety of reasons were given for the deterioration in the couple's marriage. Madonna's intensive touring schedule and Ritchie's own film projects had meant that the pair had for some time begun to lead increasingly separate lives, often communicating only through their personal assistants. Ritchie, meanwhile, had reportedly become disillusioned with Kabbalah, and this, it was said, had increased the rift between them. The final blow reportedly came when Madonna announced that she wanted the family to relocate to the USA against Ritchie's wishes.

Rosenberg explained to the press that relations between the couple were still cordial, and that they expected to agree a divorce settlement without going through the courts. There were still significant details to be agreed, however. Apart from the financial settlement, the main area for potential disagreement was over the children's education, with Ritchie keen for his son Rocco, in particular, to be privately educated in England and raised as a Londoner rather than a New Yorker, as Madonna wished.

Madonna hired top British divorce lawyer Fiona Shackleton, who had represented Prince Charles and Paul McCartney in their respective divorces from Princess Diana and Heather Mills. Just over a month later, on November 21, in London's High Court, the couple were granted a 'quickie' divorce. The settlement was said to include a payment to Ritchie of between $76 million and $92 million. According to a statement issued by Rosenberg, this included their country home, Ashcombe, in Western England, and their London pub, The Punchbowl. The couple eventually agreed to share custody of their children.

Meanwhile, the Sticky & Sweet Tour continued, with Madonna explaining that she was grateful for the distraction provided by a heavy workload. "I'm sad about my personal life," she told the Associated Press in November, "but I feel very blessed and very lucky that I have the opportunity to do what I do in my professional life. It would be horrible if I was just thinking about getting a divorce and had nothing to do."

A month later, the couple were temporarily reunited and spent part of the Christmas vacation together with 12-year-old Lourdes, eight-year-old Rocco, and three-year-old David. Madonna then took the three children to the Maldives to see in the New Year.

While Madonna and Guy were still married, the news emerged that Madonna was keen to adopt another child from Malawi: a four-year-old girl named Chifundo 'Mercy' James. "Many people—especially our Malawian friends—say that David should have a Malawian brother or sister," she explained. "It's something I have been considering, but would only do if I had the support of the Malawian people and the Government."

Madonna had first met the little girl in 2006, when she was just 13 months old and living in the same orphanage as David Banda. There she learned that Mercy's 18-year-old mother had died soon after she was born, and that the girl's father's whereabouts were unknown. Ritchie's alleged lack of support for the plan to adopt Mercy reportedly provided another divisive factor in the collapse of their marriage, although matters became further complicated when Madonna's newly single status was seen as a potential obstacle in the adoption process.

She was reportedly incensed that her divorce might mean the application was rejected. "Madonna has always been a tough independent woman and is now, more than ever, of the opinion that she doesn't need a man for anything in her life," a friend of the singer told the *Sun* newspaper. "If she falls at the last hurdle because of her marital status, it will be hard to swallow. She is already talking about starting a campaign for single mums to be allowed to adopt the world over. She believes that if you have love to offer, the fact you are divorced, widowed, or unmarried should not be seen as a barrier."

The adoption application was further hindered by the fact that, once again, Madonna had not fulfilled the Malawian Courts' stipulation that those wishing to adopt should first live in the country for at least 18 months. Eventually, however, an Appeal Court decided to override those criteria on the basis that "every child has the right to love." "We are supporting her because she is supporting over 25,000 orphans in this country through Raising Malawi," Malawian Information Minister Patricia Kalaiti told the *Times*. "We can also see that she is looking after David so well and she really loves this country."

"This is who I am / You can like it or not," Madonna sang on 'Like It Or Not.' "You can love me or leave me / 'Cause I'm never gonna stop." In these two short lines, Madonna summarized what for many has been her most enduring legacy—a resolute determination to succeed on her own terms, regardless of what rules she broke or whose nose she put out in the process. And indeed, nearly 30 years on from her first record release, there are no signs of her stopping any time soon.

Madonna has become a diva renowned for playing the music industry at its own game and on her own terms, but she also realized early on that could not achieve longevity by resting on her glamorously gilded laurels and that an ability to adapt her music and style was essential. Although she herself has dismissed the media's obsession with her seemingly endless capacity for reinvention, understandably feeling that there is more to her than a gift for chameleon-like image changes, the concept has nevertheless unquestionably been one of the defining hallmarks of her career. The very notion of Madonna has become irredeemably linked with her now-iconic series of images, from the black-lace punk of her early days through the silver screen icon of the 'Vogue' period, to the 70s disco of 'Hung Up' and her most recent incarnation as a raunchy electro-pop diva.

But with so much focus on her changing visual image, what is perhaps more often forgotten is her phenomenally impressive track record as a songwriter. Despite her 'look at me' stance, she has always backed up her neon-flashing provocatease with quality songwriting and artistic verve. For most of her career, along with a shrewd awareness of the need to keep the public on their toes, Madonna has succeeded through a combination of sheer drive, business acumen and writing talent.

Since she first emerged in the early 80s, the musical landscape has of course changed radically. The success of televised talent searches has led to the predominance of highly marketed and increasingly homogenous teen-pop. Interestingly, however, the female pop acts who stand out are often those who owe more than a little to Madonna herself, with Lady Gaga the most obvious example. But Gaga is just the latest of several generations of female stars for whom Madonna paved the way, from Gwen Stefani, Christina Aguilera, Shakira and Britney Spears to Alison Goldfrapp.

Despite changing musical trends, Madonna has always found ways to remain current. She has cleverly associated herself with new talent, whether in the form of producers and co-writers like Nellee Hooper, Stuart Price, Paul Oakenfold and Timbaland or cutting-edge designers and photographers. Her long-term working relationships with boundary-pushing photographer Steven Klein and the equally edgy video director Jonas Akerlund have likewise played a key part over the last decade in ensuring that Madonna is never far from the shock register.

But whereas earlier on in her career, Madonna used shock tactics to challenge people's ideas about women and sexuality, since discovering the teachings of Kabbalah, she has become more interested in influencing people's notions about how to live their lives in the broader sense. "In the beginning of my career, I just did whatever I wanted to," she explained in 1998. "If it made me feel good, if it was fun, that was cool. Now I feel like everything we do—the movies we make, the music, the stuff that's on television—affects society in a potent way. I feel a sense of responsibility because my consciousness has been raised and I would like to impart the wisdom I have to others without being corny or preachy."

This has not meant however that Madonna has any intention of backing down in her capacity to thumb her nose at people's expectations. She has repeatedly defied critics who have skeptically decreed her too old to remain at the top. As far back as 1998, before the release of *Ray Of Light,* comments began to appear about her age and they resurfaced again when she signed her historic deal with Live Nation a decade later. Some observers believed that, as the deal covered her next ten years of albums and live shows, Madonna had received by far the better part of the bargain, assuming that her years of success were surely behind her. But Madonna proved them wrong in 1998 and seems likely to do so again and again.

"I'm not going to be defined by my age," she told *Elle* magazine in 2008. "Why should any woman? I'm not going to slow down, get off this ride, stay home, and get fat. No way!" And indeed why should she slow down? After all, if Tina Turner and Cher can continue filling stadia well past their 60s, why not Madonna? The idea of her retiring to enjoy her millions and live a life of indolent poolside luxury is clearly anathema to her and recently, in addition to her music and acting, she has made various forays into fashion design.

In late 2006, international high street fashion chain H&M announced the launch of its 'M By Madonna' line. But rather than just lending her name to the collection, as some celebrities might have done, Madonna worked closely with H&M's Head Of Design, Margareta Van Den Bosch, inviting her to view her own wardrobe for inspiration. The plan was to create a collection which not only reflected Madonna's own combination of elegance and femininity but which was also wearable and fashionable. There was to be something for everyone: from evening tops to lumber jackets, tailored blazers and pencil skirts to blouses and kimono dresses.

Each of the pieces had a discreet 'M' motif on the linings, zips, and buttons, and the colors were largely neutral. There was also a range of accessories, including square-toed patent heels, clutch bags, skinny belts, and sunglasses. "Madonna has an impressive feel for fashion and trends," Van Den Bosch said. "She is a total professional, inspiring and enthusiastic. She was involved in even the smallest details of every design."

The promotional campaign was shot by Steven Klein and showed Madonna looking soft and feminine in key pieces from the collection, notably a black-and-white kimono dress. The clothes were instantly successful, with hundreds of people waiting outside H&M stores worldwide in the hope of being the first to buy their own piece of Madonna fashion. Many braved freezing temperatures from six in the morning in London, while in Stockholm the entire line sold out in a matter of minutes.

In light of her first collection's success, it was perhaps no surprise that in the summer of 2011 Madonna launched a second foray into fashion, this time with a teenage collection for Macy's called Material Girl, inspired by and co-designed with her daughter Lourdes. Among the clothes, footwear, handbags, and jewelry, many pieces were inspired in typically self-referential style by Madonna's own early fashions with an abundance of studs and lace and (of course) a bustier. "If you're a Material Girl," she explained, "you're a girl with a sense of humor."

Back in the world of adult fashion, Madonna subsequently designed a range of eyewear for her long-standing friends and collaborators Dolce & Gabbana, which she advertised herself with an accompanying campaign photographed by Steven Klein.

For Madonna, fashion has always also been inextricably linked in her mind with the movies. Ever since taking her seat behind the camera for *Filth And Wisdom*, she was keen to return to directing. She finally did so with the high profile yet ill-received *W.E.*, a historical drama about American divorcée Wallis Simpson and her relationship with King Edward VIII starring Abbie Cornish and James D'Arcy.

As if all that was not enough to be getting along with, she also launched her own chain of gyms, Hard Candy Fitness, in Mexico City and Moscow in 2011, and there are reportedly plans afoot to 'extend the brand' worldwide. Most recently, it has been rumored that Madonna is interested in buying a nightclub in London. Given her capacity for shrewd deal-making in her musical career, all the evidence would suggest that she is likely to be equally successful in other business endeavors.

In what little spare time she has, Madonna has also made a name for herself as a serious art collector and in the past she has mentioned that she'd like to learn to paint, but so far she has hesitated in making her own moves in the art world. "People say I should just do it," she once told Q magazine. "But I think not, because what if I suck? I'd be so disappointed."

Although financial motivation may be little more than a distant memory, she still clearly has a hunger to explore new avenues. And why shouldn't she? "I can't imagine not working," she once said. "Obviously I'm going to change and grow and be interested in different things. But I can't remember when I wasn't doing this. I mean, when I was a teenager, I was throwing myself into dance and doing crazy musicals, and I have not stopped since then. I cannot imagine not being creative in some way. I can't live without it. I don't know what I'll do, but I'll do it."

Whatever Madonna does, it seems likely she'll approach it in the same way she has handled her career from the start—on her own terms. As William Orbit once presciently observed: "Madonna's on this journey, and if you're smart you'll get on board for the ride. But it doesn't matter if you do or you don't, because she's going to get there anyway."

ENDNOTES

The numbers below indicate the pages on which the relevant quotes are used in the book.

CHAPTER 1
THE EARLY YEARS
5   "He wanted to be upwardly mobile" Denise Worrell, *Time* (May 27 1985)
6   "She was really funny" Christopher Ciccone, *Life With My Sister Madonna*
6   "a very lonely girl" Michael Gross, *Vanity Fair* (December 1986)
7   "We were one of the only" Mick St Michael, *Madonna … In Her Own Words*
7   "one of many proofs" Christopher Ciccone, *Life With My Sister Madonna*
7   "I wasn't rebellious" Michael Gross, *Vanity Fair* (December 1986)
8   "one of the best students" Robert Matthew-Walker, *Madonna: The Biography*
8   "I've never met anyone" Christopher Ciccone, *Life With My Sister Madonna*
9   "I was kind of taken" Christopher Anderson, *New York Magazine* (October 14 1991)
9   "That's necessary" Lucy O'Brien, *Madonna: Like An Icon*
10   "the bug in her ear" Christopher Anderson, *New York Magazine* (October 14 1991)
11   "She was fun, you know" Douglas Thompson, *Madonna: Queen Of The World*

CHAPTER 2
THE ARRIVAL
14   "I got so excited" Colin Devenish, *Rolling Stone* (August 2005)
15   "Madonna is great" Rikky Rooksby, *The Complete Guide To The Music Of Madonna*
15   "I was really scared" Lee Randall, *The Madonna Scrapbook*

16   "she came up to me" Christopher Anderson, *New York Magazine* (October 14 1991)
16   "the street cred she needs" Christopher Ciconne, *Life With My Sister Madonna*
17   "I thought he might" Barney Hoskyns, *New Musical Express* (November 5 1983)
17   "I wanted to push her" Douglas Thompson, *Madonna: Queen Of The World*
17   "I thought she had" Rikky Rooksby, *The Complete Guide To The Music Of Madonna*
18   "not-so-great but affecting" J. Randy Taraborelli, *Madonna: An Intimate Biography*
20   "You're either on this" Rikky Rooksby, *The Complete Guide To The Music Of Madonna*
20   "It's changing now" Barney Hoskyns, *New Musical Express* (November 5 1983)
21   "Though her voice sounded thin" Grek Kot, *Chicago Tribune* (May 13 1990)
21   "The sparse grooves and electro effects" Gavin Martin, *Uncut* (2001)
22   "The picture inside the dust sleeve" Denise Worrell, *Time* (May 27 1985)
23   "The way we dress" Kris Needs, *Flexipop!* (May 1983)
23   "For Madonna it was meant" madonnatribe.com (2006)
23   "She came to me" madonnatribe.com (2006)
24   "I remember when she" Lee Randall, *The Madonna Scrapbook*
24   "She sounded black" Christopher Anderson, *New York Magazine* (October 14 1991)

25 "At least I don't have" Phil Sutcliffe, *Q* (September 2003)

25 "The first expensive thing I bought" Lee Randall, *The Madonna Scrapbook*

25 "In America, Warners don't know" Barney Hoskyns, *New Musical Express* (November 5 1983)

CHAPTER 3
LIKE A VIRGIN

26 "I now know what I want" Barney Hoskins, *New Musical Express* (November 5 1983)

26 "It's funny about" Douglas Thompson, *Madonna: Queen Of The World*

28 "stand next to God" *The Face* (February 1985)

29 "I was hanging out" Daryl Easlea, *Everybody Dance*

29 "One morning Bernard was" Daryl Easlea, *Everybody Dance*

30 "chosen all the songs" Mick St Michael, *Madonna. In Her Own Words*

30 "They were ironic and provocative" Austin Scaggs, *Rolling Stone* (October 29 2009)

31 "God forbid irony should" J. Randy Taraborrelli, *Madonna: An Intimate Biography*

31 "represents the first time" Danny (Shredder) Weizmann, *LA Weekly* (1990)

31 "turning crass product into" John Leland, *Spin* (August 1985)

32 "I was surprised with how" Mick St Michael, *Madonna. In Her Own Words*

34 "I said: do you want" Daryl Easlea, *Everybody Dance*

37 "Few people knew that" Daryl Easlea, *Everybody Dance*

37 "*Like A Virgin* was a fluke" Daryl Easlea, *Everybody Dance*

CHAPTER 4
INTO THE GROOVE

39 "Madonna was someone" Christopher Anderson, *New York Magazine* (October 14 1991)

40 "There was so much" Mick St Michael, *Madonna ... In Her Own Words*

40 "I thought I was going to" J. Randy Taraborelli, *Madonna: An Intimate Biography*

42 "Susan wasn't a character" Andrew Motion, *Madonna* (MM Books 2001)

43 "That whole tour was crazy" Boz Scaggs, *Rolling Stone* (October 29 2009)

44 "In the first week" Robert Matthew-Walker, *Madonna: The Biography* (Pan 1989)

47 "Madonna is tiny" Michael Francis

49 "nailed her signature sound" Lucy O'Brien, *Madonna: Like An Icon*

49 "the supreme archetype" Sal Cinquemani, *Slant* (March 9 2003)

50 "a very pure expression" Allan Metz and Carol Benson, *The Madonna Companion*

50 "She was very much in love" Mick St Michael, *Madonna ... In Her Own Words*

50 "a great reworking" Dave Marsh, *The Heart Of Rock & Soul*

52 "We had a spirited discussion" Fred Bronson, *The Billboard Book Of Number 1 Hits*

53 "Immediately they're going to say" Stephen Holden, *New York Times* (July 10 1986)

54 "For the first time" Dave Marsh, *The Heart Of Rock & Soul: The 1001 Greatest Singles Ever Made*

58 "Fewer sales and less attention" Davitt Sigerson, *Rolling Stone* (July 17 1986)

CHAPTER 5
VIDEO STAR

60 "If I didn't have a video" Rikky

Rooksby, *The Complete Guide To The Music Of Madonna*

64 "From the time we" Mick St Michael, *Madonna ... In Her Own Words*

64 "an incredible actor" Carol Clerk, *Madonnastyle*

64 "I admit it" Carol Clerk, *Madonnastyle*

65 "my stunned admiration" Camille Paglia, *Sex, Art, And American Culture*

65 "I had some very specific ideas" Fred Bronson, *The Billboard Book Of Number 1 Hits*

66 "You'll see a different look" Brett Milano, *Chicago Tribune* (July 26 1987)

67 "very hands-on" Carol Clerk, *Madonnastyle*

70 "It was just grueling" Mick St Michael, *Madonna ... In Her Own Words*

CHAPTER 6
IN THE MIDNIGHT HOUR
72 "write about growing up" *The Face* (February 1985)

72 "I wrote what I felt" Lucy O'Brien, *Madonna: Like An Icon*

73 "I've been dealing with" Mick St Michael, *Madonna ... In Her Own Words*

73 "She was upset and in tears" Lucy O'Brien, *Madonna: Like An Icon*

73 "TIME IS MONEY" Guy Pratt, *My Bass And Other Animals*

74 "To me total control" Mick St Michael, *Madonna ... In Her Own Words*

76 "When I think of controversy" Glenn O'Brien, *Interview* (June 1990)

77 "She's always willing" Mick St Michael, *Madonna ... In Her Own Words*

77 "Beg me not to go with boys" Rikky Rooksby, *The Complete Guide To*

The Music Of Madonna
77 "growing up I thought" *Daily Express* (August 10 1986)

78 "Catholicism gives you an" Denise Worrell, *Time* (May 27 1985)

78 "own personal zeitgeist" Austin Scaggs, *Rolling Stone* (October 29 2009)

78 "Sometimes I'm racked with guilt" Bill Zehme, *Rolling Stone* (March 23 1989)

78 "You know how religion is" Glenn O'Brien, *Interview* (June 1990)

79 "I do believe religion" Carol Clerk, *Madonnastyle*

79 "some aspect of morality" Guy Pratt, *My Bass And Other Animals*

80 "Madonna's command of massive" Camille Paglia, *Sex, Art, And American Culture*

80 "If you don't express yourself" Rikky Rooksby, *The Complete Guide To The Music Of Madonna*

81 "Ever since I've known Prince" Carol Clerk, *Madonnastyle*

82 "It's very much drawn" Mick St Michael, *Madonna ... In Her Own Words*

86 "full of lava lights" Guy Pratt, *My Bass And Other Animals*

86 "My first couple of albums" Rikky Rooksby, *The Complete Guide To The Music Of Madonna*

86 "the tribulations of the last" Lloyd Bradley, *Q* (April 1989)

86 "proof that not only" J.D. Considine, *Rolling Stone* (April 6 1989)

86 "most accomplished and mature" Kreg Kot, *Chicago Tribune* (May 13 1990)

86 "Ex-Boy Toy Turns Herself" Jonathan Takiff, *Atlanta Journal Constitution* (March 24 1989)

87 "The overall emotional content" Mick St Michael, *Madonna ... In Her Own Words*

CHAPTER 7
I'M BREATHLESS

89 "I've created five different worlds" Glenn O'Brien, *Interview* (June 1990)

89 "There were these male dancers" Luc Sante, *The New Republic* (August 20/27 1990)

90 "The look of the tour" Luc Sante, *The New Republic* (August 20/27 1990)

91 "her vocals on 'Express Yourself'" *Variety* (May 30 1990)

92 "It took me so long" Mick St Michael, *Madonna ... In Her Own Words*

94 "The record company went bananas" Fred Bronson, *The Billboard Book Of Hits*

96 "It's easy to forget" Gene Sculatti, *The Immaculate Collection* liner notes

97 "truly avant-garde" Camille Paglia, *New York Times* (December 14 1990)

97 "Why is it that" *People* (December 17 1990)

97 "Madonna can turn catastrophes" Lynn Hirschberg, *Vanity Fair* (April 1991)

97 "People can say I'm" Robert Matthew-Walker, *Madonna: The Biography*

99 "unrevealing puff piece" Robert Matthew-Walker, *Madonna: The Biography*

99 "I'll film you without make-up" Lucy O'Brien, *Madonna: Like An Icon*

CHAPTER 8
THE MAVERICK

104 "I want a real record label" Mick St Michael, *Madonna ... In Her Own Words*

104 "Although Time Warner executives" Stephen Holden, *New York Times* (April 20 1992)

105 "My goal, of course" Carol Clerk, *Madonna Style*

105 "incorporate them into my" Andrew Motion, *Madonna*

105 "The news that Madonna" Barney Hoskins, *Times* (November 13 1991)

106 "My drive in life" Lynn Hirschberg, *Vanity Fair* (April 1991)

106 "He doesn't give you" Mick St Michael, *Madonna ... In Her Own Words*

108 "I'm dealing with sexual liberation" Mick St Michael, *Madonna ... In Her Own Words*

108 "an oversized, overpriced" Richard Harrington, *Washington Post* (October 21 1992)

108 "presenting portraits of sexual freaks" John Champagne, Pamela Robertson, *Guilty Pleasures*

108 "There is the feeling that" Martin Amis, *Observer* (October 11 1992)

108 "I called my book *Sex*" Mick St Michael, *Madonna ... In Her Own Words*

109 "She was learning that" Andrew Motion, *Madonna*

109 "I divide my career" Bob Guccione Jr, *Spin* (January 1996)

110 "All the writing was done" Rikky Rooksby, *The Complete Guide To The Music Of Madonna*

114 "simultaneous brilliance and baloney" Phil Sutcliffe, *Q* (December 1992)

114 "The biggest disappointment" Mick St Michael, *Madonna ... In Her Own Words*

116 "the birth of neo-soul" Daryl Easlea, bbc.co.uk (June 30 2009)

117 "She reminds me of" Carol Clerk, *Madonna Style*

118 "It was an effective way" Stephen M. Silverman, *People* (June 15 2004)

CHAPTER 9
DANGEROUS GAMES

122 "It had such a different" Richard Zoglin, *Time* (January 20 1997)

CHAPTER 10
DON'T CRY FOR ME

CHAPTER 11
BEAUTIFUL STRANGER

173 "'Ray Of Light' is just" musicomh.com (March 2006)
174 "We hadn't met before" Lucy O'Brien, *Madonna: Like An Icon*
174 "Like any toddler" Johnny Black, *Q* (August 2002)
175 "She stepped out" Paul French, *Q Special Edition* (2003)

CHAPTER 12
HEY, MR DJ

179 "It's a real statement" *Jane* (March 2000)
180 "I think gay men" *Next* (April 11 2000)
180 "too corny for words" *Next* (April 11 2000)
181 "Everything in life moves" *Billboard* (September 15 2000)
181 "There's the frivolous side" *The Face* (August 2000)
182 "He has a great wit" *Ladies Home Journal* (July 2005)
182 "stimulated by the cool" *US Weekly* (October 2 2000)
183 "For a lot of people" *V* (July 2000)
183 "I'm always searching for something" *Billboard* (September 15 2000)
184 "I was intent on making" *Billboard* (September 15 2000)
184 "You notice that what" *Crash* (May 2000)
184 "I just kind of threw" *US Weekly* (October 2 2000)
185 "We were working on that" *Billboard* (September 15 2000)
187 "a song about loving someone" *The Face* (August 2000)
187 "swallowing that bitter pill" Ingrid Sischy, *Interview* (March 2001)
188 "Everyone thinks and writes" Ingrid Sischy, *Interview* (March 2001)
190 "Mom, are you going to get married?" *US Weekly* (October 2000)
191 "There was a certain direction" Lucy O'Brien, *Madonna: Like An Icon*
191 "I never want to repeat myself" Ingrid Sischy, *Interview* (March 2001)
192 "I want to arrive on a spaceship" drownedmadonna.com (2006)
193 "I'm looking forward" Ingrid Sischy, *Interview* (March 2001)
194 "Her music for that moment" madonnatribe.com (2005)
195 "doing things girls aren't allowed to do" Andrew Motion, *Madonna*
195 "It's basically one note" Paul French, *Q Special Edition* (2003)

CHAPTER 13
DIE ANOTHER DAY

198 "It's a great part" Christopher Ciccone, *Genre* (October 2002)
198 "I liked the challenge" Alan Riding, *New York Times* (September 8 2002)
199 "I just thought it was" Alan Riding, *New York Times* (September 8 2002)
199 "I think it would have been" Alan Riding, *New York Times* (September 8 2002)
200 "Because people were expecting" Alan Riding, *New York Times* (September 8 2002)
200 "The song I wrote for" Christopher Ciccone, *Genre* (October 2002)
202 "we as Americans are completely" Eddy Zoey (BNN, 2003)
204 "I want to write about something" Eddy Zoey (BNN, 2003)
204 "The songs just come to me" Eddy Zoey (BNN, 2003)
205 "Very cerebral, very philosophical" Simon Garfield, *Observer Music Monthly* (November 2005)
205 "I wanted to wake people up" *Friday Night With Jonathan Ross* (BBC1, May 2 2003)
209 "Was that planned or was it" *The Oprah Winfrey Show* (September 16 2003)

209 "I feel really protective of her" Ingrid Sischy, *Interview* (March 2001)

210 "If you read the classic" Callie Northagen (Home Shopping Network, November 24 2006)

210 "I didn't really know what" *The Today Show* (NBC, June 2005)

211 "When morning came" Madonna, *The English Roses* (Calloway, 2003)

212 "I feel like it's a privilege" Callie Northagen (Home Shopping Network, November 24 2006)

212 "It felt really good to publish" *Ladies' Home Journal* (July 2005)

CHAPTER 14
RE-MAKE, RE-MODEL

214 "Madonna has created a new" David Segal, *Washington Post* (June 15 2004)

215 "I like the idea of being restrained" madonna.com (2005)

216 "I wanted to make a statement" madonna.com (2005)

217 "If I'm going to take people" *Vogue* (August 2005)

217 "I refer to an entity" Madonna, *I'm Going To Tell You A Secret*

218 "My dad sent me an email" Neil Strauss, *Rolling Stone* (December 1 2005)

218 "I got married for the wrong reasons" Madonna, *I'm Going To Tell You A Secret*

218 "All I'm saying is" Adam Mattera, *Attitude* (November 2005)

220 "That was my favorite moment" Adam Mattera, *Attitude* (November 2005)

221 "I think it's an amazing event" *Now* (June 29 2005)

221 "was the antidote for the stress" Simon Garfield, *Observer Music Monthly* (November 2005)

223 "You meet somebody" Simon Garfield, *Observer Music Monthly* (November 2005)

223 "I try to keep working with" Eddy Zoey (BNN, 2003)

223 "It was more relaxed" Simon Garfield, *Observer Music Monthly* (November 2005)

223 "Once we decided we were" *Andrew G's Excellent Adventure* (Channel V, November 29 2005)

224 "*Confessions* brought back the time" Neil Strauss, *Rolling Stone* (December 1 2005)

225 "We just wanted to experiment" *Mixmag* (December 2005)

225 "I've told him that" Adam Mattera, *Attitude* (November 2005)

225 "Every one of their songs" *Andrew G's Excellent Adventure* (Channel V, November 29 2005)

226 "It's like putting your finger" Adam Mattera, *Attitude* (November 2005)

227 "He's flawless" Keith Caulfield, *Billboard* (October 23 2005)

227 "I toyed with the idea" Keith Caulfield, *Billboard* (October 23 2005)

228 "It's like: now that I have" Keith Caulfield, *Billboard* (October 23 2005)

228 "Because Stuart DJs" Simon Garfield, *Observer Music Monthly* (November 2005)

228 "You know within the first" *Mixmag* (December 2005)

229 "Pharmaceuticals and my will" *Harper's Bazaar* (April 2006)

CHAPTER 15
TRUE CONFESSIONS

231 "I want to make people feel" Neil Strauss, *Rolling Stone* (December 1 2005)

235 "You're a person with resources" *I Am Because We Are* (Madman Films, 2008)

236 "He's a brilliant, lovely guy" Ingrid Sischy, *Interview* (April 2008)

236 "He cares deeply about everybody"
    Ingrid Sischy, *Interview* (April 2008)

237 "People always ask me" *I Am
    Because We Are* (Madman Films,
    2008)

237 "When I went there" *I Am Because
    We Are* (Madman Films, 2008)

237 "I wanted to tell the truth" Simon
    Doonan, *Elle* (May 2008)

238 "There are no accidents" *Newsnight*
    (BBC, November 1 2006)

238 "I kept saying: who's that baby"
    Today (NBC, November 1 2006)

239 "I didn't expect to be accused"
    Today (NBC, November 1 2006)

240 "All the criticism is ultimately"
    Today (NBC, November 1 2006)

CHAPTER 16
THE NEW DEAL

247 "It's kinda like 'Holiday'" *Daily
    Mirror* (April 13 2007)

247 "I would go from sitting" Jefferson
    Hack, *Dazed & Confused* (April
    2008)

247 "personifies the mood I was in"
    Warner Bros press release (April 2008)

249 "still trying to make those hits" Jane
    Stevenson, jam.canoe.ca (April 25
    2008)

250 "It's not like we hit it off" Rich
    Cohen, *Vanity Fair* (May 2008)

250 "That's not how you mean" *Jo
    Whiley Meets Madonna* (BBC Radio
    1, May 2008)

250 "When I heard the music" Jane
    Stevenson, jam.canoe.ca (April 25
    2008)

250 "tapping into the global
    consciousness" Ingrid Sischy,
    Interview (April 2008)

251 "could trick you into thinking"
    Warner Bros press release (April
    2008)

251 "We'd sit down and we'd start"
    Ingrid Sischy, *Interview* (April 2008)

252 "It's about waking up" *TAFF* (May
    2008)

252 "smooth operator" Simon Doonan,
    Elle (May 2008)

252 "I think Pharrell is a natural"
    Jefferson Hack, *Dazed & Confused*
    (April 2008)

253 "By the time we got to" Warner Bros
    press release (April 2008)

CHAPTER 17
STICKY & SWEET

256 "She's not afraid" Jacob Bernstein,
    Women's Wear Daily (August 5
    2008)

257 "so I could have a great time" Ingrid
    Sischy, *Interview* (April 2008)

262 "Many people—especially our" *The
    Nation* (March 17 2009)

263 "Madonna has always been" Simon
    Rothstein and Emma Cox, *The Sun*
    (May 6 2009)

263 "We are supporting her" Mabvuto
    Banda, *Times* (March 31 2009)

265 "In the beginning of my career" *Spin*
    (April 2008)

265 "I'm not going to be" Simon
    Doonan, *Elle* (May 2008)

267 "People say I should" Danny
    Eccleston, *Q* (March 1998)

267 "I can't imagine not working" Liz
    Smith, *Good Housekeeping* (April
    2000)

267 "Madonna's on this journey" Danny
    Eccleston, *Q* (March 1998)

BIBLIOGRAPHY

Ciccone, Christopher *Life With My Sister Madonna* (Pocket Books 2009)

St Michael, Mick *Madonna ... In Her Own Words* (Omnibus 1999)

Matthew-Walker, Robert *Madonna: The Biography* (Pan 1989)

O'Brien, Lucy *Madonna: Like An Icon* (Corgi 2008)

Thompson, Douglas *Madonna: Queen Of The World* (John Blake 2001)

Rooksby, Rikky *The Complete Guide To The Music Of Madonna* (Omnibus 2004)

Randall, Lee *The Madonna Scrapbook* (Bobcat 1992)

Taraborelli, J. Randy *Madonna: An Intimate Biography* (Sidgwick & Jackson 2001)

Easlea, Daryl *Everybody Dance: Chic & The Politics Of Disco* (Helter Skelter 2004)

Motion, Andrew *Madonna* (MM Books 2001)

Francis, Michael *Star Man: The Right Hand Man Of Rock'n'Roll* (Simon & Schuster 2003)

Madonna, *I'm Going To Tell You A Secret* (Warner Music Vision, 2005)

Metz, Allan, and Carol Benson *The Madonna Companion* (Schirmer 1999)

Marsh, Dave *The Heart Of Rock & Soul: The 1001 Greatest Singles Ever Made* (Pan 1989)

Bronson, Fred *The Billboard Book Of Number 1 Hits* (Billboard 2003)

Clerk, Carol *Madonnastyle* (Omnibus 2002)

Paglia, Camille *Sex, Art, And American Culture* (Random House 1992)

Pratt, Guy *My Bass And Other Animals* (Orion 2007)

Champagne, John, and Pamela Robertson *Guilty Pleasures: Feminist Camp From Mae West To Madonna* (Duke University Press 1996)

White, Timothy *Music To My Ears: The Billboard Essays—Portraits Of Popular Music In The 90s* (H Holt 1997)

Plus the following publications, broadcasters, websites, and resources: ABC-TV, absolutemadonna.com, allmovie.com, allmusic.com, *Aperture*, *Atlanta Journal Constitution*, *Attitude*, BBC, bbc.co.uk, *Billboard*, BNN, CBS-TV, Channel 4 (UK), Channel V (Australia), *Chicago Tribune*, *Crash*, *Daily Mirror* (UK), *Dazed & Confused*, drownedmadonna.com, *Elle*, *Entertainment Weekly*, *The Face*, *Flexipop!*, *Genre*, *Guardian* (UK), *Harper's Bazaar*, Home Shopping Network, ilikemusic.com, The Internet Movie Database, *Interview*, jam.canoe.ca, *Jane*, *LA Weekly*, *Ladies Home Journal*, *Larry King Live*, mad-eyes.net, madonna.com, madonnalicious.com, madonnatribe.com, *Melody Maker*, *Mixmag*, *Mojo*, MTV, musicohm.com, *The Nation*, NBC-TV, *New Musical Express*, *New Republic*, *New York Magazine*, *New York Times*, *Now*, *Observer* (UK), *Observer Music Monthly*, *The Oprah Winfrey Show*, *People*, *Q*, *Q Special Edition*, raisingmalawi.org, *Rolling Stone*, *Slant*, *Spin*, *The Sun*, *Sunday Times* (UK), *TAFF*, *Time*, *Times* (UK), *TV Guide*, *Uncut*, *US Weekly*, *USA Today*, *V*, *Vanity Fair*, VH-1, *Village Voice*, *Vogue*, *W*, Warner Bros, *Washington Post*, *Women's Wear Daily*, yahoo.com.

SELECTED DISCOGRAPHY

ALBUMS

Madonna *(July 1983)*
1. Lucky Star
2. Borderline
3. Burning Up
4. I Know It
5. Holiday
6. Think Of Me
7. Physical Attraction
8. Everybody

Like A Virgin *(November 1984)*
1. Material Girl
2. Angel
3. Like A Virgin
4. Over And Over
5. Love Don't Live Here Anymore
6. Dress You Up
7. Shoo-Bee-Doo
8. Pretender
9. Stay

True Blue *(June 1986)*
1. Papa Don't Preach
2. Open Your Heart
3. White Heat
4. Live To Tell
5. Where's The Party
6. True Blue
7. La Isla Bonita
8. Jimmy Jimmy
9. Love Makes The World Go Round

Who's That Girl *(July 1987)*
1. Who's That Girl (Madonna)
2. Causing A Commotion (Madonna)
3. The Book Of Love (Madonna)
4. 24 Hours (Duncan Faure)
5. Step By Step (Club Nouveau)
6. Turn It Up (Michael Davidson)
7. Best Thing Ever (Scritti Politti)
8. Can't Stop (Madonna)
9. El Coco Loco (So So Bad) (Coati Mundi)

Like A Prayer *(March 1989)*
1. Like A Prayer
2. Express Yourself
3. Love Song
4. Till Death Do Us Part
5. Promise To Try
6. Cherish
7. Dear Jessie
8. Oh Father
9. Keep It Together
10. Spanish Eyes
11. Act Of Contrition

I'm Breathless *(May 1990)*
1. He's A Man
2. Sooner Or Later
3. Hanky Panky
4. I'm Going Bananas
5. Cry Baby
6. Something To Remember
7. Back In Business
8. More
9. What Can You Lose
10. Now I'm Following You (Part I)
11. Now I'm Following You (Part II)
12. Vogue

Erotica *(October 1992)*
1. Erotica
2. Fever
3. Bye Bye Baby
4. Deeper And Deeper
5. Where Life Begins
6. Bad Girl
7. Waiting
8. Thief Of Hearts
9. Words
10. Rain
11. Why's It So Hard

12. In This Life
13. Did You Do It
14. Secret Garden

Bedtime Stories *(October 1994)*
1. Survival
2. Secret
3. I'd Rather Be Your Lover
4. Don't Stop
5. Inside Of Me
6. Human Nature
7. Forbidden Love
8. Love Tried To Welcome Me
9. Sanctuary
10. Bedtime Story
11. Take A Bow

Evita *(November 1996)*
1. Requiem For Evita
2. Oh What A Circus
3. On This Night Of A Thousand Stars
4. Eva And Magaldi/Eva Beware Of The City
5. Buenos Aires
6. Another Suitcase In Another Hall
7. Goodnight And Thank You
8. I'd Be Surprisingly Good For You
9. Perón's Latest Flame
10. A New Argentina
11. Don't Cry For Me Argentina
12. High Flying, Adored
13. Rainbow High
14. And The Money Kept Rolling In (And Out)
15. She Is A Diamond
16. Waltz For Eva And Che
17. You Must Love Me
18. Eva's Final Broadcast/Latin Chant
19. Lament

Ray Of Light *(March 1998)*
1. Drowned World/Substitute For Love
2. Swim
3. Ray Of Light
4. Candy Perfume Girl
5. Skin

6. Nothing Really Matters
7. Sky Fits Heaven
8. Shanti/Ashtangi
9. Frozen
10. The Power Of Good-Bye
11. To Have And Not To Hold
12. Little Star
13. Mer Girl

Music *(September 2000)*
1. Music
2. Impressive Instant
3. Runaway Lover
4. I Deserve It
5. Amazing
6. Nobody's Perfect
7. Don't Tell Me
8. What It Feels Like For A Girl
9. Paradise (Not For Me)
10. Gone

American Life *(April 2003)*
1. American Life
2. Hollywood
3. I'm So Stupid
4. Love Profusion
5. Nobody Knows Me
6. Nothing Fails
7. Intervention
8. X-Static Process
9. Mother And Father
10. Die Another Day
11. Easy Ride

Confessions On A Dance Floor
(November 2005)
1. Hung Up
2. Get Together
3. Sorry
4. Future Lovers
5. I Love New York
6. Let It Will Be
7. Forbidden Love
8. Jump
9. How High
10. Isaac

11. Push
12. Like It Or Not

Hard Candy *(April 2008)*
1. Candy Shop
2. 4 Minutes
3. Give It 2 Me
4. Heartbeat
5. Miles Away
6. She's Not Me
7. Incredible
8. Beat Goes On
9. Dance 2night
10. Spanish Lesson
11. Devil Wouldn't Recognize You
12. Voices

SINGLES

'Everybody' *(October 1982)*
'Burning Up' *(March 1983)*
'Holiday' *(September 1983)*
'Lucky Star' *(September 1983)*
'Borderline' *(February 1984)*
'Like A Virgin' *(November 1984)*
'Material Girl' *(January 1985)*
'Crazy For You' *(March 1985)*
'Angel' *(April 1985)*
'Into The Groove' *(July 1985)*
'Dress You Up' *(July 1985)*
'Gambler' *(October 1985)*
'Live To Tell' *(March 1986)*
'Papa Don't Preach' *(June 1986)*
'True Blue' *(September 1986)*
'Open Your Heart' *(November 1986)*
'La Isla Bonita' *(February 1987)*
'Who's That Girl' *(June 1987)*
'Causing A Commotion' *(August 1987)*
'The Look Of Love' *(November 1987)*
'Spotlight' *(April 1988)*
'Like A Prayer' *(March 1989)*
'Express Yourself' *(May 1989)*
'Cherish' *(August 1989)*
'Oh Father' *(October 1989)*
'Dear Jessie' *(December 1989)*

'Keep It Together' *(January 1990)*
'Vogue' *(March 1990)*
'Hanky Panky' *(June 1990)*
'Justify My Love' *(November 1990)*
'Rescue Me' *(February 1991)*
'This Used To Be My Playground' *(March 1992)*
'Erotica' *(October 1992)*
'Deeper And Deeper' *(December 1992)*
'Bad Girl' *(February 1993)*
'Fever' *(March 1993)*
'Rain' *(July 1993)*
'Bye Bye Baby' *(November 1993)*
'I'll Remember' *(March 1994)*
'Secret' *(September 1994)*
'Take A Bow' *(December 1994)*
'Bedtime Story' *(February 1995)*
'Human Nature' *(June 1995)*
'You'll See' *(October 1995)*
'One More Chance' *(March 1996)*
'Love Don't Live Here Anymore' *(March 1996)*
'You Must Love Me' (October 1996)
'Don't Cry For Me Argentina' *(February 1997)*
'Another Suitcase In Another Hall' *(March 1997)*
'Frozen' *(February 1998)*
'Ray Of Light' *(May 1998)*
'Drowned World/Substitute For Love' *(August 1998)*
'The Power Of Good-Bye' *(September 1998)*
'Nothing Really Matters' *(March 1999)*
'Beautiful Stranger' *(June 1999)*
'American Pie' *(March 2000)*
'Music' *(August 2000)*
'Don't Tell Me' *(November 2000)*
'What It Feels Like For A Girl' *(April 2001)*
'Die Another Day' *(October 2002)*
'American Life' *(March 2003)*
'Hollywood' *(July 2003)*
'Me Against The Music' *(October 2003)*
'Nothing Fails' *(November 2003)*
'Love Profusion' *(January 2004)*
'Hung Up' *(October 2005)*

'Sorry' *(February 2006)*
'Get Together' *(June 2006)*
'Jump' *(October 2006)*
'4 Minutes' *(March 2008)*
'Give It 2 Me' *(June 2008)*
'Miles Away' *(October 2008)*
'Celebration' *(July 2009)*
'Revolver' *(December 2009)*
'Gimme All Your Luvin'' *(January 2012)*

COMPILATIONS

You Can Dance *(November 1987)*
1. Spotlight
2. Holiday
3. Everybody
4. Physical Attraction
5. Over And Over
6. Into The Groove
7. Where's The Party

The Immaculate Collection
(November 1990)
1. Holiday
2. Lucky Star
3. Borderline
4. Like A Virgin
5. Material Girl
6. Crazy For You
7. Into The Groove
8. Live To Tell
9. Papa Don't Preach
10. Open Your Heart
11. La Isla Bonita
12. Like A Prayer
13. Express Yourself
14. Cherish
15. Vogue
16. Justify My Love
17. Rescue Me

Something To Remember
(November 1995)
1. I Want You
2. I'll Remember
3. Take A Bow
4. You'll See
5. Crazy For You
6. This Used To Be My Playground
7. Live To Tell
8. Love Don't Live Here Anymore
9. Something To Remember
10. Forbidden Love
11. One More Chance
12. Rain
13. Oh Father
14. I Want You (Orchestral)

Pre-Madonna *(June 1997)*
1. Laugh To Keep From Crying
2. Crimes Of Passion
3. Ain't No Big Deal (1997 Edit)
4. Everybody (1997 Version)
5. Burning Up
6. Ain't No Big Deal (1981 Version)
7. Everybody (1981 Version)
8. Stay (1981 Version)
9. Don't You Know
10. Ain't No Big Deal (1997 Extended
    Version)

GHV2 *(November 2001)*
1. Deeper And Deeper
2. Erotica
3. Human Nature
4. Secret
5. Don't Cry For Me Argentina
6. Bedtime Story
7. The Power Of Good-Bye
8. Beautiful Stranger
9. Frozen
10. Take A Bow
11. Ray Of Light
12. Don't Tell Me
13. What It Feels Like For A Girl
14. Drowned World/Substitute For Love
15. Music

INDEX

Word in *italics* indicate album titles unless otherwise stated. Words in 'quotes' indicate song titles.

PICTURE CREDITS

The pictures used in this book came from the following sources. **Jacket** Richard Corkery/NY Daily News Archive/Getty Images; **145** Michael McDonnell/Hulton Archive/Getty Images; **146** Warner Bros/Getty Images; **147** David McGough/DMI/Time Life Pictures/Getty Images; **148** Popperphoto/Getty Images; **149** Ebet Roberts/Redferns; Time Life Pictures/Getty Images; **150–1** Frank Micelotta/ImageDirect; **152** Kevin Winter/DMI/Time Life Pictures/Getty Images; **153** Getty Images (2); **154** Frank Micelotta/ImageDirect; **155** Kevin Mazur/WireImage; **156** Kevin Mazur/WireImage; **157** Kevin Kane/WireImage; **158** Kevin Mazur/WireImage; **159** Stringer/AFP/Getty Images; Donald Kravitz/Getty Images; **160** Kevin Mazur/WireImage/Getty Images